The Gourmet's Tour de France

27 GREAT FRENCH RESTAURANTS AND THEIR FAVORITE RECIPES

Text by:	*Henry Viard*
Recipes written and adapted by:	*Ninette Lyon*
Photographs by:	*Gilles Peress*
	Miguel Rio Branco
Editorial advisor:	*Laurent Stark*

A New York Graphic Society Book / Little, Brown and Company   Boston

New York Graphic Society Books are
published by Little, Brown and Company (Inc.)
Published simultaneously in Canada by Little,
Brown and Company (Canada) Limited

First published in France by Editions
Hologramme, Neuilly
First English language edition

Printed in Japan

Library of Congress Cataloging in Publication
Data

Viard, Henry.
    The gourmet's tour de France.

    "A New York Graphic Society book."
    Includes index.
    1. Restaurants, lunch rooms, etc. --France--Direc-
tories. 2. Cookery, French. I. Title.
TX910.F8V53 1984   641.5'0944   84-2027
ISBN 0-8212-1563-9

Contents

Introduction			6
The Restaurants	Ile-de-France	Beauvilliers - Paris	10
		Fouquet's - Paris	16
		Le Grand Véfour - Paris	22
		Hôtel de Crillon - Paris	28
		Maxim's - Paris	34
		Taillevent - Paris	40
		La Tour d'Argent - Paris	46
		La Vieille Fontaine - Maisons-Laffitte	52
	Picardy	L'Hostellerie du Château - Fère-en-Tardenois	58
	Champagne	Château Boyer les Crayères - Rheims	64
	Alsace	L'Auberge de l'Ill - Illhäusern	70
	Burgundy	Georges Blanc - Vonnas	74
	Lyons region	Paul Bocuse - Collonges-au-Mont-d'Or	80
	Savoy	L'Auberge du Père Bise - Talloires	84
	Provence-Côte d'Azur	Château de la Chèvre d'Or - Eze-Village	90
		Château du Domaine Saint-Martin - Vence	96
		Grill de l'Hôtel de Paris - Monte Carlo	102
		Le Métropole - Beaulieu-sur-Mer	108
		Le Moulin de Mougins - Mougins	114
		L'Oasis - La Napoule	120
		Oustau de Baumanière - Baux-de-Provence	126
		La Réserve de Beaulieu - Beaulieu-sur-Mer	132
	Languedoc	L'Enclos Montgranier - Sommières	138
	Aquitaine	Les Prés d'Eugénie - Eugénie-les-Bains	144
		Saint-James - Bouliac	150
	Touraine	Château d'Artigny - Montbazon	156
	Normandy	Château d'Audrieu - Tilly-sur-Seulles	162
27 Gourmand Localities			168
Some Famous Gourmands			170
General Comments about the Recipes			172
Recipe Index			174

Introduction

Our gourmand* is more than two thousand years old. His library, in which Montesquieu has as large a place as wine, befits a respectable citizen; his dictionary was written by Alexandre Dumas, and his Hall of Fame is that of the gourmet or the cigar-lover. Guillaume Apollinaire offers him word-pictures of pot-bellied bottles and Thomas Jefferson the first French vineyard map.

Our gourmand is not at all surprised that some of today's finest restaurants bear the names of ancient culinary celebrities because a long-standing habit of his is to leaf through the recipes of Archestratus, Taillevent or Beauvilliers.**

If he does not possess the early printed works or the original editions, the reprints help to plug this gap; he "devours" Brillat-Savarin, venerates Lucien Tendret, and knows everything about Monselet. He consults the modern authors, Jean-François Revel or Jean-Paul Aron, and his pantheon includes Guillaume Tirel, better known as Taillevent, Laguipière, dead in the snows of Russia with the troops of Murat for whom he had created so many dishes, Antonin Carême, the chef of Talleyrand, kings, emperors, Edouard Nignon with the **Heptameron of Gourmets** clasped to his bosom, Antoine Augustin Parmentier, pharmacist-baker and the potato's press agent. The age of Louis XIV is represented by Massialot, Menon, La Varenne, and the **Gascon Cook**. Grimod de la Reynière, the model for tasters and writers, or Viard, the professional, imperial, royal and, finally, republican chef represent the nineteenth century and thus bring us full circle with centuries of recipes from Apicius to Platina.

Our gourmand has attended the School of Medicine at Salerno and before that was a courtier at the Medici court, which, with its two queens (Catherine and Marie), completely turned our Renaissance cuisine topsyturvy.

Our gourmand is more than two thousand years old.

His Gallic ancestors, master pork butchers, have passed on to him a heritage of specialties still found all over the provinces where his gourmand relatives perpetuate the cult of Mr. Porker: chitterlings from Vire or Guéméné, raw or smoked ham from the Ardennes, parsley-dressed ham from the Beaujolais region, cooked ham from Paris, the countless dried and fresh sausages from the four corners of the country, the blood sausages, the chitterling sausages, the pâtés and the rillettes.

Each village has its own recipe and in each village chefs and pork butchers argue the merits of such and such a product and its creation. Each method is a consummate art in itself and bears witness down the centuries to the persistence of breeding and agricultural techniques in the same local area.

France has offered its hospitality to and absorbed peoples from all over Europe – the Saxons, the Franks, the Arvernis, the original Burgundians. The Vikings gaped openmouthed at the rich grazing lands of Normandy and settled along its rivers. The Roman legionary planted his vines and transformed the country into one almost continuous vineyard.

This infusion of different bloodlines has gone on for centuries and our eating habits, our love of good food has constantly been nurtured, modified and enriched.

The spices of the Middle East, indispensable enough to have been the true motivation for the Crusades, have been replaced by those from overseas, and the million returnees from Algeria offered our palates a cuisine far more sundrenched than that of Provence.

Our gourmand is more than two thousand years old. Sometimes easily, sometimes by stratagem, he has adopted so many vegetables, fruits or animals brought in by sea rovers and explorers, missionaries and soldiers that our herbarium, our barnyard, our farms over the centuries have become a paradise for the guinea hen, the potato, the ear of corn, the eggplant and watercress. New species *have been grafted onto the original flora and fauna of the country to the point that a contemporary of Rabelais would be hard pressed to recognize the herbs, roots and fowl to be found on our modern menus.*

Our gourmand is more than two thousand years old. He traveled with Marco Polo in search of Cipango and brought back pasta. He succumbed to the charms of vanilla from orchid aceae. With Madame de Sévigné he drank coffee at the Café Procope and cocoa from Bayonne. He has reinvented the "new cuisine" innumerable times and made that of Florence the most French in the world. He lamented with Voltaire over the disappearance of yesteryear's cuisine while continuing both to simplify and complicate the existing one. Following in the footsteps of Urbain Dubois or Antoine Carême, he created dishes with architectural skill; he has lunched with Talleyrand, dined with Gouffé at the Jockey Club, partaken of a champagne supper in the company of the Regent and a few carefully chosen beauties; he has created and destroyed styles, restaurants and reputations.

In two thousand years, our gourmand has helped the Romans seed our coasts with oysters, consuming a considerable number of them in the process. He has sung the praises of the snail and frogs' legs. But local loyalties are strong in France. A southwestern housewife would as soon renounce her faith as replace goose fat with olive oil from Provence. The same holds true for her Norman counterpart and her devotion to cream. And a man from the west would feel backed to the wall if asked to choose between Charentes and Isigny butter. France is truly a country with an embarrassment of riches.

Geese have become symbols, with their livers bearing witness to a kind of gourmand ecumenism. Thus, when the Norman chef Clause prepares for the Maréchal de Contades in Strasbourg a goose raised in the southwest, he stuffs the bird with truffles from Périgord or the Comtat Venaissin.

In this way, the fundamental products are combined into a single cuisine. Through its own qualities, each province, each region influences its neighbor and the neighbor the whole country.

Our gourmand knows this and will travel all over town to purchase sole or a leg of lamb, will buy only coffee roasted over coke by an artisan who takes pride in his profession, and will go all the way to Lyons for his chocolate. He has a brother and a thousand sisters each one of whom has a special address for such and such a product, a specific winegrower for his or her bottle of Pommerol or Côtes du Rhône, a baker, known all over the world, like Poilâne, or simply on his street or in his district.

Over the past two thousand years, our gourmand has refined his taste for preserved goose, never inventing any recipe but trying them all. He is a chauvinist and an opportunist, an unconditional fan of beurre blanc *in an inn on the banks of the Loire and of the Gewürztraminer which he receives at Christmas from an Alsatian cousin. He comes from everywhere; he recalls that he invented the barrel to hold cider from the Auge valley, Pauillac vintages, beer from the département du Nord, the spirits of Arnaud de Villeneuve or Gilles de Gouberville, and the favorite wines of Henri IV, who seems to have had one in every wine-growing region. He suffered with his cousin and his uncle when mildew and phylloxera attacked their vines. They talk about the event as they would of a barbarian invasion. They observe the classification of 1855 as one would the Tablets of the Law.*

The young chefs of today such as Alain Sanderens, Joël Robuchon, Guy Savoy, Alain Chapel, and Christian Ignace follow in the tradition that formed Auguste Escoffier or Georges Garin, and our gourmand is aware of their skill and talents.

He was heartbroken with Vatel that time the seafood shipment arrived too late; he has cried over the sight of broken Baccarat glass or a failed sauce. He visits every winery, every kitchen; he is aware of the alchemy of every dish and the miracles of Camembert, he knows the 365 cheeses, their seasons and the importance for Roquefort of the air in the Causses.

Despite fifty generations of Frères Provençaux, Velloni, Larue and Véry, he still debates the merits of the American lobster or its Breton rival.

His geography for a tour of France encompasses the stars in the Guide Michelin or the chefs' hats awarded by Gault and Millau, his chateaux are those that bottle Médoc; he is proud to be a Burgundian and lets you know it.

Our gourmand is two thousand years old; Curnonsky was his ancestor and Fernand Point his cousin. Perhaps he is now somewhat removed from his provincial past, but he still dreams of Mères Lyonnaises and can rummage through his memory or that of others for old terms for new dishes and vice versa. Thus, while the Grande Cuisine has been divided up, heaven only knows how or why, into High, Bourgeoise, and New categories, it still offers everything to satisfy the appetites and fantasies of all gourmands. It is the culmination of centuries of research, refinements, adaptations, and anonymous inventions.

It is rooted in the fabric of French life; it is redolent of hazelnuts and the herbs of Provence; it has the elegance of Versailles and the simplicity of fresh or salt-water fish soups; it has absorbed all cultures, gallicized the Italian ravioli into raviole, accepted clams, rediscovered the bittersweet flavors of the Middle Ages believed lost for all time. One need only cite blood sausages with apples, venison with cranberries, duck with orange sauce as proof that, like rivers, culinary styles run underground for periods of time only to surge forth once more to mellow the earth and the great chefs.

It is also a celebration, dazzling with its accouterments: the Limoges or Vieux Rouen china, the Baccarat glassware or Sèvres porcelain. Christofle silverware goes well with Valenciennes lace tablecloths, the decanters filled with the ruby redness of Bordeaux or Burgundy or the golden glow of the Sauternes, Sylvaners or Château-Chalons.

In these twenty-seven restaurants, the grace of the decor blends with the beauty of the natural setting, the chefs and the hosts have created an art of living which is a noble continuation of culinary art.

Our gourmand is over two thousand years old.

Translator's Note :
* The word gourmand as used by the author means simply someone who loves the pleasures of the table, and it should not be construed as designating a glutton. I have chosen to use the word in the translation in the sense given to it by the author.

** For this and other names mentioned here, see the "Famous Gourmands" list on page 170.

The Restaurants

Beauvilliers

*Edouard Carlier, esthete-gourmand and organizer of
Montmartre's celebrations, restaurateur enamored
of luxury, of multitudes of flowers, with his restaurant close
by the stairways leading to the top of that celebrated hill,
offers the elegant graces of his cascading terraces.*

The first restaurant in Paris was opened in 1784 by Antoine Beauvilliers, former victualling officer to the Comte de Provence, the future King Louis XVIII, a king who was both gourmet and glutton. According to Grimod de la Reynière, Beauvilliers was a stickler for detail as regards decor, the welcoming of the diners, the wine cellar and the cuisine he served. Endowed with a fabulous memory, he recognized every face and remembered every name. He was quite a sight, moving around his dining room, keeping a weather eye on his waiters and displaying a remarkable knack of knowing just what dish to recommend to an undecided customer. Beauvilliers' restaurant closed in 1793 and did not reopen until the stormy period of the Revolution had passed into history. In 1814, this kindly and illustrious epicure published *L'Art du Cuisinier,* the first page of which adorns the menu of Edouard Carlier's restaurant in Montmartre – a restaurant dedicated to the memory of this host of two hundred years ago. The loyalty of Beauvilliers to his king is matched by that of Carlier to his model, up to the pastel green plates, replicas of those once produced by the Manufacture de Clignancourt, which was the property of the Comte de Provence. The saying went that everything was green at Clignancourt and blue at Sèvres.

Installed in a former bakery that had been called the Muse des Arts, Edouard Carlier has created not simply a restaurant but three Louis-Philippe-style dining rooms in a Balzac setting that unites comfort, intimacy, romanticism, and delicacy.

Carlier boldly chose to cover the walls of the restaurant with fabrics in colors considered to be insipid: cobalt blue satin and willow green satin. These colors are found again in the lacquer work. But they are brought to life by the abundance of flowers, bouquet masterpieces, at times setting off a table or a corner of the room.

More vivid are the tablecloths in tawny colors lit by Florentine lamps, so flattering to the beauty of the women diners. The chairs, made from aged fruit-tree woods in Venice and replicas of 1830 models, seem to have just come out of the workshop of a Cremonese violin maker.

Little wonder that the celebrities in the arts, the theatre and business who throng to the three dining rooms are charmed by the elegance and decoration of their surroundings. One of the rooms is hung with eighteenth- and nineteenth-century engravings of the now-vanished windmills of Montmartre. Another features portraits of Beauvilliers' contemporaries, painted by such artists as Louis-Léopold Boilly, Raffet, or Gavarni, while the third is given over to the floral theme with its paintings of bouquets and its orange-blossom bridal wreaths under glass bell jars. All this makes as much for a worldly never-never land as for a refuge of an impassioned and highly authentic gastronomy. Edouard Carlier, from the Département du Nord, was born in Flanders, beside the Escaut River. A passionate artist, a refined aesthete, possessed with a truculence tempered by an excellent education, Carlier began his career as an art book publisher. For family reasons, he gave this up to return to Quarré-les-Tombes in the Morvan region to take over the management of the Auberge des Brizards, an inn run by his parents. He quickly turned this modest restaurant into a worldly rendezvous point for a most discerning clientele. One of his innovations was open-air dinners at which poetry recitals took place.

Endowed with an innate public relations sense and a knack for combining the paradox with the practical joke, Carlier once undertook to assemble in the village all the Brizards in the world from the direct descendant of Marie Brizard (of the famous liqueur family) to distant cousins from abroad. But he really attained his full gastronomic growth when he established himself in the former domain of Marie-Adelaide Beauvilliers, the mother superior of the Montmartre Abbey. How she would have adored the "concocted dishes", the "created dishes", the "rediscovered dishes", the "fish dishes", the "roasts", the "cold and hot entrées" on the menu of the Beauvilliers.

When the weather turns fine, the tables in the flower-bedecked outdoor dining area are stormed by a horde of diners who wish to savor the restaurant's exceptional cuisine. Dishes with mouth-watering names like *les petits apprêts, éperons, entrées de bouche,* a *poêlée d'escargots petits gris aux mousserons* (snails), a *persillade de lapereau dans sa gelée au fin bois* (young rabbit), etc. The cheese platter at Beauvilliers also becomes a work of art, especially because of the geometric forms of the goat cheeses that are a particular pride and joy of Carlier. To the delicacy of the food he serves, refined to the extreme, Carlier adds an attention to detail, to the object and to the elegance of his waiters symbolized by their Charvet ties. To sum it all up, Carlier remains faithful to the nth degree to the elitism of an Antoine Beauvilliers to the concept of celebration, to friendship and to participation.

As attentive to the quality of the bread delivered as he is to the choice of bouquets–the pride of the restaurant–under the roguish eye of a decolletée demoiselle Edouard Carlier, ever concerned with refined elegance, chose Charvet ties for his youthful, well-trained serving staff. His care in composing everything into veritable pictures, and his choice of colors are reflected in the shelves of the bar featuring jugs and wineglasses conveying a Venetian somnolence or in the cameo of a platter of goat cheeses.

1   52 rue Lamarck 75018 Paris (small dining rooms, flower-decorated outdoor dining areas, dogs not allowed). Closed all day Sunday and Monday at lunchtime and from August 28 to September 26. Must-see sights in the area: Montmartre Hill, the vineyards, the romantic streets sung about by Aristide Bruant, the Place du Tertre with its painters, the City Hall of the "Free Community," the Vieux-Montmartre Museum, the Sacré-Cœur Basilica, the St-Pierre Church (12th century). This colorful neighborhood, the birthplace of cubism and home of many noted artists at the beginning of the century, is still a very lively spot after dark.
Visa card honored   Tel : (1) 254.19.50

Turbot in red wine sauce with eggplant purée

Tronçon de turbot en meurette de vin d'Hermitage

<u>Serves 6:</u>
6 pieces of turbot weighing about
  8 oz (220 g) each
3 small eggplants (aubergines)
2 tablespoons peanut oil
1 bottle red wine, an Hermitage or a
  Burgundy
half a clove garlic, finely chopped
1 clove garlic, crushed
2 sprigs thyme
1 bay leaf
2 carrots, diced
2 shallots, diced
2 tablespoons butter, for the fish
a small amount of coarse salt
salt and freshly ground white pepper
12 baby onions, peeled
1 tablespoon of butter, for the onions

First make an eggplant purée as follows: cut each of the eggplants in half lengthwise and score the pulp in quarters with the tip of a knife. Place the eggplants in a lightly oiled baking dish, spoon a little extra oil over each one, cover with a piece of aluminum foil and place in a 410 °F (210 °C) oven for 30 minutes. Remove from the oven, let cool briefly, then scoop out the pulp with a spoon and discard the skins. Place the pulp in a blender with the chopped garlic, salt, and pepper and blend to a purée. Reserve.

In a large uncovered saucepan bring the wine to a boil, then add the diced shallots and carrots, the thyme, bay leaf, and crushed garlic. Boil rapidly for about 15 minutes or until the wine has reduced and thickened to the point where it coats a spoon. Remove from the heat and strain the sauce.

Place the pieces of fish in a roasting pan, dot with butter and sprinkle over a little coarse salt. Place in the 410 °F (210 °C) oven and bake for 7 to 8 minutes.

Cook the baby onions in a frying pan, covered, over low heat with a tablespoon of butter.

To serve, warm the eggplant purée if it has cooled, spoon some onto each plate, place a piece of fish next to it, spoon over the sauce, garnish with the baby onions, and serve.

Grilled red mullet escabèche

Filets de rougets grillés en fine escabèche

<u>Serves 6:</u>
12 red mullet weighing about 4 oz (100 g) each
6½ tablespoons (10 cl) olive oil
6 fresh basil leaves, thinly sliced
6 dried chili peppers, crushed
juice of 2 limes
salt and pepper
2 zucchini (courgettes)
1 red bell pepper
olive oil for the vegetables

Fillet the fish and use tweezers to remove any remaining bones. Lightly oil the fillets and grill or broil them, turning each over once.

Place the remaining olive oil, lime juice, basil, chili peppers, salt, and pepper in a mixing bowl and combine, using a whisk.

Place the cooked fillets on a serving platter and, while they are still warm; pour the sauce through a strainer over them. Leave the fish to marinate in the sauce for 2 hours in a cool place.

Cook the zucchini and the red pepper in separate pans over low heat with a little oil until they have softened. Cut the pepper into thick strips. Set them aside.

Place the fillets in a star pattern on a large serving platter. Place zucchini between the pieces of fish and in the center of the dish; put

some of the red pepper in the center as well. Spoon a little of the marinade over the fish, and serve.

Stuffed calves' kidneys with truffles and spinach

Petite rognonnade de veau aux truffes et feuilles d'épinards cuits minutes

Serves 6:
2 whole calves' kidneys
7 oz (200 g) veal shoulder, cut into pieces
2 large veal scallops
2 egg yolks
2 large shallots, finely chopped
2 truffles
1 3/4 cups (40 cl) dry sherry
5 - 6 tablespoons heavy cream
2 pieces of thin fat membrane (lace fat)
3 1/2 tablespoons (50 g) butter
2 oz (60 g) fresh foie gras, cubed (optional)
1/2 lb (250 g) fresh spinach
salt and pepper
truffles as a garnish (optional)

Soak the lace fat in cold water for an hour. Remove all the fat from around the kidneys, then cut each one in half lengthwise. Remove the gristle and fat from inside each kidney. Carefully peel each truffle and reserve the shavings. Place the pieces of veal shoulder in a food processor or meat grinder and chop fine. Add the egg yolks, 2 teaspoons of shallots, the truffle shavings, 6 tablespoons of sherry, 2 tablespoons of cream, salt and pepper; stir to combine. Place a spoonful or two of this stuffing on one half of each kidney, then cover it with the other half to enclose the stuffing.

Place the veal scallops on a cutting board and spread half the remaining stuffing over each one. Slice the truffles and place them in a neat line on top of the stuffing. Wrap each kidney in a veal scallop, wrap this in lace fat to hold its shape, then tie each wrapped kidney with kitchen string.

Heat 2 tablespoons of butter in a frying pan and brown the kidneys over moderate heat.

Add the rest of the shallots, pour in the remaining sherry and cream, add the foie gras (if using it) and continue cooking 10 to 15 minutes. Remove the kidneys from the pan, untie them and cut each into 8 slices. Boil the cooking liquid to reduce and thicken it, then work it through a sieve to make the sauce. Keep warm. Cook the spinach in a frying pan with the remaining butter, a little water, salt, and pepper for no more than 4 minutes. Spoon some of the sauce onto each dinner plate, place the slices of kidney in the middle, spoon over a little sauce, garnish with sliced truffles (if using them), place some of the spinach on each side of the plate, and serve.

Lemon pie with white rum

Tarte au citron douce-amère

Serves 6:

For the pastry dough:
1 3/4 cups (250 g) flour
1/2 cup (125 g) butter - pinch of salt
2/3 cup plus 2 tablespoons (125 g) confectioner's sugar
4 - 5 tablespoons dry white wine

For the filling:
6 lemons
1 1/4 cups (250 g) granulated sugar
5 whole eggs
1/2 cup (12 cl) white rum
7/8 cup (200 g) softened butter

Make short pastry using the ingredients given here. Roll out the dough and lay it in a lightly buttered pie pan. Prick the dough with a fork in several places, cover with aluminum foil shaped to fit into the crust, then fill the foil with dry uncooked beans or lentils. Place in a 400 °F (200 °C) oven and bake for 10 minutes. Remove from the oven and lift out the foil containing the beans.

Slice the lemons and remove the seeds. Place the slices in a food processor and chop to a pulp. Pour the pureed lemons into a mixing bowl, and add the sugar, eggs, rum, and the softened butter, broken into little pieces. Beat well to combine.

Pour the lemon filling into the pie crust and bake in a 300 °F (150 °C) oven for 40 minutes. The filling should be nicely browned when done. Remove from the oven and allow to cool before serving. Serve cold.

FOUQUET'S

Rendezvous point or last bastion of good eating on the Champs-Elysées,
Fouquet's has a mission that combines elegance
and the gourmand's way of life.
Jenny-Paule Casanova conscientiously watches over her father's
establishment and perpetuates the most Parisian of all institutions.

Two hundred years ago Ambassador Thomas Jefferson could gaze from the embassy garden across the street upon the most beautiful thoroughfare in the world–the Champs-Elysées. No triumphal arch crowned its end. No obelisk had as yet been erected in the square from which it begins. The present site of the United States embassy was then occupied by the town house of La Reynière, the wealthy pre-Revolutionary financier. And on the Champs-Elysées the other town houses had not yet been replaced by the airline companies, banks, and movie houses. Already, however, it was the route taken by the elegant to go from the Tuileries to the Bois de Boulogne. Eighty years ago it was frequented by hansom cabs and the drivers made a point of stopping for refreshment at a tavern run by a certain Mr. Fouquet. He "Americanized" his name by adding an apostrophe *s* to it and the setting with an American bar. He thus followed the style set by Maxim's combining English chic with a touch of a Yankee accent.

Given its marvelous location, Fouquet's was destined not to remain simply a coachmen's tavern. Léopold Mourier, who succeeded the founder, Louis Fouquet, expanded the premises, decorated its walls with mahogany panels, and installed a grill-room. The racetrack habitués from Auteuil, Longchamp, and even Saint-Cloud became regular customers either in search of a good tip or to toast a victory with a flood of champagne.

The upper floor was opened in 1913. At that time, Fouquet's was already known as a restaurant offering very classic, restrained, and refined elegance. It was fashionable to lunch or dine there, the food having acquired renown both in Paris and abroad. Theodore Roosevelt made a point of inviting Aristide Briand to join him for a meal there. National and international political leaders became regular customers. Raymond Poincaré or Winston Churchill rubbed elbows with famous aviators or sports figures. The leaders of the motion picture world quickly took up Fouquet's, and many of France's most important films were created in the euphoric afterglow of a Fouquet's meal. Raimu held court there from a corner which he claimed as his personal realm. This long association with the cinema made it natural for Fouquet's to be chosen as the site for the awarding of the Césars, the French version of the Oscars. What a cast could be assembled from a simple recital of the Fouquet's regulars! The outdoor table area on Avenue George V is the most elegant one in Paris with its bevy of female stars and starlets, each one more beautiful, more famous (or hoping to be) than the other. The James Joyce Room reminds us that authors were in the habit of dropping in for a quick one. Then came the Drouant era. For a period of almost fifty years the entire world, from Marlene Dietrich (who used to have a Fouquet's cheese platter sent to her each day in New York) to Arthur Rubinstein, from the Duc Louis Decazes to Jean Gabin, made it a point to dine at the elegant establishment on the Avenue des Champs-Elysées. Certain tables at Fouquet's took on greater importance than the offices of cabinet ministers. When, in 1976, Maurice Casanova moved over from the Left Bank to run Fouquet's, the tradition was continued with even more feasts and gala evenings than before. From this last monument to the pleasures of the table on the upper portion of the Champs-Elysées, Maurice Casanova and his daughter, Jenny-Paule, are fighting against the invasion of "fast food" shops and mediocrity. Fouquet's has known how to preserve a style from a time of leisurely dining. The marvelous Christofle serving trolleys, the carvers, the headwaiters and the wine stewards for its exceptional cellar all combine to perpetuate the great tradition of the deluxe restaurants. There are in fact several Fouquet's. The covered outside dining area, which runs from the Champs-Elysées around to the Avenue George V, is the most beautiful and most famous one in Paris. In the renovated second-floor dining room with its Louis XVI style wall brackets, sumptuous floral decorations and purple drapes, the menu of chef Pierre Ducroux is a subtle combination of the great classic dishes and an evolving cuisine. The fact that Ducroux, although Paris-born, comes from an old Burgundian family might explain his fondness for wine sauces. After a period at the Plaza Athénée, he has been a Fouquet's fixture since 1956. Working at all the culinary trades, Ducroux was sauce-cook for ten years before taking over as chef in 1980. However, everything begins at the bar. This meeting point, this shrine of the cocktail and good cheer is presided over in an irreproachable manner by Raymond. Television celebrities like Bernard Pivot and Jacques Chancel have turned it into their canteen and José Artur's Pop Club is broadcast nightly from the premises. All that Fouquet's represents for the gourmand itinerary we owe to the determination and the discernment of Maurice Casanova and to the perfect mastery of his daughter, Jenny-Paule, who, despite her youth, is already one of the great ladies of the restaurant trade.

2 89 Avenue des Champs-Elysées 75008 Paris (small dining rooms for meetings, dogs allowed). Open all year except for upper floor, which is closed on Sundays and Saturdays and during August. Must-see sights: the Champs-Elysées with its 24-hour hustle and bustle, the Arc de Triomphe (a fascinating museum at its top), Avenue George V with its famous couturiers, the Crazy Horse Saloon, the banks of the Seine, the excursion boats (embarkation point at the Alma bridge) and the Grand Palais museum.
AE - Diners - Visa cards honored
Tel. (1) 723.70.60

The Fouquet's team is made up of faces known to all its regular customers: bartenders, the humidor man, headwaiters, wine stewards, carvers and waiters as well as those working in the bustle of the spotless kitchens or in the calm of the offices. The elegant outdoor dining area or the second-floor dining room, which seems to offer the Arc de Triomphe as a part of its decor, calls upon the services of people like Joël Minot showing off the restaurant's famous **bar en croute** *(bass baked in a crust) or Roland Fuchs carving succulent slices of ham on the resplendent silver Christofle serving trolley. This team has its traditions, its customs, and even its initiation rites. The attire of each one, be it the immaculate white jacket or the tuxedo, has an exact significance and a hierarchy to be respected. The dining room is the site of the feasts of the Parisian and movie world* **Who's Who** *and, somewhere in the room, a gossip writer may be hiding, hoping to eavesdrop on some juicy scandal or state secret. But Fouquet's is most of all its bar, the spot for confiding secrets, concluding fabulous deals, and giving full rein to one's wildest dreams. Hours of endless waiting for the writer, the singer, or the actor seeking inspiration while Didier presides over it all with his silver cocktail shaker.*

Smoked haddock salad

Salade de haddock aux épinards

Serves 4:
1 lb (600 g) smoked haddock
2 ¼ lbs (1 kg) fresh spinach (small leaves)
½ cup (125 g) butter, softened
4 ¼ cups (1 L) milk
2 tablespoons (3 cl) heavy cream
1 teaspoon coarsely ground peppercorns
2 shallots, sliced thin
3 tablespoons (5 cl) dry white wine
2 tablespoons (3 cl) white wine vinegar
3 tablespoons fresh chives,
 cut into half-inch strips
1 clove garlic, peeled - salt and pepper

If the haddock is very salty, soak it overnight in half the milk before cooking it. Discard the milk. To cook, place the fish in a large pan with the rest of the fresh milk and water to barely cover. As soon as the liquid boils, the fish is cooked. Remove the fish from the pan with a slotted spoon and drain on a paper towel. Carefully remove any bones from the fish, then gently separate the flesh into little wedge-shaped pieces. Keep fish warm.

For sauce: place thin-sliced shallots into a small saucepan (preferably an enameled one), add white wine, vinegar, pepper and boil. When liquid has been reduced to about a quarter of its original volume, add the cream and whisk, lower the heat, and, little by little, whisk in all but 5 teaspoons of the softened butter. Remove from the heat, add salt if needed, and strain the sauce. Reserve.

Remove the stems from the spinach. Heat the remaining butter in a frying pan until it just starts to lightly color; add the spinach. Insert the prongs of a fork into a clove of garlic and use this to stir the spinach as it cooks. Cook just long enough to soften the spinach.

To serve, carefully arrange some spinach leaves at the edges of each dinner plate, then place the fish in the center of the plate. Season fish with pepper, then spoon over the sauce. Sprinkle chives onto each plate. Serve warm.

Sea bass baked in salt

Bar en croûte de sel

Serves 4:
1 sea bass weighing 4 lbs (1.800 kg) cleaned
 but not scaled
3 ¼ lbs (1.500 kg) coarse sea salt
5 cups (700 g) flour - 8 egg whites

For the butter sauce :
2 shallots, finely sliced - 4 small tomatoes
1 teaspoon coarsely ground or cracked
 pepper
3 tablespoons (5 cl) dry white wine
3 tablespoons (5 cl) white wine vinegar
8 teaspoons (4 cl) heavy cream - salt
1 cup (250 g) butter, softened
4 tablespoons fresh chervil leaves

Place the salt, flour, and egg whites in a mixing bowl and beat to form a soft "dough" (add more egg whites if necessary).

Line a baking dish with aluminum foil, spread a layer of dough ⅛ inch over the foil, (it should be about the length and width of the fish). Place the fish on top of the dough and cover it completely with the remaining dough to seal it inside. Bake in a hot oven (375-400°F/180-200°C) for 25 minutes.

Make a foamy butter sauce as follows: place the shallots, wine, vinegar, and pepper in a small saucepan (preferably an enameled one) and bring to a boil. Once the liquid has reduced by three quarters, add the cream, whisk, and boil for a second or two, then lower the heat and whisk in the butter little by little. Remove from the heat and add salt as needed. Don't strain the sauce when serving with sea bass as cooked here. Place half the sauce in a clean saucepan and add the chervil to it.

When the fish has finished cooking, the dough should have hardened into a crust around it. Cut it open with kitchen scissors and discard the crust. Take the skin off the fish, then remove the bones from the fillets, place the fillets on the dinner plates with a little plain foamy butter sauce on one side and the chervil sauce on the other. Decorate each plate with a little tomato cut to look like a rose, and serve.

Veal steaks with Marsala

Médaillon de veau au Marsala

Serves 4:
4 tenderloin veal steaks, about 6 ½ oz (180 g)
 each
3 tablespoons (5 cl) Marsala
1 truffle weighing 1 oz (30 g), cut into 8 slices
2 tablespoons truffle juice
4 large mushrooms - juice of 1 lemon
4 tablespoons fresh chervil leaves
8 artichoke bottoms, quartered
⅞ cup (200 g) butter
6 tablespoons (60 g) flour - salt and pepper

Cook the mushrooms over high heat in a frying pan with 1 ½ tablespoons of butter and a little lemon juice. Once they have softened, remove from the heat, pour into a sieve, reserving their cooking liquid in a separate bowl. Keep warm. Melt 7 tablespoons butter in a frying pan and cook artichoke bottoms until they have softened and begun to brown. Remove from heat, reserve.

Heat 2 tablespoons butter in another frying pan until it sizzles. Lightly salt and pepper the veal steaks and dust with flour. Cook over low heat for 10 minutes per side, until golden brown. Remove from the pan and keep warm.

Pour off the butter, then pour into the pan the Marsala, truffle juice, the liquid from cooking the mushrooms, and 3 tablespoons of water. Scrape the bottom of the pan to detach the meat juices, then boil the liquid until reduced by half to make the sauce. Once reduced, taste for seasoning, add the remaining butter and the juice of half a lemon. Strain. To serve, place veal on serving platter. Put first two slices of mushroom on each piece of veal then cover this with two slices of truffle. Arrange the other pieces of veal on platter in this manner. Spoon over the sauce. Sprinkle fresh chervil over veal. Garnish with the pieces of artichoke.

Duck breast with lime sauce and peppery pineapple

Magrets de canard au citron vert, compote d'ananas au poivre

Serves 4:
4 large duck breasts, boned
butter for cooking
4 small tomatoes (optional)
a few watercress leaves (optional)

For the sauce:
4¼ cups (1 L) duck stock
⅔ cup (150 g) granulated sugar
⅔ cup (15 cl) white vinegar
juice of 4 limes
salt and pepper

For the pineapple:
2 pineapples
6½ tablespoons (10 cl) white vinegar
3½ tablespoons (5 cl) red wine vinegar
6 tablespoons (80 g) granulated sugar
2 tablespoons (15 g) whole peppercorns

For the candied zest:
zest of 4 limes
zest of 1 orange
equal amounts of sugar and water

Make the sauce as follows: place the vinegar and sugar in a small saucepan and boil until the mixture begins to caramelize. Add the lime juice and cook 10 minutes, then add the duck stock and cook slowly, uncovered, for at least an hour more to reduce. Season with salt and pepper as needed. Reserve.

Cut off all the pineapple rind and any hard spots in the pulp. Cut the pineapple in half lengthwise, then halve each piece lengthwise again. Cut out the hard central core. Save any juices that come from the fruit. Cut the pineapple into large chunks. Place the two kinds of vinegar, the peppercorns and the sugar in a saucepan and simmer for 30 minutes, then add the pineapple and continue cooking for 20 minutes. Remove from the heat and set aside.

Cut the lime zest and orange zest into julienne strips. Make a sugar syrup with equal parts water and sugar. Cook the strips in the sugar syrup until they have softened and become candied. Set aside.

Heat a little butter in a frying pan and cook the duck breasts over low heat for 12 to 15 minutes (they should be rare).

To serve, spoon some sauce onto each plate. Slice the duck breasts and place on top of the sauce, spoon a little sauce over the meat, then sprinkle the candied zest over as well. Place some of the pineapple on each plate and decorate (if desired) with a tomato cut like a flower and some fresh watercress leaves, and serve.

Snow eggs with pink caramelized almonds

Œufs à la neige aux pralines roses

Serves 4:
4¼ cups (1 L) milk
8 egg yolks
8 egg whites
1 vanilla bean
1¾ cups (400 g) granulated sugar
⅔ cup (100 g) pink caramelized almonds

Make the sauce as follows: beat the egg yolks and sugar until the mixture is lemon-colored. In a saucepan, heat ⅓ cup of sugar with the milk and the vanilla bean. Bring to a boil, then pour onto the egg yolk mixture, whisking constantly. Pour the mixture back into the saucepan and reheat, stirring constantly until it reaches 185 °F (85-90 °C); the mixture will coat a spoon when it is cooked enough. Remove from the heat and pour the sauce through a strainer into a clean bowl. Stir the sauce to cool it, then place in the refrigerator.

To cook the egg whites, first beat the whites until they are quite stiff. Fold in ⅓ cup of granulated sugar. Fill a large saucepan two thirds full of water and bring to a boil. Use one or two large spoons to shape the beaten whites into balls, then slide the "eggs" into the water and poach (do not boil) for 1 minute; turn each "egg" over and continue poaching 2 minutes longer. Lift the "eggs" out with a slotted spoon and drain on a clean towel.

To serve, spoon some of the cream onto each plate, place several "snow eggs" on top, and sprinkle with pink caramelized almonds.

Pour a little light caramel made with water and the remaining sugar over each egg, and serve.

LE GRAND VÉFOUR

History and grande cuisine *meet under the arcades of the Palais Royal
in Le Grand Véfour. Raymond Oliver and his chef, Yves Labrousse,
have modernized this Directoire restaurant
and restored it to its ancient glory,
without ever making concessions to passing fashions.*

There are several stories that are told of Le Grand Véfour. All of them relate to that perfect square in the Palais Royal gardens. The columns of its covered walks have lost their past animation. The eccentrically-dressed "Incroyables" and "Merveilleuses" are no longer there, seeking fortune and sometimes finding it, like Joséphine de Beauharnais meeting Bonaparte in the shop of Corcellet, grocer to the Parisian smart set. And yet the charm and the dreamy beauty of the spot remain intact, undisturbed by the solar gun that used to be fired every day at noon.

The first of our stories involves the fantastic growth of gastronomy during the period of transition from monarchy to republic. In the space of thirty years and in an area covering only a few hundred feet, all the great restaurants of the early nineteenth century came into being. All the famous names to which our cuisine owes its renown were to be found under the arcades of Philippe-Egalité: Very, Méot, Les Frères Provençaux, Beauvilliers, Le Bœuf à la Mode and many others. But, above all, there was Le Grand Véfour, the only one to have survived to the present day with its original delightful décor intact. Grimod de la Reynière dined there, as did Fragonard. In fact, the artist ate his last ice cream in the restaurant and Raymond Oliver has honored his memory by featuring on the menu a crêpe bearing his name.

Our second tale concerns history. The history of the Palais Royal is closely intertwined with that of France and Le Grand Véfour. Just reading Raymond Oliver's *Cuisine de Mes Amis* serves to evoke all those who, over the centuries, sat under the restaurant's painted ceilings, dreamily contemplating the glass protecting the silk paintings or the soft light of the gardens and the Galerie de Beaujolais. Jean Cocteau converses with Colette in imaginary dialogues. Balzac dines there. Madame Tallien exercises her feminine wiles on Barras. Everything is frozen in time; the suppers of the modern era are exact duplicates of those of the time of the Directoire. The prestigious restaurant seemed destined to become a culinary waxworks if, in 1948, an exceptional personality, Raymond Oliver, had not undertaken to breathe new life into it.

His tall figure is now slightly stooped and his hair has turned white, but the inimitable husky southwestern accent and the magnetism have not diminished. Raymond Oliver was a television pioneer with his series of highly popular cooking lessons. It was in large measure due to him that the very personal cuisine

he proposed remained an unrestricted one, mixing the modern with the traditional, the *blanquette de volaille* in the old manner, the *petits légumes* (mixed garden vegetables), which twenty years later have become popular dishes. We are indebted to him for the current *grande cuisine* passion, and the pursuit of the joys of the table that has seized our contemporaries. It was he who forced chefs to become stars. Paul Bocuse simply expanded the phenomenon. Raymond Oliver never allowed himself to become giddy with his success. He served only one mistress – *la cuisine.* All the while he crisscrossed the globe, assembling a fabulous culinary library (around 6,000 volumes), Oliver created a new-style cuisine. Others rushed to follow the trail blazed by him. The Véfour was duplicated in London, Tokyo, and Stockholm. This passion for cuisine runs in the Oliver family. His son Michel succeeded him on television and created Les Bistrots de Paris restaurants. His daughter, Stéphane, now operates the marvelous Petite Cour restaurant, and his grandson is already well launched on a culinary career. And Raymond, who has trained so many great chefs, continues to inspire the cuisine of Yves Labrousse, the current chef at the Véfour. Like so many others at the restaurant, Labrousse has spent his entire professional career there. Starting as a busboy, he made his way up the ladder and today he is master of the Véfour's kitchens. The same path has been followed by the wine stewards and the headwaiters. François Mesnage, now director of Le Grand Véfour, has never worked anywhere else. Such fidelity can become a consuming passion, as evidenced by Guy Courtois, who has set himself the task of writing a history of the Véfour, working at it with the diligence of a medieval monk. Yves Labrousse, therefore, has the responsibility of continuing in the footsteps of Oliver.

The *Guide Michelin's* unjust sanction at the time of the "changing of the guard" at Le Grand Véfour has in no way diminished the enthusiasm of its customers faithful to the *cassolette de homard Palais-Royal* or *côtes d'agneau Albarine* (small lamb chops stuffed with foie gras and veal kidneys in a casing braised in a white wine, cream, and shallot sauce). Honey vinegar, sweet garlic, and lamprey are a few of the products rediscovered by Raymond Oliver. And the *œuf au plat Louis Oliver* (fried egg), created in memory of his father, modified and codified by Raymond Oliver as a gesture of filial devotion, is the favorite dish of Langon, his home town.

MAISON FONDÉE EN 1760

3 17 rue de Beaujolais 75001 Paris (air-conditioned, dogs not allowed). Closed in August, Saturday nights from September 1 to April 30, and Sundays from April 30 to September 1. Must-see sights: the Palais Royal, the arcades and the gardens, the old streets of the neighborhood, notably the covered passages (Choiseul, Véro-Dodat), the Louvre palace and museum, the Decorative Arts museum, the Tuileries gardens, the Carousel Triumphal Arch, the Molière Fountain, and the theatre of the Comédie Française. AE cards honored
Tel.(1) 296.56.27

Oliver also displays this fidelity as regards the wines of Bordeaux and especially to the admirable Sauternes of his childhood. The light at Le Grand Véfour seems to take on the color and glints of an Yquem. "The culinary art has the poignancy of the ephemeral," wrote Raymond Oliver, regretting the oblivion into which the great chefs sink after their moment of glory. But this would be setting little value on Raymond Oliver's contribution to the art of the cuisine, his writings and Le Grand Véfour.

At the time of their recent acquisition of this admirable establishment, the Taittinger group stated their intention to maintain the restaurant's unique character while giving it the means for surpassing itself and being inventive. Raymond Oliver remains honorary president of Le Grand Véfour, a restaurant which he brought back to life.

In this miraculously preserved setting opening onto the gardens of the Palais Royal, painted ceilings and silk paintings recreate the charm and elegance of time past. But time has not stopped with the Directoirate and the fall of the Empire. In the cellars of Le Grand Véfour, the wines from La Guyenne, particular favorites of Raymond Oliver, are the objects of special care by Dominique Derozier, the wine steward.

Frogs' legs soufflé

Soufflé de grenouilles

Serves 4:
7 oz (200 g) frogs' legs
½ cup (85 g) flour
6 ½ tablespoons (100 g) butter, total
5 egg yolks
5 egg whites
6 ½ tablespoons (10 cl) dry white wine
3 ¼ cups (75 cl) fish stock
4 shallots, finely sliced
1 small bouquet garni
salt and pepper

For the Poulette sauce:
6 ½ tablespoons (10 cl) dry white wine
2 generous cups (50 cl) fish stock
3 egg yolks
¾ cup (20 cl) heavy cream
1 tablespoon finely chopped fresh herbs
   (parsley, chervil, chives, tarragon, etc.,
   mixed together)
salt and pepper

Melt a tablespoon of butter in a saucepan, add the shallots, and cook over low heat for 5 minutes. Add the frogs' legs, salt, and pepper and continue cooking over moderate heat 5 minutes more. Add the white wine and boil to reduce by half, then add the fish stock (or water) and the bouquet garni. Simmer for 5 minutes then lift out the frogs' legs with a slotted spoon and drain. While still warm carefully remove the bones.

In a clean saucepan melt ⅓ cup butter and stir in ⅓ cup flour. Once the flour begins to brown, pour the strained cooking liquid from the frogs' legs into the pan little by little, whisking constantly as it is being added. Cook a minute or two, then remove the pan from the heat and beat in the egg yolks one by one. Beat the egg whites until stiff, then fold them carefully into the soufflé base, which should have cooled until it is just warm.

Lightly butter individual soufflé dishes; dust the side of each dish with a little flour, then spoon in some of the soufflé mixture. Place some of the boned leg meat into each dish, and finish filling with the soufflé mixture (you can make more layers if you prefer, but end with the soufflé mixture).

Cook the soufflés in a 475 °F (250 °C) oven for 12 minutes.

Make the Poulette sauce as follows: place the white wine and fish stock in a saucepan, bring to a boil, and allow to reduce by two thirds. In a mixing bowl, beat the egg yolks and cream together. When the wine-stock mixture has reduced, remove it from the heat and whisk in the egg-cream mixture. Season with salt and pepper, return to low heat, and cook gently, stirring constantly, for about 5 minutes, or until the sauce has thickened enough to lightly coat the spoon. Do not allow to boil. Strain into a sauceboat and stir in the finely chopped herbs.

When the soufflés are done, remove them from the oven, spoon a little of the sauce over each one, and serve immediately with the rest of the sauce on the side.

Puff pastry with oysters, scallops, and spinach

Feuilleté d'huîtres et de Saint-Jacques aux épinards

Serves 4:
10 ½ oz (300 g) puff pastry
½ lb (250 g) fresh spinach,
   stemmed and washed
32 fresh oysters
8 large sea scallops, preferably with coral
   still attached
3 tablespoons (5 cl) white vermouth
2 generous cups (50 cl) fish stock
⅞ cup (20 cl) heavy cream
2 teaspoons flour
3 tablespoons (40 g) butter
3 egg yolks
salt and pepper

Roll out the puff pastry and cut it into pieces the shape and size of a scallop shell. Brush the pastries with one egg yolk beaten with a spoonful of water then place them on a greased and lightly floured baking sheet and bake in a 450 °F (240 °C) oven for 20 minutes.

While the pastry is cooking, put the spinach in a large pot of salted water. As soon as the water comes back to a boil after adding the spinach, drain it and cool it in cold running water. Squeeze out all the water from the spinach, put it into a saucepan with a tablespoon of butter, and keep warm.

Heat the fish stock in a saucepan with the vermouth; do not let it boil. Add the scallops and the oysters and poach for a few seconds only, then lift out both and keep warm while making the sauce. Boil the liquid in the saucepan over high heat to reduce by three quarters; add the cream and cook a minute or two more, then, off the heat, whisk in the remaining two egg yolks. Heat the sauce to warm but do not boil.

To serve, cut each piece of pastry in half horizontally through the middle and place the bottom half on each dinner plate. Cover the pastry with spinach, then place the oysters and scallops on top and spoon some of the sauce over them. Cover with the top piece of pastry, then place the dinner plates in a very hot oven for a few seconds to reheat, and serve.

Another way of serving this dish is first to place the spinach on the plates, then fill each pastry scallop with the seafood and spoon over the sauce; in this case the plates should be placed quickly under a broiler to brown the sauce lightly, as shown in the photo.

Filet mignon with green pepper sauce

Mignonettes au poivre vert

<u>Serves 4:</u>
8 small filets mignons (about 3 oz (70 g) each)
4 teaspoons cognac
2 carrots, finely sliced
2 onions, finely sliced
3 tomatoes, peeled, seeded, and chopped
1 tablespoon flour
1 bouquet garni
2 cups (50 cl) water
6 ½ tablespoons (10 cl) white wine
4 ½ teaspoons (25 g) green peppercorns
4 ½ tablespoons (65 g) butter
salt

Make a vegetable stock as follows: heat 2 tablespoons of butter in a saucepan, add the carrots and onions and lightly brown. Sprinkle a little flour into the pan and stir to combine, then add tomatoes, bouquet garni, wine, and water. Salt lightly but do not add pepper; simmer the stock for 1 hour over low heat, then strain and reserve.

Gently crush the green peppercorns with a rolling pin. Salt the steaks, then roll them in the peppercorns. Heat a tablespoon of butter in a frying pan and cook the steaks over high heat just long enough to brown well on both sides, if you like your steak very rare.

Place the steaks on hot dinner plates and add the cognac to the pan they cooked in; boil to reduce, then add 1 ⅓ cups of the stock prepared earlier and continue boiling to reduce still more. Take the pan off the heat and whisk in the remaining butter, then spoon this over the steaks and serve, garnished with souffléed potatoes.

Oriental oranges

Oranges orientales

<u>Serves 4:</u>
4 large oranges
1 ¼ cups (250 g) granulated sugar
1 cup (25 cl) water
4 tablespoons (6 cl) kirsch or Cointreau
2 tablespoons (3 cl) grenadine
8 candied violets

Remove the zest from 4 large oranges and cut them into thin julienne strips. Place the zests in a saucepan with cold water, bring to a boil, then drain immediately. Cool the zests under cold running water then place them in a clean saucepan with the sugar and 1 cup cold water. Heat the water until it almost boils, then reduce the heat and simmer until the syrup has thickened and the zests have softened. Remove from the heat and let the syrup cool a short time before adding the kirsch or Cointreau and the grenadine (for color).

Finish peeling the oranges completely and cut each in half through the middle. Remove any seeds and the whitish core, then place them in a bowl with the syrup and candied zest and leave to marinate in the refrigerator for several hours before serving.

To serve, place two orange halves on each plate, spoon over the syrup and the zests, and decorate with candied violets just before serving.

HÔTEL DE CRILLON

*Behind the noble façade of the Crillon
on the Place de la Concorde is one of the most luxurious
and refined hotels in Paris. In the patio,
Chef Jean-Paul Bonin and his second-in-command, André Signoret,
take a breather.*

There are two or three spots in the world that are famous for their architecture and their history. The Place de la Concorde is one of them. The superb view of the Seine, the admirable stretch of the Champs-Elysées prolonging the vista from the Louvre and the Tuileries gardens or that from the Palais Bourbon on the other side of the Concorde bridge toward the Eglise de la Madeleine closing off the upper end of the elegant rue Royale, fitted in between the Corinthian columns of the two palaces designed by Gabriel, all belong to the common heritage of mankind. And the Obelisk of Luxor erected in the middle of the Place like a pointer in the center of Paris, regulates, day and night, the continuous swirl of traffic, lights, and noises.

The colonnaded Hotel Crillon, gabled pavilion with a triangular pediment decorated with allegorical figures, occupies the western portion of the Place at the corner of the rue Boissy d'Anglas. Behind this façade, the architect, Louis Trouard, constructed a sumptuously decorated town house. For a time the building was rented to the Duc d'Aumont, but in 1788 it became the property of François Félix Dorothée de Berton de Balbes, Comte de Crillon. Except for the period of emigration following the Revolution, the Crillon family remained the owners. In 1902, the building was purchased by the Société du Louvre, now controlled by the Taittinger Group, and they converted it into the most luxurious hotel in Paris. This aristocratic residence, with its sumptuously decorated and furnished rooms and suites, its salons with their gilded walls and ceilings, unique examples of eighteenth-century decorative art, has been the site of the most important international conferences, and host to kings and heads of state from all over the world. It is one of the last great Parisian hotels still under French ownership.

Is this the reason why in the former Salon des Ambassadeurs, with its indefinable air of Paris during the Age of Enlightenment, the restaurant of the Hôtel de Crillon seems to be the quintessence of several arts?

The immaculate whiteness of the tablecloths, exquisite china of Sonia Rykiel, and sparkling silverware reflect the candlelight and centuries of good living. The balletlike comings and goings of the headwaiters and waiters in their frock coats and white gloves add a touch of the unreal to the elegance of the dining room that looks out on the Place through its high windows. The second Michelin Star recently awarded was fully merited, if a little slow in coming. Jean-Paul Bonin, the chef, and his team of thirty-five cooks and bakers have made a habit of collecting honors and winning competitions.

Bonin, a bearded thirty-seven-year-old Burgundian, has behind him a long career of service in prestigious restaurants. The Richmond in Geneva, the Réserve in Beaulieu, the Pavillon Henri IV, Lamazère, Le Relais Bisson, and Le Bristol in Paris are a few in which he displayed his talents. For him and his second-in-command, André Signoret, the important things are to transform produce without altering its taste and that "cuisine is a moment of joy that is offered to the diner." The choice of produce, which is made according to the season, and its appearance, since the cuisine of Jean-Paul Bonin is also a feast for the eyes, play a very important role in the preparation of a meal. Thus, the goat cheeses will be purchased directly from a famous goat-raising farm specializing in them at Hurigny in Burgundy, and the fish will be the most beautiful ones to be had at the now-central markets of Rungis. And the reception and the inspection of the various purchases make for a most impressive ceremony.

Desiring to transmit his sensitivity to others and to bring it into harmony with the service offered, especially as regards the wines, performed brilliantly by wine steward Jean-Claude Maitre, Bonin has known how to gather around him a solidly reliable team on which various members (assistants, busboys, or waiters), perhaps in imitation of him, are also bearded.

Philippe Roche, the guiding spirit of this hotel, a discreet and elegant Parisian trained in the world's most important luxury hotels, is the dynamic force behind the rebirth of the Crillon. Knowing the importance of its table to a hotel's success, he, a fine gourmet, has placed his full confidence in Bonin. The Maître Cuisiniers association selected Bonin as the Chef of the Year in his first year at the Crillon. Inventiveness, lightness, prevailing naturalness, delicacy, and cooking precision are the attributes of his cuisine. Rediscovering through a reading of Edouard Nignon a *brouet de homard au fumet de truffes* (a lobster dish scented with truffles) or creating a *mousse de gingembre à la mangue et baies de cassis* (a ginger mousse with mangoes and black-currant berries), Bonin has proved himself to be one of the masters in the new generation of chefs, restoring the taste for gastronomy to the Crillon's faithful clients. Rarely has such an outpouring of joy greeted an event, bearing witness to the esteem felt by all.

*Reflected in the glass doors of the Hôtel de
Crillon are the dome of the Invalides and a
glimpse of the Place de la Concorde, graced by
Gabriel's two palaces, with their classical lines of
colonnades and gabled wings. In the gilded and
marbled precincts of the Salon des Ambassadeurs,
now serving as the hotel's dining room, the
balletlike precision of the headwaiters on Jean-
Paul Bonin's team is also impressive to behold.*

4   10 Place de la Concorde 75008 Paris (air
conditioned, 159 rooms, 46 suites, rooms
for receptions and seminars, dogs admitted at extra charge). Open all year. To be
seen nearby: the Place de la Concorde and
the famous view of the Champs-Elysées,
the Tuileries gardens, the Jeu de Paume
museum (with its collection of im-
pressionist paintings) and the Louvre
Museum. The visitor can admire the window displays and buy gifts on rue Tron-
chet, rue de Rivoli, and rue du Faubourg
Saint-Honoré.
AE - Diners - Visa cards honored
Tél. (1) 265 24 24

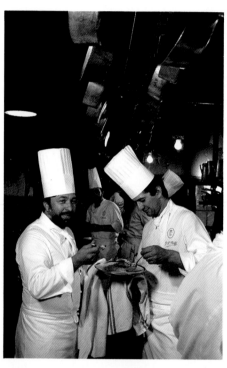

Red and white quail eggs in cream sauce with herbs

Crème fines herbes aux œufs de caille et vin rouge

Serves 4:
24 quail eggs
1 cup (25 cl) chicken stock
1 egg yolk
6 ½ tablespoons (10 cl) whipped cream
4 tablespoons freshly chopped chives and
  chervil, mixed
¾ cup (20 cl) red wine
¾ cup (20 cl) water
2 teaspoons white vinegar
1 tomato - salt and pepper
chives, to garnish

Place the egg yolk and the chicken stock in a saucepan and heat gently, whisking constantly, to thicken. Do not allow to boil. Once the sauce has thickened, pour it into a mixing bowl and continue whisking over ice until it has cooled completely; then fold in the whipped cream and freshly chopped herbs.
Poach half of the quail eggs in a saucepan with red wine and the other half in a saucepan with the water and vinegar. Poach the eggs a total of 1 minute then lift out and drain on a clean towel.
Peel and seed the tomato and cut it into julienne strips.
To serve, spoon some of the sauce onto each of the dinner plates then place six eggs on each plate, alternating the red eggs with the white. Garnish the plates with the tomato strips and a few sprigs of chive and serve.

Porgy with garlic and tomato sauce

Daurade rôtie à l'ail doux, sauce vierge

Serves 4:
2 sea bream/or porgies weighing about
  1 ½ lbs (700 g) each
3 medium tomatoes
4 heads garlic
⅞ cup (20 cl) olive oil
1 bunch fresh basil
⅞ cup (20 cl) fish stock
salt and pepper

Fillet the fish and place them in a dish with half the olive oil, add several sprigs of fresh basil, and marinate for 1 hour.
Make a tomato sauce. Peel and seed the tomatoes. Work half of them through a sieve to make a fine puree and chop the rest coarsely, using a knife. Place all the tomatoes in a saucepan with the remaining olive oil, four or five basil leaves finely sliced, three cloves of garlic finely chopped, salt and pepper. Place the saucepan in a larger pot full of hot water (a bain-marie) and simmer the tomatoes very gently so that they will slowly warm through but not cook.
Peel the remaining cloves of garlic and drop them into a pot of boiling water; cook until soft, then drain.
Boil the fish stock rapidly to reduce and thicken to a glaze, then roll the cooked garlic cloves in the glaze to coat them.
Cook the fish fillets in a roasting pan in a very hot oven for 7 minutes, basting them with their marinade as they cook.
Spoon some of the tomato sauce onto each dinner plate, place the fish next to it, garnish with the whole cloves of garlic, and serve.
Note: snow peas quickly blanched or lightly sautéed can also be used as a garnish as shown in the photo.

Turbot with lobster mousse and cabbage

Blanc de turbot rôti, mousseline de homard

Serves 4:
4 lb (1.800 kg) turbot, filleted
1 lb (450 g) lobster
6 ½ tablespoons (10 cl) heavy cream
1 egg yolk
3 ½ tablespoons (50 g) clarified butter
salt and pepper
1 shallot
1 tablespoon (15 g) butter
⅞ cup (20 cl) fish stock
6 ½ tablespoons (10 cl) whipped cream
1 lb (400 g) green cabbage
3 tablespoons (5 cl) vinaigrette, made with
    walnut oil
chervil

Make a lobster sauce as follows: after boiling your lobster, remove the meat from the tail and claws and save the shells. Use the meat for making the mousse and the shells to flavor the sauce. Coarsely chop the shells with a cleaver and lightly brown them in a saucepan with a little butter, then add the shallot and fish stock. Cook for 5 minutes, then strain the sauce into a clean saucepan, add the cream, and whisk in the butter little by little. Keep warm but do not boil.
Steam the cabbage and slice fine.
Make the lobster mousse. Work the lobster meat through a sieve into a bowl over ice. Stir in the egg yolk then gently fold in the whipped cream. Season with salt and pepper. Used clarified butter to lightly grease four individual dishes of a capacity of about 3 tablespoons each. Fill them with the mousse and place them in a baking dish full of boiling water (the water should come halfway up the sides of the dishes). Bake in a slow oven for 12 minutes. Brush the turbot fillets with the remaining clarified butter, place them on a grill in a roasting pan and bake slowly, basting frequently. Reheat the cabbage by steaming again quickly, then season it with a vinaigrette made with walnut oil.

To serve, turn out the mousses onto the dinner plates, place the cabbage around them, and the turbot around that. Spoon some of the sauce onto each plate, decorate with fresh chervil, and serve.

Lamb with zucchini and tomatoes

Jumelé d'agneau, corolle de courgettes et tomates

Serves 4:
4 slices of lamb from the filet,
    about 3 oz (80 g) each
4 rib lamb chops
2 zucchini (courgettes)
2 tomatoes, peeled and seeded
2 heads garlic
⅔ cup (150 g) butter
1 ⅔ cups (40 cl) lamb stock
4 tablespoons heavy cream
thyme
salt and pepper · chervil

Slice the zucchini into ¾ inch-thick slices and drop into a pot of lightly salted boiling water. Boil for a minute or two, then cool in icewater and drain.
Slice the tomatoes. Lightly butter 4 small baking dishes and fill each one with overlapping pieces of zucchini and tomato. Season with salt, pepper, thyme, and a tablespoon of cream each, then bake uncovered in a moderate oven.
Peel the cloves of garlic, drop them into rapidly boiling water, then drain immediately. Place them in a saucepan with enough of the lamb stock to barely cover, and cook slowly until the stock has reduced and glazes the garlic.
Heat 6 ½ tablespoons of butter in a large frying pan and cook the lamb just long enough to brown nicely on both sides (it should be served rare). Remove from the pan and

keep warm. Pour back into the pan any juices that come from the meat and add the rest of the lamb stock, scraping the bottom of the pan with a wooden spoon. Boil to reduce, then whisk in the remaining butter little by little.
To serve, slide the vegetables from the baking dishes onto each plate; place one piece of each cut of lamb on each plate, and garnish with the garlic. Spoon over the sauce, garnish with chervil and serve.
Note: the photo shows another version of this recipe made by roasting a lamb tenderloin, slicing it, and serving it with a sauce made by deglazing the roasting pan. Here fresh broad beans are used as a garnish instead of garlic.

MAXIM'S

*Pierre Cardin has taken on the task of preserving the monument the world
knows as Maxim's. He has renovated, redecorated,
and at times imitated, with exceptional success,
the establishment on the Rue Royale. But he wisely chose not to try to give
new costumes to its famous pages and doormen.*

Its very name evokes something delightfully naughty in the minds of beautiful women all over the world. Ever since Franz Lehar set one of the acts of *The Merry Widow* in its dining rooms and Georges Feydeau created that incredible character La Môme Crevette, *La Dame de Chez Maxim's,* innumerable films and plays have used the restaurant as their setting or simply cited its name. The Maxim's legend, often intertwined with history, evokes for us the marvelous way of life during *La Belle Epoque,* the frock coats and white ties of Sem's sketches, the beauties, trailing the scent of ilang-ilang behind them as they pass in their Worth, Paquin, or Poiret gowns, names like Liane de Pougy, Emilienne d'Alençon, Caroline Ortero or Irma de Montigny, on whom the dandies and Jockey Club members lavished or exhausted their fortunes.

The legend is also the astounding rise of the former café of Maxime Gaillard. Americanized into Maxim's by Arnold de Contades on the night of the Prix de Diane horse race (May 20, 1893), the restaurant quickly became *the* place to which one had to go and be seen. Anyone who was anyone simply had to be a "maximilian." Nothing has changed. The current personification of the legend is Roger Viard ("dear Roger"), unforgettable successor to Albert as the director of Maxim's. His has been a career devoted to the subtle game of deciding which diner took precedence over another, the creation of a special atmosphere, the way of setting up a dining room, the art of focusing attention on the beautiful women present, the task of assigning each diner according to his merits to the grill, the bar, or the "Omnibus." He still keeps a weather eye on the correct elegance of the arriving guests. It is a life that barely left its mark upon him save for a graying at the temples and perhaps an increased irony and urbanity in his look as reflected in the restaurant's frieze of mirrors.

The literary aspect of the legend runs from Alphonse Allais to Françoise Sagan; the show business world gathers at Maxim's to celebrate opening nights or Golden Record awards. The beautiful interior decoration of Louis Marnez, the bronze leafwork of Alexandre Brosset, the copper vines and plants of Léon Souvier have been restored to their original sparkle. The cloth-backed wall paintings filled with nymphs, dancing figures, fruits and flower-bedecked pools have recovered their original freshness and the ceilings are just so many mirrors to reflect the glances of the beautiful women diners and the light of the small rose-colored lamps on each table. Following in the wake of the

fifty-year reign of the Vaudables, the new monarch is Pierre Cardin. It is comforting to know that two such monuments as Maxim's and the Château Margaux vintage wines have been conserved, nay saved, by two foreigners concerned with preserving the heritage of France. What André Mentzelopoulos did for the top-rated Château Margaux vintage, Pierre Cardin, couturier of genius of Italian descent, is doing for the culinary landmark on the rue Royale. The visitor is so impressed with the imitations truer-than-the-original Cardin has had made for the second and third floors and by silver art objects from his own collection in the display cases that he or she would be willing to swear that everything at Maxim's dates from *La Belle Epoque.* Nowadays, it is fashionable, especially when one has never been there and undoubtedly will never go, to mutter that people go to Maxim's not so much to dine as to be seen. This sort of talk is an insult to the memory of Alex Humbert, chef at Maxim's for decades. And it enrages Michel Menant, Humbert's successor, who worked with him from 1964 to 1968. Menant was with the great Soustelle at Lucas Carton, as well as working at the Normandy in Deauville. The Club des Cent, which conferred a certificate of excellence on Menant and whose members regularly dine at Maxim's, is not the type of organization to award honors to just anyone. Were these highly strict judges seduced by the quail's eggs with caviar, *la crème de tortue blond au coulis de tomate,* the surprising mixture of shellfish and sole fillets in truffle sauce, the highly classic Bresse fowl with fresh morel mushrooms in cream sauce? Or did they adore the daring of the Bresse fowl with cucumbers or the rustic quality of the duckling cooked in cider with Normandy apples or were they lost in reverie before a *crêpe Veuve Joyeuse* (Merry Widow pancake)? I, for one, believe they simply appreciated the way that the great classic dishes of Maxim's could have been lightened and modernized while respecting their essential qualities just as is done in the theatre with the great authors. And what restaurant is more theatrical than Maxim's? Being chosen or recognized by Roger Viard has just as much importance as it did in the era of Albert.

The faces change but not the names. The grandsons come to dine where their grandfathers did, the beautiful women are as numerous as in the past. Dior and Cardin gowns have replaced those of Worth and Poiret, but our new crop of beauties have the same look about them. The mahogany-paneled walls glow

Roger Viard, successor to Albert as director of Maxim's, and chef Michel Menant have succeeded in winning the complete confidence of Pierre Cardin. Knowing the courtesy of the first and the skills and talent of the second, this is not surprising. Be it in the "Omnibus" or in the dining rooms with their marvelous Belle Epoque decorations, the spirit of Maxim's has been preserved and even magnified. Everything at Maxim's encourages participation in the festivities: the soft lamplight so flattering to the women's faces, the mahogany and lacquered interior decorations, and the host of waiters ready to serve the restaurant's renowned dishes.

5   3 rue Royale 75008 Paris (air-conditioned, dogs not allowed). Closed on Sundays. Must-see sights nearby: the rue Royale, the Madeleine Church, the Place de la Concorde, the Tuileries Gardens, the splendid view offered by the Champs-Elysées, the Grands Boulevards, the Place Vendôme with the shops of world-famed jewelers, the Opéra, constructed by Charles Garnier, symbol of the Napoleon III style, with its Chagall ceiling, and the Louvre Palace with its museum, one of the largest in the world.
AE - Visa - Diners cards honored
Tel: (1) 265.27.94

softly and, as Paul Valéry put it, the beveled mirrors reflect "the glaucous light evoking a submarine stranded on the sea bottom."

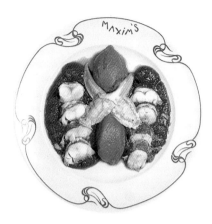

Lobster with bell pepper mousse and tomato sauce

Médaillon de homard à la mousse de poivrons

Serves 4:
4 lobsters about 1 lb (400 g) each
2 lbs (800 g) green bell peppers
1 lb (500 g) tomatoes
6 ½ tablespoons (10 cl) heavy cream, whipped
6 ½ tablespoons (10 cl) olive oil
3 sprigs fresh basil
4 qts (4 L) court bouillon
salt and pepper

Drop the lobster headfirst into a large pot of rapidly boiling court bouillon. Bring back to a boil and cook for 5 minutes. Remove the pot from the heat and leave the lobsters in the liquid until they cool and can be handled easily. Remove the meat from the shells.

Seed and slice the bell peppers, then cook them in a frying pan with a tablespoon of oil. Once the peppers have softened, puree them in a blender. Sieve the puree and season with salt and pepper. Once the puree has cooled completely, place it over ice and carefully fold in the whipped cream. This must be done over ice so that the cream holds its shape.

Peel, seed, and chop the tomatoes. Cook them in a saucepan with a tablespoon of olive oil. Once they are soft, work them through a sieve and leave to cool before seasoning with freshly chopped basil, salt, pepper and the remaining olive oil.

To serve, cut the lobster tail into thick slices (about ¼ inch thick) and slice the claw meat (or leave whole, if preferred). Use a tablespoon to form the pepper mousse into egglike-shapes and place them on the dinner plates. Spoon the tomato sauce around the mousse, put the pieces of lobster on top of it, then serve.

Duck with raspberry vinegar, turnips, and glazed onions

Caneton au vinaigre de framboises avec petits navets et oignons en compote

Serves 4:
2 ducks weighing about 5 ½ lbs (2.500 kg) each
4 ¼ cups (1 L) duck stock
2 cups (200 g) raspberries
2 shallots, finely chopped
2 ¼ lbs (1 kg) turnips, peeled
1 lb (400 g) baby onions, peeled
⅔ cup (15 cl) raspberry vinegar (or sherry vinegar)
6 ½ tablespoons (100 g) butter
7 teaspoons granulated sugar (8 sugar lumps) (for onions)
2 tablespoons granulated sugar (for turnips)
salt and pepper

Roast the ducks for about 35 minutes; they will still be rare inside. Slice off the breast meat and cut off the legs and thighs. Keep warm.

Melt a tablespoon of butter in a large pot, add the duck carcasses and shallots. Cook over moderate heat to lightly brown, then deglaze the pot with half the raspberry vinegar. Scrape to detach any meat juices on the bottom of the pot, then add the duck stock and boil to reduce by half. Add the fresh raspberries and continue cooking until the sauce has a nice color.

In the meantime, thinly slice the turnips and cook them in 3 ½ tablespoons of butter and 1 tablespoon of sugar, salt, pepper, and a little water until they are soft.

Cook the onions just like the turnips but remove them from the pan when they are only halfway done. Add to the pan 7 teaspoons of sugar and boil to make a syrup. Place the onions back in the pan with the remaining vinegar and finish cooking and glazing.

Just before serving, place the breast meat and the legs of the duck on a charcoal grill (or under the broiler) with the skin facing the flame to brown nicely.

Serve the pieces of duck on dinner plates surrounded by the glazed onions and turnips. Spoon over the sauce and serve.

"Merry widow" crêpes

Crêpes "Veuve Joyeuse"

Serves 6:

For the batter:
½ cup (75 g) flour
1 tablespoon (15 g) granulated sugar
2 ½ tablespoons (35 g) butter, melted
2 eggs
1 cup (25 cl) warm milk
pinch of salt

For the filling:
3 tablespoons (30 g) flour
1 heaped cup (220 g) granulated sugar
1 cup (25 cl) milk
1 vanilla bean
3 large lemons
3 egg yolks
8 egg whites

Make a crêpe batter by whisking together the flour, sugar, eggs, and salt. Pour in the warm milk and continue whisking until smooth. Lastly, stir in the melted butter. Leave the batter to rest for at least an hour before making the crêpes.

Make the crêpes in small (6-inch) crêpe pans; it will be unnecessary to grease the pans because of the butter in the batter. Keep the crêpes warm once they are cooked.

Remove the zest from the lemons and chop fine. Squeeze the lemons and place the chopped zest in the juice for 15 minutes, then drain.

Make a pastry cream as follows: place the vanilla bean in the milk, bring to a boil and leave to infuse for about 5 minutes. Beat the sugar and the egg yolks until the mixture is lemon-colored, stir in the flour, then whisk in the hot milk little by little. Add the zest, place the mixture in a saucepan, and boil for 1 minute, stirring constantly. Remove the vanilla bean and place the cream in a large mixing bowl. Stir occasionally as it cools. Beat the egg whites until stiff and carefully fold them into the cream once it has cooled.

Fill each crêpe with some of the cream and fold to enclose, as shown in the photo. Place them on a lightly buttered baking sheet and bake in a 425 °F (220 °C) oven for 8 minutes. Serve straight from the oven.

Tulip pastries with raspberry mousse filling

Mousse glacée à la framboise, servie en tulipes

Serves 12:

For the pastry:
1 ½ cups (200 g) flour
1 ½ cups (200 g) confectioner's sugar
½ cup (125 g) butter, melted
6 egg whites

For the mousse:
8 egg yolks
scant 2 cups (400 g) granulated sugar
⅔ cup (15 cl) water
2 ¼ cups (600 g) pureed raspberries
  (or wild strawberries)
3 ⅓ cups (80 cl) heavy cream
1 teaspoon powdered vanilla
1 cup (25 cl) raspberry
  (or wild strawberry) sauce
raspberries (or wild strawberries)
  to garnish

Begin by making the tulip pastries. Sift the flour into a mixing bowl and whisk in the confectioner's sugar and egg whites, working the batter as little as possible. Last, whisk in the melted butter to make a smooth batter.

Make twelve thin crêpe-like circles of the batter, approximately 6 inches across, on a lightly buttered baking sheet. Bake in a 475 °F (250 °C) oven for 5 to 10 minutes (the edges of each pastry should just begin to brown). Shape the pastries into cup-like tulips as soon as they come from the oven. To do this, place a hot pastry over a glass or bowl that has been turned upside down. Cover with a slightly larger glass or bowl. It takes only a minute for the pastry to stiffen. Remove it from under the glass and continue shaping the pastries in this manner. To make a raspberry mousse for filling the tulips, first boil the sugar and water in a saucepan until the syrup registers 240 °F (115 °C) on a candy thermometer (soft-ball stage).

Beat the egg yolks and carefully pour the hot sugar syrup onto them, whisking constantly. Continue whisking until the mixture cools, then stir in the pureed raspberries and vanilla.

Beat the cream until stiff, then fold it gently into the raspberry mixture. Place in the freezer for 30 to 40 minutes before serving.

To serve, whisk the cream once or twice, then spoon it into a pastry bag and pipe it into the tulip pastries. Garnish with some fresh raspberries and serve with a bowl of raspberry sauce on the side or simply as is.

TAILLEVENT

Jean-Claude Vrinat is identified in people's minds with Taillevent,
and the sober elegance of the restaurant
owner harmonizes with the very pure lines of the town house
on the rue Lamennais. He has succeeded in maintaining this beautiful
establishment at the pinnacle of excellence.

"In Taillevent let us see where he speaks of fricassee." Thus spoke François Villon. The fact that one of France's earliest culinary writers is cited and glorified by one of its greatest poets is ample proof of the importance of Guillaume Tirel, known as Taillevent. It follows, then, that it is only natural for one of the country's finest restaurants to be named after him. This temple of cuisine, installed in a town house, pays a further tribute by featuring on its menu a *blanc-manger* (blancmange) taken out of Taillevent's *Le Viandier*. Nobility is the first word that comes to mind when speaking both about the restaurant and its owner, Jean-Claude Vrinat. It was Jean-Claude Vrinat's father, an omnivorous reader of ancient works on cuisine, who decided to call his restaurant on rue Saint-Georges *Le Taillevent*. The restaurant's success helped him to decide in 1950 to move to larger, more luxurious quarters in an elegant town house near the Place de l'Etoile. Constructed by the Duc de Morny, the half-brother of Napoleon III, the building was for a time the Uruguayan embassy. Thus, diplomats stationed in Paris were well aware of its location. The same held true for the restaurant guides. Michelin awarded it a second star in 1954 and a third one in 1973. These honors were a just reward for an astonishing team – Jean-Claude Vrinat and his chef, Claude Deligne. At the outset however, Jean-Claude Vrinat seemed destined for a totally different career. Holder of a diploma from France's most distinguished business schools, he could have easily become a higher-echelon executive with a large company. But his love for cuisine won out. And yet when you enter Taillevent, you are won over by his air of being a cabinet minister's right-hand man or a top official at some multinational. Smiling, elegant, his face adorned by a pair of tortoise-shell-rimmed glasses, he is the perfect host. He is also a fine gourmet and a highly demanding wine connoisseur, as is proved by his perfect cellar, rich in quality but reasonable in price.

Like his father, he also reads the great culinary writers in search of ideas. The *cervelas de fruits de mer aux truffes et aux pistaches* (mixed seafood with truffles and pistachio nuts) hardly sounds like a creation of Antonin Carême, but it is. Aided by the culinary skill of Deligne, Vrinat has purified, lightened, and transformed it. Claude Deligne is an exceptional individual. Originally from Bordeaux, the fortyish chef has excellent restaurant credentials. His father was a pastry-cook under the father of Raymond Oliver, Louis. Deligne worked in a whole series of renowned but terrifying establishments at a time when such an apprenticeship was just a cut above penal servitude. Times have changed. Today chefs have a right to speak out about how a restaurant should be run. And Deligne takes full advantage of this right. His approach to the classic dishes, his way of simplifying them, of modernizing them in the finest sense of this word constitute the great force of his talent. The continuity and the afterglow of a cuisine antedating the Medicis are not limited at the Taillevent to a *blanc-manger*. Here and there the menu also proposes a Regency sauce, a walnut oil salad dressing gives an old-fashioned flavor to a golden liver mousse. Herbs like lemon balm, tarragon, or fresh mint perfume different dishes. Basil enhances the flavor of a sole, and the cabbage in a *salmis de pigeonneau* (ragout of squab) gives it just the right rustic note. The decor of the restaurant seems to have been created as a showcase for this cuisine. The smooth and unmarked stone of the first room, the soaring line of the sparkling gilded staircase or the second room's tawny wood panels, brightened by eighteenth-century paintings, divided in as many imaginary paradises as there are tables: everything here exudes an Olympian calm. A diner always retains vivid memories of a meal eaten at Taillevent. Reservations have to be made months in advance; it is probably the only restaurant in the world for which vacations are planned according to the period during which the three-star establishment on rue Lamennais is open.

It represents an art of living, an end goal of a civilization that is nevertheless put to the test at every meal, with every dish. This accounts for the amazement of its guests, who are never disappointed as they rediscover on every occasion the perfectionism of Vrinat and Deligne. Both the restaurant-owner and his chef are reserved men, little given to ostentatious show and junketing. They are true to reputations divided between tradition and novelty. A new gourmand order will have to be created for Jean-Claude Vrinat bearing the name of the chef of Charles VI (Taillevent). The medal of this order could show a coat of arms composed of three cauldrons bordered by six roses. Vrinat's absolute classicism is that of precision. It is a concern for perfection in the smallest detail. It recalls the nobility of the paintings of Poussin or the lighting in those of Le Nain. It is the ritual array of a supper at Versailles without the overabundance and the exaggeration of the dishes. Unlike the restraint of the rest of the meal, the moment of the dessert is marked by an explosion of

It is impossible to dissociate Jean-Claude Vrinat from chef Claude Deligne when speaking of the success and the quality of Taillevent. The slenderness of Vrinat contrasts sharply with the solidity of Deligne. Both of them have known how to create a Taillevent-style cuisine from a combination of classicism and modernism, offered in a restrained manner amidst a profusion of statues, gilt ornaments, painting by Dutch masters, light and polished wooden panelings. A perfection tempered by comfort and often hidden, or at least discreetly displayed, art treasures.

6 15 rue Lamennais 75008 Paris (air-conditioned, dogs not allowed). Closed Sundays and holidays, from March 26 to April 4 and from July 23 to August 23. Must-see sights nearby: the Champs-Elysées with luxurious shopping arcades, the Arc de Triomphe, the Place de la Concorde, the embankments of the Seine (river sightseeing trips on the excursion boats), the Monceau park with the Pavillon Ledoux, the beautiful view on the Avenue Foch, the Bois de Boulogne (strolling, or boating on the lake).
Tel: (1) 561.12.90

thousands of fruits, sauces, and liqueurs and the diner leaves with a taste of honey on his lips.

Poached eggs with asparagus

Œuf pochés aux asperges

Serves 1:
6 large green asparagus spears
3 eggs
3 sprigs of fresh chervil
⅔ cup (15 cl) heavy cream, whipped
salt and pepper

For the hollandaise sauce:
4 egg yolks
juice of ½ lemon
½ lb (250 g) butter, clarified
salt
cayenne pepper

Peel the asparagus and break off the end of each one (this is tough and often bitter). Cook the asparagus in salted boiling water until they are tender, then cool immediately in cold water to keep them green. Cut each asparagus spear about 2 inches below the tip. Reserve the tips and place the rest in a blender to puree. Work the puree through a sieve, then set aside.

Make a hollandaise sauce as follows: place egg yolks and lemon juice in the top of a double boiler and heat, stirring, until the yolks begin to thicken. Whisk in the butter little by little to make a thick sauce. Season with salt and cayenne pepper.

Stir, first the warm sauce, then the whipped cream, into the pureed asparagus, season with salt and pepper, and keep warm in the double boiler.

Poach the eggs and drain on a towel. Use scissors to trim the ragged edges from around each egg.

To serve, spoon some of the sauce onto a dinner plate, place the eggs and asparagus tips on the plate, garnish with fresh chervil leaves.

Note: rather than being pureed, the ends of the asparagus can simply be sliced and served as in the photo.

Squab with cabbage

Pigeons au chou vert

Serves 6:
6 young pigeons (squab), about 1 lb (450 g) each
1 large green cabbage
5 ½ oz (150 g) bacon
12 shallots, peeled and sliced
1 cup plus 1 tablespoon (250 g) butter
1 tablespoon olive oil
3 tablespoons (5 cl) white wine
1 ¼ cups (30 cl) chicken stock
salt and pepper
parsley, chopped

Remove the outer leaves from the cabbage; use only the central tender "heart" for this recipe. Slice the cabbage as finely as possible and reserve.

Cut the bacon into "strips" about an inch long and ⅛ inch wide. Place them in a saucepan with cold water, bring to a boil, and drain immediately.

Melt ¾ cup of butter in a large frying pan, add the shallots and cook over moderate heat for 2 minutes, then add the bacon strips and cook a minute more. Add the cabbage to the pan, season with salt and pepper and cook slowly 8 to 10 minutes, stirring occasionally. If the cabbage begins to dry, add a little water to the pan. Cover and keep warm.

Salt and pepper the pigeons. Place in a roasting pan with the remaining butter and oil. Roast in a 550 °F (300 °C) oven for 10 minutes, turning the birds over after 5 minutes. Take from the oven, remove the breast meat and the legs from each bird, and set aside in a warm place.

Chop the carcasses with a cleaver, and put them back in the roasting pan to brown on top of the stove. Skim off the fat from the pan and deglaze the pan with white wine. Boil until all the wine has evaporated then add the chicken stock, and boil for 5 minutes. Add salt and pepper if needed and strain the sauce into a clean pan.

Either serve the pigeon and cabbage on separate plates, or place the cabbage in the center of a dinner plate with the pigeon around it. Spoon over the sauce, sprinkle with a little parsley, and serve.

Chocolate Marquise

Marquise au chocolat

Serves 8:
½ lb (250 g) cooking (baking) chocolate
¾ cup (175 g) butter, softened
⅔ cup (100 g) confectioner's sugar
5 egg yolks
5 egg whites
pinch of salt

For the sauce:
4 ¼ cups (1 L) milk
⅔ cup (100 g) ground pistachios
1 ¼ cups (250 g) granulated sugar
8 egg yolks

Melt the chocolate in a double boiler, add the sugar and beat with a fork or electric mixer, then beat in the butter, broken into pieces. Stir in the egg yolks one at a time.

Add a pinch of salt to the egg whites and beat until very stiff. Remove the top of the double boiler from the heat and carefully fold the egg whites into the rest.

Rinse a loaf pan in cold water, then fill it with the chocolate mixture. Place in the refrigerator for at least 12 hours before serving.

To serve, wrap the cake mold in a towel that has been soaked in boiling water, then turn out the marquise onto a serving platter. Serve whole or in slices with a pistachio sauce made as follows: mix the ground pistachios with the milk in a saucepan and bring to a boil. Remove from the heat once the milk has boiled. Beat the egg yolks and sugar until the mixture whitens, then pour the milk onto them, whisking as it is added. Place the mixture in a double boiler and heat, stirring constantly, until the sauce thickens. Allow the sauce to cool before serving with the marquise.

Almond cream with fruit

Blanc-manger

Serves 10:
1 lb (500 g) blanched almonds
2 cups and 2 tablespoons (50 cl) milk
1 cup and 2 tablespoons (250 g)
  granulated sugar
2 cups and 2 tablespoons (50 cl) heavy cream
1 drop almond extract
1 generous tablespoon gelatin
3 tablespoons water
1 pear
2 peaches
sugar syrup (equal amounts of sugar and
  water, boiled together)
2 slices fresh pineapple
¾ pt (200 g) strawberries
strawberry or raspberry sauce

Twenty-four hours in advance pound the almonds in a mortar with the sugar. Bring the milk to a boil and leave to cool completely, then pour it onto the almond-sugar mixture and leave overnight.

The next day, strain the mixture through a sieve pressing all the milk out of the almonds (only the flavored milk is used in this recipe). Bring the milk to a boil in a large saucepan, then remove from the heat. Dissolve the gelatin in the water, stir into the milk, and add the almond extract. Cool over ice.

Peel the pear and the peaches. Remove the pits from the peaches and core the pear; cut the fruit into wedges. Place in a saucepan with some sugar syrup, add the slices of pineapple, and poach. Leave to cool, then dice the pieces of fruit.

Beat the cream until stiff and fold carefully into the almond milk, then stir in the pieces of candied fruit and strawberries. Spoon the cream into lightly oiled ramekins or small bowls and refrigerate for 4 hours.

Turn out just before serving. Serve with strawberry or raspberry sauce.

La Tour d'Argent

*From the bottom to the top of the Tour,
from Alain Faugères, doorman and guardian of its treasures,
to Claude Terrail and his chef,
Dominique Bouchet, each in his way contributes to making
the four-hundred-year-old Tour d'Argent the most famous restaurant in France.*

A great dinner must also be a spectacle and the most beautiful gourmand theatre is located in Paris. Everyone at the Tour d'Argent is letter-perfect in his role of contributor to a perfect festive atmosphere. A scenic designer would be hard-pressed to match the setting. How could he or she hope to even equal its backdrop of Notre-Dame, the Louvre and the Seine representing the Paris of dreams, history and beauty. The spectacle is played out on several levels, on several stories. The tables become orchestra or loge seats as, on the podium, the "canardiers" (the duck-preparers and servers) perpetuate the tradition established by Frédéric when he created the famous Tour d'Argent-style duck. The individually numbered ducks from Challans are still sacrificed to the press in accordance with an immutable ritual. On the ground floor, the arriving guests find themselves in the Museum of the Table. History is there before their eyes in the form of the Table of the Three Emperors, unoccupied but, at the same time, so alive that the beholder believes that he is at the Café Anglais on June 7, 1865, waiting for William I of Germany, Tsar Alexander II, the Tsarevitch, and Bismarck to arrive. The menu still displayed in the middle of the table adds to the feeling of being witness to a moment of history. In the bar, a fire crackles in the fireplace and casts its glow on the clear wooden panels, the tapestries and the collections of glasses and autographs.

From the time of Henri III everyone who was anyone in France came to the Tour d'Argent, learning the use of the fork on its premises. Henri IV imposed the *poule au pot* (chicken in a pot) before it was replaced by the numbered duck. The Duc de Richelieu had beef prepared there in thirty-six ways, and Madame de Sévigné sipped the first cups of coffee and cocoa served in France. Philippe d'Orléans, the Regent of France, dined in its private dining rooms in the company of the beautiful Aïssés and Junon Parabère. La Pompadour tasted her first glass of champagne, a beverage highly popular with the guests at the Tour d'Argent.

Later came the Duc de Morny, the illegitimate son of Hortense de Beauharnais; or Napoleon III, incognito, encountering Hortense Schneider, Offenbach's favorite actress or Marguerite, a very special friend of the emperor. Alexandre Dumas, Alfred de Musset, George Sand, and Honoré de Balzac represented literature's contribution to the clientele of the Tour. Recently, the menu commemorating the four-hundredth anniversary of the restaurant included a list of celebrities who had honored the Tour d'Argent by their presence. The list started with Woody Allen and Charlie Chaplin and continued with Ursula Andress, Maria Callas, Maurice Chevalier, Winston Churchill, Charlton Heston, Cyd Charisse, Zino Davidoff, Maurice Druon, Her Gracious Majesty Queen Elizabeth II of England, and the living god Emperor Hirohito of Japan, the Duke of Edinburgh, Henry Kissinger, Philippe de Rothschild, Pierre Salinger, Ornella Mutti, Richard Nixon, David Rockefeller, Henri Troyat, Jean Dutourd, André Malraux, Raymond Oliver, Alain Senderens, and about one hundred others.

But the curtain is about to go up and the elevator whisks you up to the dining room. There, with the perennial blue carnation in his buttonhole, the director and perfect host, Claude Terrail, presents his spectacle, the "spectacle" of the Tour d'Argent. The woodwork and ceilings are from time to time illuminated by the spotlight beams of the passing excursion boats on the Seine. There is always a dazzling display of lights and colors: the moiré effects of the lacquers, the silvery highlights of the place-setting plates and the menu; the grace and harmony in the silent, precise movements of the splendidly attired headwaiters, the delights of the harmonious floral bouquets and sparkling china. Everything awaits the moment when, resplendently presented under silver serving-dish covers, the culinary masterpieces of chef Dominique Bouchet arrive at the tables. Carlo is a headwaiter of the old school. He, along with Claude Terrail, knows exactly how to "set up" a dining room, to seat everyone without committing errors in protocol, to recognize an oil magnate who hasn't set foot in the restaurant for over twenty years, to attach a name to the seven thousand faces he has retained in his memory, and then go on to his duties of cutting, slicing, seasoning, and setting alight the liqueur poured over a dessert. Yes, this unforgettable spectacle is still performed at the Tour d'Argent.

David Ridgway is the current wine steward of the cellar at the Tour d'Argent, one of the most beautiful and richest in Paris. This Englishman from Surrey is responsible for watching over hundreds of thousands of bottles, those of the Wine Museum, which is another spectacle offered to its guests by the Tour. The visit to the museum is accompanied by the music of Jean-Baptiste Lully or Marc-Antoine Charpentier. It is thrilling to be shown a Lafite 1811 or La Fine Clos du Greffier 1788, bottled one year before the storming of the Bastille. The choice of the

The Ducru Beaucaillou 1928 shown here is just one of more than four hundred thousand bottles to be found in the cellars of the Tour d'Argent. They are worthy of being part of the spectacle. Everything is spectacular here with the backdrop of the Seine and Notre-Dame as seen from corner tables, the most sought-after ones at the Tour. Another part of the spectacle is the ritual operations of the "canardiers" as they prepare and serve the house specialty – the Tour d'Argent duck. Very shortly, they will be serving the millionth one since Frédéric decided to number them.

7 15 Quai de la Tournelle 75005 Paris (rooms for reception, dogs allowed). Closed on Mondays. To be seen on premises and nearby: the Small Museum of the Tables, a visit to the wine cellar and a historical spectacle concerning wines; the Ile of Saint-Louis, the church of Saint-Louis-en-l'Ile (seventeenth century) with its beautiful collection of Italian school painting on wood; the Ile de la Cité, Notre-Dame, the Conciergerie, the flower market; the banks of the Seine, the bookstalls, the sculpture museum on the Quai Saint-Bernard; the Latin Quarter.
AE - Diners cards honored.
Tel. (1) 354.23.31

talented and enthusiastic Dominique Bouchet as chef has changed many things at the Tour d'Argent. While the *canard Tour d'Argent* remains sacrosanct, a goodly number of new dishes have been introduced to delight the palates of the diners. The astonishingly youthful Claude Terrail keeps an eye on everything and everyone. This solicitude also extends to the raising of the restaurant's ducks on the farm of Clovis Burgaud at Challans. He knows everything about the ducks, their history which goes back to Philip IV of Spain, and their marsh, fed by the canals of the lake of Grand-Lieu.

But, above all, he is aware of the intertwined history of "his" Tour and Paris. He has an intimate knowledge of the old Parisian neighborhoods and is fiercely proud of the view the Tour commands over the most beautiful city in the world. As proof of his love for Paris, he has established two other restaurants in the Place des Vosges: La Guirlande de Julie and Marc Annibal de Coconas, named for a resident of the Place and friend of Queen Margot. At the Tour d'Argent the history of Paris passes before the eyes of the beholder.

Sweetbreads and lobster in aspic

Marbré de ris de veau et homard en gelée

Serves 4:
12 oz (350 g) veal sweetbreads
1 ½ tablespoons (20 g) butter
1 ½ oz (40 g) truffles, sliced
⅞ cup (20 cl) beef consommé
1 carrot, sliced
1 onion, sliced
meat from tail and claws of one 1 lb (450 g) boiled lobster
2 tablespoons gelatin
6 tablespoons (10 cl) cold water
3 tablespoons (5 cl) port
1 teaspoon fresh tarragon leaves, chopped
salt and pepper

For the red and green mayonnaise:
mayonnaise
catsup
Tabasco sauce
Cognac
spinach

Soak the sweetbreads for several hours in cold water. Parboil them, drain, and wrap in a towel. Place a plate on top of them and a weight (about a pound) on the plate. Leave to cool completely.

Place the carrot and onion in a roasting pan with a little butter. Unwrap the sweetbreads, slice them, and place on top of the vegetables; cook in a 500 °F (260 °C) oven for 15 minutes. Turn the sweetbreads over after 8 minutes. Remove from the oven and set aside on a plate. Dissolve the gelatin in 6 tablespoons of cold water. Heat the consommé but do not boil; add the port and gelatin and stir. Remove from the heat and add the tarragon.

Fill a terrine with the slices of sweetbread, lobster, and truffles. The terrine should be about three quarters full. Pour in the meat jelly and refrigerate for 4 hours.

To serve, turn out the terrine and slice the aspic. Serve with a green salad in a separate bowl and a little red and green mayonnaise on either side of the aspic. Color the mayonnaise as follows:

Red mayonnaise: simply add a bit of catsup, Tabasco sauce, and a few drops of Cognac to ordinary mayonnaise.

Green mayonnaise: chop some spinach, then boil it for a few minutes in just enough water to cover. Strain, squeezing the spinach to extract all the water. Discard the spinach. Bring the water to a boil, boil 1 minute, then strain into a fine sieve; color the mayonnaise with the green coloring left in the sieve.

Duck à la Tour d'Argent

Caneton Tour d'Argent

Serves 4:
2 large ducks weighing about 3 ½ lbs (1.600 kg) each
3 tablespoons old Madeira
4 tablespoons Cognac
½ cup (12 cl) highly seasoned beef consommé
juice of ½ lemon
salt and pepper

Ducks slaughtered by suffocation are used for this recipe at the Tour d'Argent.

Roast the ducks in a 500 °F (260 °C) oven. Remove from the oven, detach the legs, and slice off the breast meat. Remove the skin from the breast meat and cut the meat into thick slices. Keep warm.

Chop the livers and place them in a chafing dish with the breast meat, Madeira, Cognac and lemon juice. Chop the duck carcasses with a cleaver or cut with large kitchen scissors. Place the carcasses into a large duck press and squeeze out all the juices. Add a little con-sommé to the juice. Pour the juice into the chafing dish and simmer for 25 minutes to reduce the sauce. Stir the sauce as it cooks. Serve the breast meat in the sauce, garnished with souffléed potatoes. Brown the duck legs under the broiler and serve later with a green salad.

Lamb with chanterelles and tarragon sauce

Rosettes d'agneau à l'estragon

Serves 4:
2 racks of lamb, about 2 ¼ lbs
  (1.100 kg) apiece
1 tablespoon tarragon, freshly chopped
6 ½ tablespoons (10 cl) heavy cream
⅞ cup (20 cl) veal stock
1 lb (450 g) fresh chanterelles
3 ½ tablespoons (50 g) butter
4 shallots, finely chopped
oil
salt and pepper

Cut the meat from each rack of lamb. Cut off all the fat and gristle so as to have a cylindrical piece of only the tenderest and leanest meat from each one.

Place the cream, tarragon, and stock in a saucepan over low heat and boil slowly for 7 to 8 minutes to reduce. The sauce should be an ivory color. It will thicken as it reduces. Season with salt and pepper and keep warm.

Clean the mushrooms; wash, drain and dry on a towel. Cook them quickly in a little hot oil then lift out of the pan, pour off the oil, add the butter and shallots and put the mushrooms back into the pan. Keep warm.

Heat a little more oil in a frying pan and cook the lamb for about 4 to 5 minutes; it should be rare inside. Turn the meat frequently as it cooks. Remove the pan from the heat, cover, and leave the meat for 3 minutes before serving. To serve, cut the meat into thin slices and arrange them on the dinner plates. Place mushrooms in the center of the plate, spoon some of the sauce around the meat, and serve.

Note: if preferred, this dish may be garnished with a mixture of green beans cut into small pieces and sautéed with mushrooms, served on a bed of spinach, as shown in the photo.

Fruit gratin with champagne sauce

Gratin de fruits au sabayon de champagne

Serves 4:
2 oranges
2 peaches (optional)
2 grapefruit
12 strawberries
4 egg yolks
3 tablespoons (40 g) granulated sugar
¼ teaspoon vanilla
⅞ cup (20 cl) champagne

Peel the oranges and grapefruit. Remove all the whitish skin, then cut the wedges of fruit from between the membranes that surround them. Peel the peaches and pit them. Cut them into wedges the size and shape of the orange wedges. Cut each strawberry in half. Arrange the fruit around the edges of four oven-proof dessert plates. Set aside.

Beat the egg yolk in a double boiler for about 10 minutes, whisking in the champagne little by little. When the sauce thickens and forms a ribbon, whisk in the sugar and the vanilla. Remove from heat. Spoon some of the sauce into the center of each of the dessert plates, then place the plates under the broiler just long enough to brown the sauce. Serve immediately.

LA VIEILLE FONTAINE

*Manon Letourneur and François Clerc have set up
operations in the Vieille Fontaine, isolated in a park
which itself is surrounded by the park of Maisons-Laffitte.
There, they offer charm, a warm welcome, and the
culinary talents of the chef.*

Set in a park within the park of Maisons-Laffitte, a nineteenth-century middle-class residence, falling somewhere between that of *The Magnificent Ambersons* of Booth Tarkington as immortalized on the screen by Orson Welles and of Colette's heroine in *Le Blé en Herbe (The Ripening Seed)*, has been converted into one of the most beautiful restaurants in France. It is surrounded by one of the most elegant residential zones in the vicinity of Paris, an imposing chateau, a racecourse and, on the edges of the park, the stables with the jockeys, the stable boys, and trainers. The garden of La Vieille Fontaine, with its bridge right out of a Japanese print and a fountain transplanted from the chateau, adds a romantic touch to the domain of the proprietors, Manon Letourneur and François Clerc. The formerly uncared-for park and residence have been restored. In many instances the work on the exteriors was done by Clerc himself while Manon decorated the interior, covering the tables with delicate lace tablecloths, choosing the sparkling glassware, the dazzling Limoges china, the silverware, and the profusion of flowers for the beige and old-rose backgrounds. The romantic bay windows open onto the foliage of the grounds and the turn-of-the-century aspect of the building takes on a more mysterious air when the wispy mists cling to the surrounding trees or when the bourgeois décor of the Vieille Fontaine is illuminated.

What secrets are hidden in the eleven-hundred-gallon saltwater fish preserve, or in the cellar watched over by Hervé Besler, a wine steward enamored of the Vosne-Romanée, the Musigny, or the Château-la-Dominique (a Saint-Emilion "marvelous at the end of a meal when it is well oxygenated")? What treasures of the imagination have been expended by François Clerc to produce the *marinière de cuisses de grenouilles à la coque* (frogs' legs in sauce served in a shell) arriving at your table? He has a perpetual need to invent: he conceived the small vermeil spoons with their frog-design handles when he tried his hand at being a silversmith, as well as the serving platter decorated with three vermeil frogs or the purselike caviar serving-dish filled with the luxurious and aphrodisiac eggs of the sturgeon.

Originally from Toulouse, an orphan, François Clerc began his career at the age of twelve, working first as a kitchen helper and then as a waiter in the dining rooms at a series of luxury hotels. During his military service, he was maitre d'hôtel to a general. On his return to civilian life, he worked as a cook in several bourgeois households and in some rather undistinguished restaurants. Things continued in this manner until he met Manon, a prime mover behind several restaurant experiences. The dining room was his domain. It became that of Manon, the discreet, elegant, omnipresent hostess, always clad in long skirts and lace blouses. It was she who reawakened the love of cuisine in Clerc. But during the initial period in the dilapidated house surrounded by the seedy grounds, the clientele was limited to the jockeys and trainers living in the vicinity. François Clerc raged and fumed at the disappointing cooks working in his kitchens. It was a far cry from what he had hoped for, from what they had dreamed about. At one time, they wanted to have a Munich-style café-restaurant. The result was the Tannhaüser in Paris. But that was not enough for them. Clerc, who had never learned the techniques of classic or modern cuisine under the great chefs, without imitating or reading their writing, perhaps because he did not possess a basic culinary culture, would soon become famous as a self-taught chef despite the serious "on the job" training he had received. He discovered that any dish must be a creation, as well as the fact that everything had already been invented so it was necessary to recreate, to reinvent. He also knew that everyone could, if he had the will, produce the best product. It was a local journalist who first called public attention to Clerc, but it would be ten years before La Vieille Fontaine would receive its first chef's hat award and thirteen before the first star.

But that was just the beginning. In rapid succession, the restaurant was honored with a second and then a third chef's hat, followed by a second star. During all this time success did not harm the inspiration of one nor change the femininity and the supreme refinement of the other. Then was created the cuisine style of François Clerc, compounded of absolute regularity and quality. Experiments, Clerc carries out hundreds of them, but it is never he who imposes his will. It is rather the product that imposes itself on him. From their very origin, the stocks, the *demi-glaces* must have the flavor of the dish that is to be created. If he is thinking about a duck, he will use a duck stock instead of the usual veal ones. His customers are his friends. It was for them that he established a catering service at Saint-Germain-en-Laye. It was for them that he has constructed an impressive laboratory. One day, he and Manon decided to repeat their Maisons-Laffitte success by restoring the dormant Pavillon des Princes near the Bois de Boulogne but without in any way

8   8 avenue Grétry 78600 Maisons-Laffitte (garden, open-air terrace dining area for meals, bar). Closed on Sun. and Mon. and during the month of August. Saint-Germain-en-Laye is 8 kilometers (5 miles) away; Orly is the closest airport. Must-see sights: the park, the residential area in part given over to horseback riding and walking parties. The chateau, constructed by François Mansart (seventeenth century), the beautiful grand staircase, the King's Chamber. The stables and racecourse (created by the Comte d'Artois, the future King Charles X).
AE - Diners - Visa cards honored
Tel: (3) 962.01.78

neglecting La Vieille Fontaine. Their magic worked a second time, and Manon and François seem to possess the gift of ubiquitousness. But that is another story, as are the courses he gives in Los Angeles at Patrick Terrail's restaurant, La Maison. There, he has to find the American equivalents for the French products, but his enthusiasm is equal to the task.

All this activity is only possible thanks to the constant symbiosis between dining room and kitchen. Manon Letourneur and François Clerc believe in the elegance and the joy of offering in all its perfection a cuisine transmuted into an art.

Light old-fashioned curtains veiling the windows opening onto the greenery of the grounds; the tables covered with lace, an outdoor dining terrace recalling the calm, sedate pace of a spa; the light in the dining room drawing the eye to the precious objects it contains, highlighting the details of the silver decorations, or glinting off the reddish-gold hair of Manon. Culinary delights in secret preparation in the kitchen or lying in the cool depths of the oyster and shellfish preserve.

Caviar "alms-purses"

Aumônières de caviar

Serves 4:
7 oz (200 g) caviar
6 ½ tablespoons (10 cl) heavy cream
chives - oil - 4 tomatoes

For the crêpes:
⅓ cup (50 g) flour
2 eggs - pinch of salt
½ cup (12 cl) milk
5 teaspoons (25 g) butter, melted
3 tablespoons (5 cl) beer

Make a crêpe batter by whisking together the eggs, flour, and a little salt. Pour in the milk little by little and whisk until smooth. Add the melted butter and beer, whisk, then leave the batter to rest for 3 hours before using.

Lightly oil several blini pans and make 20 little crêpes. When they are done, place a crêpe on a plate, then fill it with 2 teaspoons of caviar and 1 teaspoon of cream. Pull the edges of the crêpe up and pinch just above the filling to close. Tie each little "purse" closed with chives.

To serve, place the "purses" on a baking sheet in a moderate oven for 3 minutes, then remove and place on dinner plates. Garnish the center of each plate with a tomato peel curled like a rose.

Scallop and spinach dainties

Douceurs de Saint-Jacques

Serves 5:
15 large sea scallops - 2 large onions
½ pound (200 g) fresh spinach, cleaned
5 tablespoons heavy cream
2 tablespoons clarified butter
1 tablespoon lemon juice - 2 tomatoes
chervil - 2 carrots - salt and pepper
tomatoes, for decoration (optional)

Slice the onions as thin as possible. Place them in a saucepan with the butter and cook *very* slowly for 2 hours. Toward the end of the cooking time, add the spinach and cook until tender. Puree the vegetables in a food mill or work them through a sieve. Season with salt and pepper and reserve.

Thinly slice the scallops then lay slices in the bottom of each of four dishes about 4 inches wide and ¾ inch deep. Finish filling the dishes with the vegetable mixture, then place in a 400 °F (200 °C) oven for 5 minutes.

Prepare a sauce by peeling and seeding two tomatoes and pureeing them in a blender, or by working through a sieve. Add cream and lemon juice to the tomatoes and season with salt and pepper.

Peel carrots and cut several thin strips from each one, then slice carrots and steam until soft. To serve, spoon some of the sauce on each plate, turn out the scallops and place in the center of the plate. Finish decorating with the strips and rounds of carrot. Place a sprig of chervil on top of the scallops and serve.

Note: thin strips of tomato can be used instead of the strips of carrot to garnish the plates.

Veal steaks with mustard sauce and mushrooms

Mignon de veau à la graine de moutarde

Serves 4:
16 veal loin steaks (filet mignon) about
   1 ½ oz (40 g) each
1 teaspoon mustard seed
2 teaspoons Meaux mustard (whole grain
   mustard)
1 cup and 1 tablespoon (25 cl) heavy cream
5 tablespoons (70 g) butter, softened
chives or chervil
lemon juice
1 clove garlic, chopped
1 lb (400 g) wild mushrooms (chanterelle,
   boletus, or oyster mushrooms, etc.)
oil - salt and pepper

Clean the mushrooms and cook over moderate heat in a frying pan with a tablespoon of butter and chopped garlic. Once they have given out their water, remove them from the pan with a slotted spoon. Keep warm.

Add the cream and mustard seed to the pan and boil for 3 to 4 minutes to reduce the sauce. Add the mustard and 3 ½ tablespoons of butter broken into little pieces. Whisk to combine. Do not boil the sauce. Add salt and pepper as needed and a little lemon juice.

Salt and pepper the veal. Cook it in an oiled frying pan about 2 minutes on a side so it will not dry out.

To serve, place the mushrooms in the center of each dinner plate, place four pieces of veal around them and spoon over the sauce. Garnish each piece of veal with a little chervil or sprinkle over some chopped chives and serve.

Note: carrots cut into thin strips and boiled can be tied with a little chive and used as a garnish, as in the photo.

Chocolate Alcazar

Alcazar au chocolat

Serves 6:
10 egg yolks
1 ½ cups (320 g) granulated sugar
9 egg whites
generous ½ cup (80 g) flour, sifted
½ teaspoon (3 g) vanilla extract
1 vanilla bean
1 cup (25 cl) milk
2 ½ teaspoons gelatin
2 ½ tablespoons water
1 cup plus 2 tablespoons (28 cl) heavy cream
½ lb semi-sweet cooking chocolate

For pastry: Whisk together 3 egg yolks and 7 tablespoons of sugar until mixture becomes lemon-colored. In another bowl, beat stiff 4 egg whites with 3 ½ tablespoons of sugar. Whisking constantly, add a third of the whites to the egg-yolk mixture, then fold in flour and rest of egg whites. Spoon this batter into a pastry bag fitted with a ¾ inch nozzle and squeeze it out onto a buttered and floured baking sheet in a circle about 8 inches wide. Bake 5 to 10 minutes in a 450 °F (220 °C) oven, then remove and allow to cool. Once it is cold, use a 2-inch deep, 8 ½ inch flan ring to cut off the edges and make a perfect circle. Remove ring and use a large serrated knife to cut the cake into two layers. Place the bottom layer back in flan ring on a serving platter and set aside the top. Add vanilla to 1 cup of milk and bring to a boil. Make a syrup by boiling ⅔ cup sugar with enough water to make a thin syrup. Add the vanilla extract and reserve. Beat 4 egg yolks and a scant ½ cup sugar to lemon color, then pour in the milk with the vanilla. Quickly

dissolve gelatin in water. Place the syrup, egg, and milk mixture over low heat and stir constantly until the cream coats a spoon. Remove vanilla, add the gelatin, and remove from the heat. Cool by whisking in bowl over ice. Beat ⅞ cup of cream until it peaks, then fold into the filling. Set aside.
Make a chocolate mousse by melting the chocolate in a double boiler, then stirring in the egg yolks and the remaining cream (boil the cream before adding to the chocolate). Remove from the heat and fold in 5 egg whites, beaten stiff. To assemble the dessert: brush the bottom half of the pastry with the vanilla-flavored syrup, cover with the vanilla filling, cover this with the remaining pastry, brush it with syrup and cover with the chocolate mousse. The mousse should come to the top of the flan ring used to build the cake. Refrigerate for at least 2 hours. Decorate with chocolate shavings or an almond paste flower, and serve with vanilla sauce.

Lime "mirror"*

Miroir au citron vert

Serves 6:
For the pastry:
3 egg yolks - 3 egg whites
6 tablespoons (80 g) granulated sugar
generous ½ cup (80 g) flour, sifted
For the rum syrup:
scant ½ cup (100 g) granulated sugar
⅓ cup (10 cl) water
5 tablespoons (5 cl) white rum
For the filling:
2 cups (500 g) pureed lime pulp
1 cup (225 g) granulated sugar
6 ½ tablespoons (10 cl) water
1 ½ cups (35 cl) heavy cream
4 egg whites - 4 teaspoons gelatin
4 tablespoons water
For the jelly:
1 ½ tablespoons (20 g) pureed lime pulp
1 teaspoon liquid glucose
⅞ cup (20 cl) water
1 ½ teaspoons powdered pectin
3 tablespoons (60 g) apricot jam
7 teaspoons (30 g) granulated sugar
2 drops green food coloring

Make the pastry. Whisk the egg yolks and 5 ½ teaspoons of sugar until they are lemon-colored. In a separate bowl beat the egg whites with the remaining sugar until stiff. Whisk a third of the whites into the yolk mixture, then gently fold in first the flour, then the remaining whites. Lightly butter and flour a 9-inch flan ring, 2 inches high, and fill it with the batter. Bake in a 425 °F (220 °C) oven 10 minutes then remove and cool on a cake rack. Once cold, cut the cake in half through the middle, clean the flan ring, oil it lightly, and place it on a serving platter. Place the bottom of the cake back in the ring. Reserve the top half for later.
Make a rum syrup by boiling the sugar and water together, then remove from the heat and add the rum. Reserve.
Prepare filling. Make Italian meringue by boiling 1 scant cup sugar with 6 ½ tablespoons of water until the mixture registers 257 °F (121 °C) on candy thermometer.
Beat the egg whites until they start to stiffen, then pour on the hot syrup little by little. Continue whisking until the mixture cools. Beat the cream and the remaining sugar until it forms peaks. Combine first the lime pulp with

the meringue mixture, then stir in the whipped cream and finally the gelatin, dissolved in 4 tablespoons water.
Brush some of the rum syrup over bottom piece of pastry, cover with half of the lime filling, put the top piece of pastry in place, brush it with rum syrup and cover with remaining filling. Place in the freezer for about 1 hour.
Make a jelly topping by combining lime pulp, water, and in a saucepan bring to a boil. In a second saucepan, boil sugar and glucose. In a third pan, heat apricot jam. When all are hot, pour contents of second pan into the first, then the add the jam and stir in the food coloring. Stir and lower the heat so the mixture is between 95 °F and 104 °F (35 °- 45 °C). Pour the jelly over the cake and place in the refrigerator. Remove the flan ring just before serving.

---

* There is no photo for this recipe.

L'Hostellerie du Château

*In the impressive setting
of the ruins of the Château de Fère-en-Tardenois,
a beautiful Renaissance residence
has been transformed into a hostelry by Gérard Blot
and a gourmand stopover point by Patrick Michelon.*

Located on the coronation route of the French kings to Rheims, Fère-en-Tardenois was more than just a stopover point. This impregnable fortress, built on a moat-surrounded height and protected by seven towers, had the look of a page out of a Book of Hours. It resisted sieges, attacks by English invaders, the cannonballs simply ricocheting off its walls thanks to their ingenious construction. The king and his court, his accompanying army of servants and cooks, were lodged either at the chateau or in the courtyard. This practice might have been the origin for its career as a hostelry, as indicated by the names given to various points within the chateau: la Tour de la Vis de Cuisine (the kitchen tower), la Tour du Fournil (the bakehouse tower) and, in the gallery, le Gobelet du Roy (the King's goblet). This last one would be a perfect name for a bar.

The chateau was transformed into an elegant Renaissance residence by Anne de Montmorency, High Constable of France. The viaduct built by Jean Bullant reminds one of the style of Chenonceaux despite its current ruined condition, which nevertheless imparts to it a romanticism worthy of Victor Hugo. A succession of wars destroyed the monumental structure; the lead of the roofs was stripped away by smelters and armorers, while some of its stones were shipped off by order of Philippe d'Orléans for use in the construction of the new Palais-Royal. Ravaged and dismantled, Fère-en-Tardenois declined into ruin and oblivion. Forgotten were the names of its owners, the kings and queens who had sojourned within its walls, bringing with them a giddy whirl of banners and sumptuous feasts. The courtyard buildings, located on a plateau, were reconstructed in pure Renaissance style in the sixteenth century. The nineteenth century saw the addition of several wings. The chateau might have fallen into ruin a second time had it not been for the happy initiative of farseeing individuals. Its restoration to the tradition of hospitality attached to the locale was the work of Gérard Blot. Trained at the Prince de Galles, the Café de la Paix, and the Hotel Meurice, this affable giant surrounded by his womenfolk (wife, mother, and sisters) has been a prime mover in the creation of this link in the Relais et Châteaux chain. The hostelry he set up at Fère-en-Tardenois has preserved the elegance and intimacy of the chateau. The discreet comfort of the bar seems to impose champagne as the obligatory drink. All the common rooms open onto the two façades; on one side are the ruins of the old chateau and its grounds, on the other the gradual fall of the valley and the horizon line of the meadows. The dining room with its majestic wall panels is the chapel in which are chanted vespers to the red wine of the Champagne province and to the surprisingly inventive cuisine. Given the sumptuousness of the surroundings, it would have been very tempting to be content with what one of my colleagues so aptly dubbed a "purring" cuisine, but that isn't the style of the chef, Patrick Michelon.

Patrick Michelon, chef of the new generation, is giving new impetus to this cuisine, which is both very rich and very light. It is a cuisine of flaky crusts and clearly defined taste sensations. There is no hesitation about using hazelnut salad oil, which goes so well with the medieval and sylvan aftertastes of dill. Full use is made of the season's bounty and innovation also plays its part.

The sea urchin, served hot in its shell, brings the scent of the ocean to the Champagne region. The ancient cuisine of banquets in the days of chivalry is rediscovered in the cockscombs served with morels and kidneys in a flaky pastry shell. The *beurre Vénus* (Venus butter) may not make lovers dream of that goddess, but it certainly delights the gourmands – it is a *beurre blanc* thickened by the liquid of this marvelous mollusk and cooking juices. As for the *bar de ligne* (bass) modestly baptized with a truffle butter, it is as regally packed with truffles as it is perfectly cooked. The vegetables themselves bespeak the rich soil of the Tardenois region, the marshes of the Somme where the broad beans grow and the ducks abound. And there is the *foie gras*, which takes on a peasant air in an unforgettable stew with cabbage and caraway seeds.

The desserts, charmingly designated as "boutehors" (send-offs), are as incredible as they are numerous and are likely to make one linger longer at the table. They include the classic *bourdaloue aux poires* (pear tart), the *délice de Nesles flambé au cointreau,* a light chocolate mousse, usually difficult to carry off with success and "marjolaine" cake, with its rustic name. For the cheese-lovers there is the platter of Brie and Thiérache, some of the most perfect ones that I have ever encountered. If a stopover at Fère-en-Tardenois was obligatory for the Kings of France on the way to the cathedral of Rheims to be consecrated as God's anointed on the throne, we lesser mortals would do well today to turn off the highway and head for this haven of calm and good living. No jousts or single combats between knights in armor. Just comfort and the joys of the table.

9 02130 Fère-en-Tardenois (rooms for receptions and seminars, guest accommodations: 12 rooms, 7 suites, tennis, horseback riding and a golf course 25 miles away). Closed in January and February. Soissons is 4 miles away and Rheims 28 miles, the airport of Roissy-Charles-de-Gaulle is 56 miles away, Paris 68 miles. To be seen nearby: the American military cemetery at Belleau Wood (1918), Soissons, the ancient abbeys, the cathedral of St. Gervais and St. Protais, housing "The Adoration of the Shepherds" by Rubens, the château.
AE - card honored
Tel: (23) 82.21.13

A strange mixture of wildness and gentleness pervades the grounds and the surrounding countryside. It is also present in the sober façade, rebuilt in the sixteenth century in the purest Renaissance style. The somber mass of the forest seems to keep guard over the ruins of the former chateau. The windows of the dining room offer the guests a panoramic view ruled off by the small panes. With a little imagination, one can catch a glimpse of a passing musketeer or a noble lady awaiting the arrival of her lover. The rooms are regally dimensioned with impressive high ceilings, but they evoke memories of a country squire inviting a few traveling companions (lawyers, nobles, local leading citizens, or worse) to come and sup with him. Like any good castle governor who has endured many sieges and battles, Gérard Blot knows the value of comfort, an agreeable setting, and the restorative virtues of a great dinner.

Eel and sweetbread pie with nettle sauce

Tourte d'anguilles et de ris de veau, beurre d'orties blanches

Serves 4:
For the sweetbread filling:
7 oz (200 g) veal sweetbreads
6 tablespoons (100 g) butter
2 whole eggs, plus 1 egg white
²⁄₃ cup (150 g) heavy cream
salt and pepper

10 ¹⁄₂ oz (300 g) veal sweetbreads
10 ¹⁄₂ oz (300 g) eel
7 oz (200 g) mushrooms
⁷⁄₈ cup (20 cl) heavy cream
10 oz (270 g) butter, softened
¹⁄₂ lb (250 g) puff pastry
1 large bunch nettles, leaves only
   (see Note)
2 shallots, finely chopped
juice of 2 lemons
salt and pepper

Make the sweetbread filling by pureeing the sweetbreads in a processor; add the butter, eggs, egg white, salt and pepper and process until smooth. Chill over ice for 2 hours, then either stir in the cream or add it in the processor. Chill for at least another hour before using (it's even better if you can make the filling the day before making the pie).
Soak the remaining sweetbreads in cold water for several hours, then drain and cut off all gristle and fat. Skin the eel, cut the meat from the bone, and parboil it for 1 minute in lightly salted boiling water. Drain and reserve.
Butter a 10-inch pie plate with 3 tablespoons of butter. Roll out puff pastry dough; use about half to line the pan and save the rest to make the top of the pie. Fill the pie with the sweetbread filling mixed with pieces of the whole sweetbread and eel. Roll out the remaining dough and make a cover for the pie. Bake in a 400 °F (200 °C) oven for 45 minutes.
Meanwhile, parboil the nettles in salted boiling water, drain, and purée by working through a sieve. Set aside.
Cook the mushrooms in a pan with 3 tablespoons of butter and a little lemon juice. Cook, covered, until they have shrunken. Lift out the mushrooms and reserve. Add cream and shallots to the pan and boil to reduce the liquid by half, then whisk in the butter little by little to make a creamy sauce. Last, whisk in the nettle purée, season with salt and pepper as needed, and serve with a slice of the pie on dinner plates garnished with one of the mushrooms.
Note: sorrel or watercress may be used instead of nettles.

Sea bass with truffles

Bar de ligne au beurre de truffes fraîches, de Richerenches

Serves 4:
1 sea bass weighing about 2 lbs (1 kg)
3 ¹⁄₂ oz (100 g) truffles
6 ¹⁄₂ tablespoons (10 cl) heavy cream
1 lb less 4 tablespoons (400 g) butter,
   very cold
8 shallots, finely chopped
8 asparagus tips
8 baby onions, peeled
4 zucchini (courgette) flowers,
   with baby zucchini (courgette) attached
   and sliced lengthwise into a fan
salt and pepper

Fillet the fish and cut the fillets horizontally to make 8 thin "scallops". Cook the fish 7 to 8 minutes in the oven, or steam just enough to cook through.
Boil the asparagus tips, baby onions, and zucchini flowers in separate pots of lightly salted water. Keep warm.
Cut 12 thin slices of truffle and set aside. Chop the remaining truffles and warm them in a saucepan with a little butter and the shallots. Add a little liquid from the truffle can and the cream, bring to a boil, and whisk in the cold butter little by little to make the sauce. Season with salt and pepper.
To serve, spoon some of the sauce onto each plate, place two pieces of fish on top, garnish with sliced truffles, and place some of the vegetables on each plate. Serve immediately.
Note: a little puff pastry filled with spinach can also be used as a garnish.

Turbot with maderized champagne

Turbot de petits bateaux au vieux champagne madérisé

<u>Serves 4:</u>

4 pieces of turbot weighing about
  7 oz (180 g) apiece
3 tomatoes, peeled, seeded, and coarsely
  chopped
2 tablespoons finely chopped shallots
1 small clove garlic, finely chopped
1 ⅓ cups (30 cl) old maderized champagne
  (or equal parts Madeira and champagne)
⅞ cup (20 cl) fish stock (preferably
  made with turbot bones)
½ lb (250 g) mushrooms, sliced
salt and pepper
2 cups and 2 tablespoons (50 cl) heavy cream
2 tablespoons chopped parsley

Place all the ingredients, with the exception of the cream and parsley, in a large pan with the turbot and bring to a boil. Poach the fish just long enough to cook, then lift it out and drain. Boil the cooking liquid to reduce by three quarters, then add the cream and continue boiling and stirring until the sauce is nice and thick. Spoon the sauce onto the dinner plates, top with a piece of turbot and garnish with parsley. Serve immediately.

Note: whole mushrooms and asparagus tips can be cooked separately and used as a garnish in addition to the sauce.

Strawberry millefeuille

Millefeuille aux fraises

<u>Serves 4:</u>

<u>For the pastry:</u>
1 ¾ cups (250 g) flour
⅞ cup (200 g) butter
2 teaspoons salt
6 ½ tablespoons (10 cl) water

<u>For the pastry cream:</u>
generous 1 ⅔ cups (40 cl) milk
2 egg yolks
scant ½ cup (100 g) granulated sugar
2 ½ tablespoons (25 g) cornstarch
⅓ cup (80 g) butter, broken into small pieces
6 ½ tablespoons (10 cl) heavy cream,
  whipped

<u>For the sauce:</u>
6 ½ tablespoons (10 cl) water
scant ½ cup (100 g) granulated sugar
½ lb (250 g) strawberries

<u>To garnish:</u>
1 lb (500 g) strawberries, sliced
8 mint leaves
confectioner's sugar

Make "inverted" puff pastry as follows: quickly combine ½ cup of flour with ⅞ cup butter. Form into a square and refrigerate. Place the remaining flour on a clean table, make a well in the center, put the salt and water into the well, and quickly combine to make a dough. Refrigerate until the dough and the butter are both cool and approximately the same temperature. Make the pastry as you would an ordinary puff pastry: roll out the dough and enclose the butter in it. Roll this out and give the dough first one turn, then a double turn, then a single turn to finish (see General Comments for explanation). Roll out the dough and cut it into four rectangular pieces just before baking. Make a pastry cream. Boil the milk. Beat the egg yolks and sugar until they are pale yellow and foamy, then stir in the cornstarch and whisk in the milk. Pour into a saucepan and cook over low heat, stirring constantly until the cream thickens. Pour the cream into a mixing bowl; stir to cool. When the cream is only just warm stir in the butter little by little, and when the cream is completely cold, fold in the whipped cream.

To make strawberry sauce, boil the water and sugar until the sugar dissolves, then leave to cool completely before blending in the strawberries (use a blender or food processor). Strain the sauce.

Cook the pastry and allow to cool. Cut each pastry horizontally in half through the middle; cover the bottom piece with the pastry cream and some freshly sliced strawberries. Spread on a little more pastry cream, then cover with the top piece of pastry. Sprinkle the top with confectioner's sugar. Garnish with the remaining sliced strawberries, the sauce, and fresh mint leaves.

CHÂTEAU BOYER LES CRAYÈRES

Nestled in the jewel-box setting of its grounds in the center of Rheims,
coronation site for French monarchs, heart of the Champagne region,
the Château des Crayères has transformed
Prince Charming and Cinderella (Gérard Boyer and Elyane)
into the masters of a fairy-tale palace.

Gérard Boyer felt hemmed in by his cottage in Rheims. The once-rural setting was being ravaged by the hectic pace of urbanization. The trees in the area had been felled, and the comfortable villas on the Avenue d'Épernay had been replaced by high-rise apartment buildings. The surroundings were no longer to the liking of this former chef at Lasserre nor were they conducive to three-star cuisine. However, it wasn't the magic wand of a fairy godmother that transformed Gérard Boyer and Elyane into the masters of a fairy-tale palace but the determination of a champagne magnate. His intention was to give Rheims a prestigious restaurant and at the same time make intelligent use of his Second Empire chateau, a somewhat rundown edifice on a fifteen-acre tract of greenery and woodland in the center of the city. It was the grand gesture of Xavier Gardinier, owner of the Lanson and Pommery companies, that permitted a miracle to happen - the restoration of the noble champenois limestone to its original whiteness. The citizens of Rheims can now dream of seeing their cathedral regain a pristine whiteness matching that of the Château des Crayères. The wood panels in the dining room of Princesse de Polignac have been restored. The verandas have been converted into a bar or winter-garden so that one and all have the opportunity to savor the wines of Rheims, Aÿ, or Cumières.

Gérard Boyer's vocation is to be the ecumenicist of Champagne, gathering together squires, country gentlemen, farmers or winegrowers. Be the gracious bubbles consumed those of Dom Perignon or Veuve Clicquot, from the heights of Hautvilliers or the winepresses of Bouzy, they are particularly suited to the cuisine of Gérard Boyer. It is a cuisine brimming over with gaiety, worthy of the suppers of the Regent or feasts orchestrated by Offenbach. The menu itself, illustrated with a grape-harvesting scene, pays tribute to the vine just as several vine stocks are still to be found on the grounds of the chateau.

Gérard Boyer is most assuredly a colorist. He plays with tones and shades and his dishes are often astonishing creations very close to modern art with their geometrical shapes and pastel colors. But the visual aspect of a dish, its aesthetics, come into play only later, after the flavors have been tested. He will not sacrifice taste to presentation. He has paid tribute to two modern culinary masters, Freddy Girardet and Jean Delaveyne, by naming two dishes after them. These two chefs, each in his generation, have marked or influenced the direction taken by

la grande cuisine. Strangely enough, this champagne menu offers very few dishes marked by regionalism. Bisseuil, a local vintage wine, is featured in a *filet de bœuf au Bissueil à la moelle* (fillet of beef with Bisseuil and squash). Although not one to scorn the *foie gras,* the lobster or the truffle, Gérard Boyer practices a cuisine characterized by great simplicity, employing vegetables with special scents (fennel compote, watercress sauce) or seeking the exotic touch in salmon scalloped with cabbage and ginger. He is instinctively drawn to seafood, especially that from Brittany, to the point of combining a *grenadin de veau* with lobster, and a most happy and successful marriage it turns out to be. No useless complications, just an almost infallible taste in the service of a perfected technique of short cooking times and light sauces. The steamed Breton lobster in Sauternes, despite its noble and rich ingredients, is an ideal example of this type of cuisine, which knows exactly when to introduce the rustic touch. It also knows how to remain soberly familial. Two or three generations back, Gérard's grandparents left their native Auvergne for Paris. They set up residence at Vincennes and opened a modestly priced restaurant frequented by draymen. The grandmother even saw to the feeding of their horses. In her honor and to commemorate the family's beginnings in the restaurant trade, the menu features a *filet d'agneau rôti grand' mère.* Because it is a closely knit family and because the father, Gaston, has always been associated with his son ever since the latter's return from working in restaurants all over the country, *La Chaumière* run by father and son (G and G) was one of the most modest three-star restaurants in France. Now transplanted to the Château, the Boyer clan has very smoothly made the transition into the aristocratic role of lords of the manor. The ever-elegant Elyane with her laughing blue eyes watches over the welcome and comfort offered to the guests. She has given the dining room and the decor of the hotel accommodations a feminine, tender note that goes very well with the artistic cuisine of the Master of Crayères. The most remarkable aspect is neither the patina that seems authentic nor the soaring staircase leading to the marvelous hotel accomodations, but the sensation that everything is in its correct place and that a decorator played no role in the end result. Just as with stately old mansions in which the successions of generations and styles have created in apparent confusion an inimitable setting - one that truly belongs. The juxtaposition of glass, steel and stone in

An imposing façade of white stone from the quarries of Rheims, the same type of stone used in constructing the cathedral, the coronation site for the Kings of France, the same stone from which was sculpted the famous Angel Musician with its enigmatic smile, and which served to create the cellars under the city for the maturing of millions of bottles of champagne. The discreet comfort of an apartment decorated with taste by Elyane, mistress of the domain, preoccupied by the elegance of the hangings or the shape of a lampshade. In the vast dining room with the white-leaded woodwork or bare stone dressed with rich tapestries and contemporary paintings,

all these details prepare the diner for the delights of Gérard Boyer's cuisine. The perfect spaces, the impeccable alignment of silverware and the china, the artful lighting. On the shelves of the display cases, the ancient earthenware dishes recall the chefs of times past. And then there is the intimate atmosphere with all its solicitous touches: the rose on a plate, the eiderdown quilt or the tapestry in the hotel room. Footsteps are muffled in the thick carpets and in the lawn. Under the centuries-old trees in the grounds, winding paths invite the guest to stroll in a romantic green universe.

10 64 Boulevard Henri-Vasnier 51100 Rheims (air-conditioned, 16 suites, rooms for receptions and seminars. Vast grounds, bar-winter garden section, tennis courts, dogs allowed). Closed Mondays and for lunch on Tuesdays and from Dec. 22 to Jan. 14. Epernay is 17 miles away, Paris 88 miles. To be seen nearby: the cathedral of Notre-Dame with its marvelous statues: the Virgin (north typanum), the Angel Musician; the Tau Palace, the Beaux-Arts museum (Poussin, Le Nain, Cranach, Corot, Renoir), the Carnegie Library (Daumier), the champagne cellars.
AE - Diners - Visa cards honored
Tel. : (26) 82.80.80

the bar-winter garden section symbolizes the alliance of different ages just as the wine cellars under the city and the vineyards join in imagination the generations of vintners who created champagne.

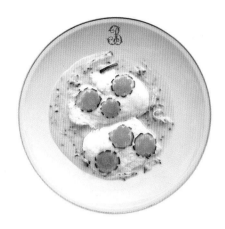

Mussel soup with orange

Soupe de moules à l'orange

Serves 8:
6 ½ lbs (3 L) mussels, scraped and
   debearded
2 shallots, finely chopped
1 leek, white part only, sliced
6 ½ tablespoons (10 cl) fish stock
4 tablespoons (6 cl) dry white wine
2 carrots, cut into julienne strips
2 leeks, white and part of the green,
   cut into julienne strips
3 stalks celery, cut into julienne strips
10 tablespoons (150 g) butter
½ cup (15 cl) heavy cream
a few pinches saffron
zest of 1 orange, grated fine
2 tablespoons orange juice
salt and pepper

Place the mussels, wine, fish stock, chopped shallots, and sliced leek in a large pot, cover, and cook over high heat until all the mussels have opened. Take out the mussels and remove each one from its shell.

Strain the cooking liquid into a clean saucepan and boil to reduce by one third. Add the cream and saffron and continue boiling to reduce the remaining liquid by about a quarter.

Boil the juliennes of carrots, leeks, and celery in lightly salted water for about 2 minutes, or until just tender. Drain, cool under cold running water, then drain thoroughly.

Place the grated orange zest in a small saucepan, cover with cold water, bring to a boil, and boil for 1 minute. Drain, cool under cold running water, and drain again thoroughly.

Whisk the butter into the sauce little by little, then stir in the julienned vegetables, the orange zest and orange juice. Season with salt and pepper as needed. Add the mussels and heat, without allowing to boil, just long enough to warm the mussels through, then serve immediately.

Turbot with mixed vegetables and champagne sauce

Filets de turbot à la julienne de légumes, sauce champagne

Serves 4:
1 turbot weighing about 3 ½ lbs (1.500 kg),
   filleted and cut into 8 pieces
1 large carrot, cut into julienne strips
4 medium mushrooms,
   cut into julienne strips
1 stalk of celery, peeled and cut into
   julienne strips
1 leek, cut into julienne strips
2 shallots, chopped fine
½ cup (12 cl) champagne
1 cup and 1 tablespoon (25 cl) heavy cream
½ lb (250 g) butter, broken into small pieces
lemon juice
salt and pepper

Melt 1 ½ tablespoons of butter in a large frying pan and cook the strips of leek, carrot, mushrooms, and celery slowly until they begin to color. Remove from the heat and reserve.

Butter a roasting pan, sprinkle in the shallots, salt and pepper, then place the fish fillets in the pan, add the champagne and bake in a 425 °F (220 °C) oven for about 8 minutes. Check to be sure the fish is cooked, then lift it out of the pan and keep warm while making the sauce.

Strain the cooking liquid from the roasting pan into a clean saucepan and boil to reduce by two thirds. Add the cream and continue boiling to reduce by a third. Whisk in the butter little by little, season with salt, pepper and a little lemon juice. Add the cooked vegetables to the sauce to reheat. Spoon some of the sauce onto each plate, place a piece of fish on top and serve.

Note: you can decorate the fish with quickly cooked slices of zucchini topped with smaller slices of carrot, as in the photo, for a more elegant presentation.

Chicken breast stuffed with truffles, served with leeks

Suprême de Bresse cuit à la vapeur et marmelade de poireaux

Serves 8:
8 chicken breasts from chickens weighing about 4 ½ lbs (2 kg) apiece
5 oz (150 g) truffles
4 ¼ cups (1 L) chicken stock
2 ¼ lbs (1 kg) leeks
1 cup and 1 tablespoon (25 cl) heavy cream
⅞ cup (200 g) butter
salt and pepper

Place a chicken breast on a cutting board and, holding a large knife parallel to the board, cut the breast *almost* in half–don't cut all the way through. Cut flaps all across the breast this way so that they will be "hinged" on one side and open like a book. Season the inside of each slice with salt and pepper, then fill each one with thick slices of truffles.

Place the chicken stock in the bottom of a steamer, bring to a boil and steam the breasts for 10 minutes. Tightly cover the top of the steamer so no steam escapes.

Clean the leeks and cut the white part, and a little of the green, into pieces about ⅜ inch long and about half as wide. Separate the leaves and wash carefully. Cook the leeks in a pan with 1 ½ tablespoons of butter until soft, but don't allow to brown. Add 6 ½ tablespoons of the cream and cook gently until it has virtually disappeared. Salt and pepper.

Once the breasts are cooked, remove them from the steamer and keep warm. Pour half the stock into a saucepan, add the remaining cream, and boil until the sauce is thick and creamy. Over high heat, whisk in the butter little by little.

Place the leeks in the center of each plate, spoon some of the sauce around them, put a breast on top of the leeks, and serve immediately.

Chocolate Alexandra

Alexandra

Serves 8:
4 egg yolks
4 egg whites
generous ⅔ cup (150 g) granulated sugar
1 lb 1 ½ oz (500 g) semi-sweet cooking chocolate
¾ cup (100 g) flour
3 ¼ cups (75 cl) heavy cream, whipped
6 ½ tablespoons (10 cl) rum-flavored sugar syrup
unsweetened cocoa

Make a cake batter as follows: whisk together the egg yolks and ½ cup granulated sugar until the mixture lightens in color. Sift the flour and gently stir into this mixture. Beat the egg whites until they begin to stiffen, whisk in the remaining sugar, then fold the egg whites into the egg-yolk mixture. Pour the batter into a buttered and floured cake pan and bake in a 275 °F (135 °C) oven until a toothpick stuck into the cake comes out clean. Remove from the oven, turn out the cake onto a rack, and allow to cool.

Make a chocolate mousse: melt the chocolate, then fold in the whipped cream. The two ingredients should be perfectly mixed to make a smooth mousse.

Cut the cake in half, horizontally, lift off the top, and place the bottom on a serving platter. Brush the bottom with sugar syrup to lightly moisten, then spread one third of the chocolate mousse over it (you can make several layers this way by cutting the cake into three if you prefer). Place the top of the cake over the mousse and cover it and the sides with the remaining mousse. Refrigerate for 2 to 3 hours. Dust the top of the cake with cocoa before serving.

This cake can be made several days in advance and kept refrigerated until ready to be served. It can be served alone or with a vanilla sauce.

L'AUBERGE DE L'ILL

*The Auberge de l'Ill, gourmand outpost on the German frontier,
Alsace in miniature set on the banks
of a peaceful and sinuous river,
almost domesticated by the art of Jean-Pierre Haeberlin,
ennobled by the cuisine of his brother Paul.*

From its source in the south of the province, the river Ill winds its peaceful way amid poplar-planted banks, watering the plains and at times flooding them. The river's long meanderings take it through Mulhouse, Colmar, and Strasbourg, where it transforms a part of the city (la Petite Alsace) into a miniature Venice. Before joining the Rhine, the course of the Ill has symbolized and irrigated the whole of Alsace. At Illhäusern, the river is sinuous and bucolic; the weeping willows plunge their thin, tender branches into it. The village, destroyed during World War II, has been reconstructed with loving care, and flowers planted in profusion perfume the narrow streets. The storks nest in the church steeple, sallying forth to gorge themselves on the frogs living along the banks of the Ill. In 1882, the Haeberlin family opened a little tavern, which they called l'Arbre Vert (the Green Tree). People from Sélestat and Colmar came there to eat *matelotes,* fried fish, or crayfish fritters, or to canoe on the river. A husband-wife team worked in the kitchen, while the great-grandfather, half part farmer, restaurant-keeper, looked after the till. Since then, five generations of Haeberlins have labored in this idyllic setting.

Paul Haeberlin is a true native son of Illhäusern. He was born there in 1923 and spent his childhood in a kitchen presided over by his mother and an aunt. It therefore was quite a simple matter to induce him to continue the family tradition. Edouard Weber, former chef to the Tsar, the Greek court, and the Rothschilds, had opened a restaurant, la Pépinière at Ribeauvillé, a few miles away. Paul went to work there as an apprentice. Weber was a strict and demanding teacher, but his student had great talents. And Paul Haeberlin polished these talents in a series of important establishments, including the then-famous Rôtisserie Périgourdine. His younger brother, Jean-Pierre, was born in 1932. Possessed of a considerable talent as a watercolorist and painter, he seemed destined for an artistic career. He had even worked for a time in an architect's atelier.

But when the Auberge, destroyed in 1940, was rebuilt in 1950, he joined his brother in the adventure of restoring the restaurant to its ancient glory. Jean-Pierre, the esthete, learned the trade of headwaiter during a training period at Poccardi in Paris. He employed his artistic talents in the transformation of the Auberge. It was he who had the idea of moving into the gardens and old building that dated from 1758 and that the city of Colmar no longer wanted. It was he who designed the menu, chose those works of art that constitute the restaurant's silver plates and buckets, the colors of the table linen and the flowers that decorate the establishment, the old earthenware frying pans and the Alsatian credenzas. Paul, who succeeded his father, concentrated his efforts on innovating, drawing upon the resources of Alsatian gastronomy for inspiration but taking into account the new preferences of the customers. In this way, he created the dishes that were to give the Auberge de l'Ill its world-renown: deer, hare – the sublime hare *à la royale des Haeberlin,* both firm and velvety smooth – or the wild duck *au sang.*

All these products of the game-filled forests and plains of Alsace are to be found on the menu during the hunting season. As demanding as he is with himself, Paul has no egotistical urge to keep his knowledge to himself. At the present time, he is teaching his culinary art to about a dozen students, who undoubtedly will be the great chefs or restaurant owners of the future. His preparations are architectural masterpieces, influenced probably by the constructions of Weber at the Imperial Court of Saint Petersburg. But even if his cuisine draws upon the great traditional styles, it is far in advance of the new cuisine.

A magician of the kitchen, Paul prefers to remain there. He detests traveling and attending cocktail parties. He has found a worthy successor in his son, Marc, thus assuring the future of the Auberge. Like his ancestors, Marc has always wanted to be a chef. He studied at the Ecole Hôtelière in Strasbourg, spent his restaurant apprenticeship at Troisgros, Paul Bocuse, Lasserre, and under Gaston Lenôtre for pastry.

The Haeberlins are an admirable family, attached body and soul to their native Alsace and its traditions. Although the two brothers have been the objects of praise and awards, they have not lost their simplicity and graciousness. It is, above all, the confidence of the public that counts for them. Endowed with the typically Alsatian virtues of industriousness and fidelity, Jean-Pierre and Paul Haeberlin have labored long to transform places, to turn a *mousseline de grenouilles* into a memorable experience, and to promote the noble wines of the province – Riesling, Tokay, Gewürtztraminer, and Sylvaner. In addition, the restaurant's location near the German border made it a showcase of French culinary art. The double award of the Croix de Chevalier de l'Ordre du Mérite in 1980 probably meant more to them than the third Michelin star acquired in 1967 or the four "toques rouges," the near perfect 19 out of 20 score from Gault

Flower-bedecked Illhäusern is a village that was reconstructed in the purest of Alsatian traditions. Strolling down its streets, the visitor comes upon a sign which a future ethnologist would certainly say dated from the nineteenth century. L'Auberge de l'Ill is located in a charming rustic garden running down to the banks of the river Ill, where weeping willows trail their graceful branches in its waters. Generations of chefs rooted in the soil of Alsace, the Haeberlins have been able to reconstitute, in a mixture of simplicity and opulence, an entire universe of traditions in a house pervaded by the human touch.

11 rue de Collonges Illhäusern 68150-Ribeauvillé (air-conditioned, rooms for receptions, garden on the banks of the river Ill, dogs admitted). Closed on Monday nights and all day Tuesday in February and from July 1 to 7. Colmar (airport) is 10 miles away, Strasbourg is 37 miles away, and Paris 324 miles. To be seen: Sélestat, the chateau of Kintzheim (10 miles), training of eagles. Colmar, with its many old houses, including la Maison des Têtes and la Maison Pfister, the Unterlinden museum (the Isenheim altarpiece), the Bartholdi Museum.
AE - Diners cards honored
Tel: (89) 71.83.23

and Millau. We gourmands derive our happiness from the delights to be found on the menu of l'Auberge de l'Ill: *boudin de cailles et de foie d'oie cuit à la vapeur* (steamed sausage of quail and goose livers), salmon soufflé, *aiguillettes de canard aux pleurotes fraîches et aux petits oignons* (duck fillets with wild mushrooms and onions), a creation of Marc Haeberlin, *sandre au Pinot noir* (pike-perch in wine sauce), *suprême de faisan Alcantara* (pheasant with *foie gras,* port wine, and truffle sauce and small quenelles of pheasant meat), peach Haeberlin (poached, served with pistachio ice cream and a champagne-flavored cream sauce), *pêches soufflées Cardinal de Rohan,* or the rhubarb-glazed soufflé in a cherry (griottes) sauce.
There is a German saying, "As happy as God in France." A simple visit to l'Auberge de l'Ill is enough to make one realize its truth.

GEORGES BLANC

*The Veyle River gives the inn of the Mother Blanc,
now rebaptized Georges Blanc, the deceptive air of Venice
in the Bressan countryside. Jacqueline and Georges Blanc
have succeeded in making the small village
of Vonnas world-famous.*

It was in 1872 that the Blanc family began its restaurant career on the market square at Vonnas. The square was quite a lively spot on market days (Thursdays) when all the riches of the surrounding countryside were on display: world-famous Bresse chickens with their blue feet, allowed to roam free in the barnyard and raised on grain, the crayfish, and the fattened pullets. It was the wife who did the cooking "La Mère". "La Mère Blanc." That name evokes together the "mothers" who offered their hospitality to the journeymen working their way around France, the mother of a family and her nourishing home cooking, and "la mère lyonnaise," heiress to a long culinary tradition running back to the cook of the Maréchal de Castellane, military governor of Lyons, who gave the name of "sapper's apron" to her recipe for a breaded beef plate because it resembled the actual apron worn by the sappers in the engineering corps. Her daughter, trained in a bourgeois establishment, insisted on using regional products: frogs, snails. In 1933, the famous culinary writer Curnonsky called her the finest chef in the world. On weekends her restaurant was packed with people who had traveled great distances to feast on her marvelous dishes. There were the wealthy silk merchants from Lyons, the diplomats from Geneva, the well-to-do bourgeoisie, and farmers from the Bresse region. Edouard Herriot, longtime mayor of Lyons and prominent national political figure, delighted in the rich and velvety-smooth dishes and the *crêpes vonnassiennes* (potato pancakes) which for three generations contributed to making Vonnas famous in the world of gourmets. The success and the pace imposed by it on restaurant keepers began to be felt by Georges Blanc's mother. So at the age of twenty-one, he was obliged to aid her with the cooking duties. Raised in a restaurant atmosphere, he was destined for a career as a chef even if he had not felt the call as a child. It is very possible that his literature oriented education is responsible for the fact that he is today one of those French chefs given to long discussions of aspects of culinary techniques. He spent several training periods at various restaurants, including la Réserve de Beaulieu, but these in no way influenced him.

The idea of carrying on the family tradition, a return to his origins, and the traditions of a slightly old-fashioned cuisine hardly excited him. The coming of the "new cuisine" revolution of the 1960s, promoted mostly by the chefs' wild enthusiasm and Gault and Millau, and its public acceptance, kindled the spark of Georges Blanc's imagination. But he knew how to adapt this "new cuisine" to the local products of the Bresse and Dombes regions, how to root it in the soil of France. His was a success in continuity, change without breaking with tradition. He lightened the sauce thickeners, diversified what was offered, and imperceptibly modified eating habits. The diner barely perceived the transition from one style of cuisine to the other. Maître Cuisinier de France, Meilleur Ouvrier de France, Chef of the Year in 1981, four "toques" and a score of 19 out of 20 from Gault et Millau, and a three-star rating in the *Guide Michelin* are some of the awards garnered by this perfectionist who wants to offer a modern cuisine, but one created of regional or traditional products. The thousand-year-old gourmand traditions of nearby Lyons, Mâcon, Bresse, and Bugey are to be found on Georges Blanc's menu.

With a deceptive Venetian or Brugeois air and embellished by a footbridge over the flower-banked Veyle River, the inn of Georges Blanc was decorated by his wife, Jacqueline, and himself with old cupboards and impressive tables which they ferreted out at local antique dealers. The diner feels completely relaxed, surrounded in the very middle of a village by an expanse of wondrous greenery.

Despite the traditional décor, Georges Blanc remains resolutely attached to the present. He has installed a helicopter landing area on the grounds and modernized the kitchen to make his culinary tasks easier. But he still knows how to take his time, how to respect the seasons as much as he does his customers. He is aware that there must be obligatory pauses during a meal, a physiological one between the fish and the meat courses, that the savors of a dish must be preserved. He will leave the scallop attached to its shell, thus proving its freshness, authenticity, and, as he puts it, different texture. He is constantly in search of anything that will add to the refinement of a dish. He will take months, seasons, and sometimes an entire year to produce a new recipe. Tests, modifications, temporary oversights: all these are part of the destiny of a dish. There is always a need to back off, to see the concept as a whole in order to offer the customer or a friend, the supreme judge, a complete, successful dish fully meeting his demanding criteria.

The tapestry that hangs on one of the restaurant's walls wasn't woven in a single day. Perhaps this is why Georges Blanc chose it to decorate his menu and thus remind us of the craftsman

12 01540 Vonnas (air-conditioned, 21 rooms, 5 suites, rooms for receptions and seminars, dogs allowed, swimming pool, tennis courts, heliport). Closed Wednesdays, Thursdays, the entire month of January, and the first week of February. Mâcon is 12 miles away, Lyons 41 miles, and Paris 256 miles. To be seen: Brou (14 miles), Gothic church with rood-screen, stalls, tombs, and stained-glass windows. Bird preserve at Dombes. Pérouges (31 miles), a medieval city, fifteenth- and seventeenth-century fortifications. The Beaujolais vineyards.
AE - Diners - Visa cards honored
Tel: (74) 50.00.10

efforts of the chef, the marvels of ingenuity and knowledge, the meticulous patience required to create a *gâteau de foie blond* (light liver loaf) or a *gougeonnette de saumon aux grenouilles au Sauternes et au curry* (salmon with frogs in a Sauterne and curry sauce). Sample this lukewarm crayfish and frog vinaigrette, these raviolis filled with liver and truffles, the *crêpes vonnassiennes* or all the spices and flavors from a time when pollution did not exist and which have been miraculously preserved by Georges Blanc. Rediscover desserts, each one more surprising than the other, a *galette bressane à la crème grand-mère Blanc.* Come taste all these wonders presented by the most sophisticated chef of the natural.

A gourmand's tiered terrine

Millefeuille gourmand en terrine terrine

Serves 8:
4 ¼ cups (1 L) port-flavored
  meat jelly
14 oz (400 g) foie gras (see Note)
3 or 4 artichoke hearts, cooked
  and thickly sliced
2 chicken breasts, still attached to the carcass
3 qts (3 L) of chicken broth
4 ½ lbs (2 kg) tomatoes, peeled, seeded
  and chopped
8 large spinach leaves
1 bouquet garni
1 clove garlic
2 shallots, finely chopped
6 ½ tablespoons (10 cl) heavy cream
1 tablespoon gelatin
3 tablespoons cold water
2 or 3 avocados, peeled, pitted, and chopped
1 lb (400 g) broad beans or green peas,
  shelled; or ½ lb (250 g) very thin green
  beans, cooked until tender
2 large truffles, sliced
2 tablespoons olive oil
salt and pepper

Prepare a meat jelly and flavor it with port. Cool until it begins to thicken, then brush some of it onto the sides and bottom of a cold 10-by-6-inch porcelain terrine that is about 4 inches deep. Refrigerate.

Drop the spinach into boiling water, boil for 30 seconds, drain, and cool. Squeeze out the water. Reserve.

Place the shallots, tomatoes, and olive oil in a saucepan over moderate heat. Cook for a minute or two then add the bouquet garni and garlic and boil to concentrate the sauce.

Remove the garlic and the bouquet, season generously with salt and pepper, and leave to cool.

Poach the chicken breasts 30 minutes in the broth, drain, and leave to cool. When they are cold, cut the breast meat into relatively wide thin scallops.

Dissolve the gelatin in cold water. Heat the cream and stir in the gelatin. Add the avocados to the cream; salt and pepper. Pour into a blender and blend until smooth. Reserve.

Line the bottom of the terrine with 4 or 5 spinach leaves, place half the foie gras on top and brush with meat jelly. Place back in the refrigerator until the jelly stiffens, then spoon half of the avocado mousse into the terrine; cover with the broad beans, peas, or green beans. Lightly press the vegetables into the mousse. Cover with meat jelly and refrigerate until it stiffens.

Place half the pieces of chicken into the terrine, cover with the tomato sauce, and lay in the remaining chicken. Brush with the meat jelly and cover with sliced truffles. Refrigerate to stiffen the jelly, then spoon the remaining mousse into the terrine mixed with the artichokes. Cover with the remaining foie gras, spinach leaves, and meat jelly. Refrigerate for 24 hours before serving.

To serve, quickly dip the terrine into a bowl of hot water and turn the contents out onto a platter. Dip a sharp knife into hot water and carefully slice the terrine. Serve with a vinaigrette that includes some peeled and seeded tomatoes and freshly chopped herbs. For a nicer presentation, you may decorate the plate with artichoke tips and some more peeled, seeded, and chopped tomato, topped with bits of truffle julienne.

Note: this terrine would no doubt be excellent made with calf's liver lightly poached in stock instead of the fresh foie gras mentioned here.

Potato crêpes

Crêpes vonnassiennes

Serves 6:
1 lb (500 g) potatoes
2 cups plus 1 tablespoon (50 cl) milk
generous ⅓ cup (60 g) flour
3 whole eggs plus 4 eggs whites
4 tablespoons heavy cream
1 ⅓ cups (300 g) clarified butter
salt and pepper

Peel the potatoes and boil in salted water. Mash them while hot, adding the milk as you do so. Leave to cool, then stir in first the flour, then the eggs one by one and the egg whites (don't beat them). Last, stir in the cream. Try to stir just enough to make a smooth "batter" about the consistency of a pastry cream. Add salt and pepper as needed.

Heat in a frying pan as much clarified butter as you would need to cook an omelette. When the butter is quite hot, use a spoon to make little mounds of the potato mixture in the pan. The mounds will spread out to make crêpe-like rounds. The crêpes should not touch each other while they are cooking.

Cook the crêpes over high heat, turning each one over once. Cook just long enough to brown both sides. Serve them on individual dinner plates or on one large platter.

These crêpes are excellent with most meats, but they can also be sprinkled with sugar and served as a dessert.

The batter can be prepared up to 24 hours before making the crêpes. If refrigerated, it should be warmed to room temperature before using.

Sea bass marinière

Bar de ligne à la marinière

Serves 4:
1 sea bass weighing about 2 ¼ lbs (1 kg),
  skinned, filleted, and sliced into
  ¼ inch thick scallops
3 ½ tablespoons (50 g) butter (for the fish)

For the sauce:
¼ lb (120 g) butter, quite cold
6 ½ tablespoons (10 cl) olive oil
2 tablespoons lemon juice
3 shallots, finely sliced
1 tomato, peeled, seeded, chopped, and
  boiled to thicken
3 tablespoons chives, tarragon, and basil,
  chopped
half a bay leaf
a pinch of thyme - salt and pepper

For the court bouillon:
half a bottle dry white wine
3 tablespoons (5 cl) water
2 carrots, sliced - 1 onion, sliced
4 shallots, sliced
1 bouquet garni
2 cloves garlic, peeled
1 lemon, peeled and sliced
salt and pepper - fresh chervil

Place the fish fillets on a buttered baking sheet and refrigerate until ready to cook. Heat the oven to 550 °F (290°C).
Begin making the sauce by placing all the ingredients for the court bouillon (except the salt and pepper) in a large saucepan. Cook for 30 minutes. Add the salt and pepper and strain. Set aside.
Heat the olive oil in a saucepan and add the shallots. Cook the shallots until soft, add the tomato, and 1 cup of the court bouillon; the sauce should not be too liquid at this stage. Add more salt and pepper as needed. Add the thyme, bay leaf, and a little lemon juice. Boil for 8 minutes to reduce.
While the sauce is reducing, place 4 tablespoons of water and the remaining lemon juice in a clean saucepan and bring to a boil. Whisk in the butter little by little to form an emulsion, then remove from the heat. Season with salt and pepper. Pour the melted butter into the reduced sauce, stirring constantly. Add the freshly chopped herbs, then adjust the seasoning to taste by adding either more oil, butter, or court bouillon. Whisk the sauce as any ingredient is added. Keep warm.
Salt and pepper the fish fillets, brush them with a little cold water and place in the oven. The water will evaporate almost immediately if the oven is very hot and the fish will be cooked through. Once the fish are cooked, place the fillets on dinner plates, spoon over the sauce, sprinkle with fresh chervil and serve.
Other fish or shellfish can be cooked and served the same way.

Frozen mousse with fresh fruit

Mousse glacée aux fruits frais

Serves 8:
1 cup and one tablespoon (250 g)
  heavy cream, whipped
2 ¼ lbs (1 kg) oranges
½ lb (250 g) strawberries
½ lb (250 g) raspberries

For the syrup:
⅞ cup (20 cl) water
1 ⅓ cups (300 g) granulated sugar
10 eggs yolks
Grand Marnier, rum, or fruit brandy, etc.

Make the syrup first. Place the water and sugar in a small saucepan and bring to a boil. Once the sugar has dissolved continue to boil, without stirring, for 3 minutes, then remove from the heat.
Beat the egg yolks in a bowl, by hand or with an electric mixer, and slowly pour in the sugar syrup. Continue beating for 10 to 15 minutes to make a thick, creamy mixture, then add a little alcohol of your choice.
Beat the cream until very stiff; spoon the egg-yolk mixture over the cream and fold to combine. The resulting mousse should be perfectly smooth. Place the mousse in the freezer and leave for 12 hours.
To serve: Place 8 champagne glasses in the freezer for an hour to chill, or simply chill dessert plates.

Use a knife to peel the oranges, then cut out the wedges from the membranes that surround each one. Cut the strawberries in half. Place two tablespoons of the mousse in the center of each plate, surround with the fruit and serve. The mousse can be molded in individual ramekins, rather than frozen in a bowl, turned out, and served as described. Fresh mint and/or a fruit sauce may also be served with this dessert.

PAUL BOCUSE

*Paul Bocuse and his wife, Raymonde, are seen here
humorously posed before a full-length portrait of the most
famous of all chefs, honoring this roving ambassador of
French cuisine and his success, faithful to his establishment
on the banks of the Saône.*

Almost as much as the Rhône, the Saône River has been a strong influence in the destiny of Paul Bocuse. It was his refuge during hard times, which he evokes when speaking of poaching expeditions with his father, or when their boat nearly sank under the weight of its load of fish. Since 1765, the Bocuse family have been restaurant keepers at Collonges-au-Mont-d'Or, a fishing village on the banks of the rich and often turbulent Saône. Their earliest customers were boatmen who transported sacks of wheat to be ground into flour at a mill dating from 1634. The first Bocuse restaurant keeper couple was composed of a husband, miller, and a wife, chef, in the tradition of the "mères lyonnaises." With the passage of time, they gradually acquired a local reputation as purveyors of al fresco meals of fried fish and Beaujolais until Paul's father, Georges, was introduced to a more elaborate cuisine in the luxury hotels of the 1920s. The Hotel de Paris in Monte Carlo, the Imperial in Menton, and the Royal in Evian were some of the stops in his progression. He met Fernand Point in his travels and the two remained good friends even when Point was at the height of his glory at La Pyramide in Vienne.

The vicissitudes of the times, marital problems, the sale of the family inn and the name (it took years of effort by Paul Bocuse to establish himself under his own name), World War II, in which he fought brilliantly with the famous Chad Battalion, a hard apprenticeship at the Restaurant de la Soierie in Lyons, all these events make the adolescence of Paul Bocuse read like a novel. But Paul learned something new from each chapter. His knowledge of fowl stems from the time he took refuge on a farm in the Bresse region to avoid being sent as a compulsory laborer to Germany during the war. Things were hard in those days. There was no royal road to success for the sons of chefs then. Today, the succeeding generations in the culinary world assume their positions running some of the most prestigious restaurants in the world by hereditary right.

But this enthusiastic hunter of hares and thrushes never shrank from any task set before him. He worked for a time at "Mère Brazier"; he even took an assumed name to get hired by Fernand Point. When he was at Lucas Carton he made friends with Jean Troisgros before returning to Point as pantry chef. After a period at Megève, he returned to Collonges. In 1959, on the death of his father, he borrowed enough money to set up on his own. He was awarded the title of M.O.F. (Meilleur Ouvrier de

France–best craftsman in his trade) in 1960. The first Michelin star came in 1961, the second three years later, and the third three years after that. It was at this time that he bought back the title "Paul Bocuse" and made it famous. But Paul Bocuse also personifies faithfulness. To his ideas: the Valéry Giscard d'Estaing truffle created for a dinner at the presidential palace is still on the menu. To his friends: this condottiere, this pilgrim in the cause of French cuisine, who loudly proclaims his preferences for beautiful women and elaborate practical jokes (a book has been written on these) is an imposing personality. His hobbies of collecting prefaces, ancient weapons, cookbooks (his own sell very well), and newspaper front pages have not separated him from his origins.

The luxury of his restaurant, its international fame or that of the annex created for special occasions, l'Abbaye, have in no way altered his love for the cuisine of the open-air market, of being able to appreciate sensually the freshness of a product, the odors of the soil, and the mellowness of a fruit.

But what is of utmost importance to the history of cuisine is that Paul Bocuse, turning away from the "mistaken ideas of a new cuisine," regretted that "the whiting has disappeared from French kitchens, swept away by a tidal wave of scallops." His menu features not only butter and cream but also a soup made daily with freshly bought vegetables (no fewer than eighteen of them), sea-perch in crust, and the admirable Bresse fowl. There are sumptuous *gratins dauphinois à la crème double* (another demonstration of his ideas) as well as "grand veneur" sauces or vernal butters concocted from shallots and chervil.

Paul Bocuse is constantly on the move. One day, he is at Disney World, the next this Red Adair of the kitchen is rushing off to help a friend get his restaurant back into working order, and then off he goes for a series of cooking lessons in Tokyo or lectures in Los Angeles. But despite all this gadding about, he is always present at Collonges. Roger Jaloux, his chef and also a M.O.F., has become so proficient at emulating the "master" that he is a second Bocuse in cuisine without his imperial stature, truculence, or highly developed communication sense. Amid the décor of full-length portraits of himself, Paul Bocuse is more than simply a showman. He has created a personal cuisine and generations of young chefs have taken Bocuse as a reference, as a landmark. Along with Raymond Oliver, he has known how to bring the chefs out of the anonymity of their kitchens where

Paul Bocuse has not forgotten his origins, the river of his childhood, the joys of hunting or strolling in the rich Bresse countryside. He is true to his birthplace of Collonges and the heritage of his ancestors. All these aspects of his character seem to be symbolized by these roosting doves in the restaurant's gardens. Of all his desires, the strongest and most significant one was that of transforming the family inn into a temple of the ultimate in culinary art. He has satisfied it, complete with a smartly attired bellboy as in the luxury hotels. Roger Jaloux, his chef, operates out of one of the most beautiful kitchens in the world, conceived and created by Paul Bocuse himself.

13 Place d'Illhäusern 69660 Collonges-au-Mont-d'Or (air-conditioned, rooms for banquets and receptions). Closed from August 4 to August 26. Lyons is 7 1/2 miles away, the airport of Satolas is 22 miles away, and Paris 292 miles. To be seen: Lyons, the "traboules" (localism for passages), the Croix-Rousse district, the Notre-Dame de Fourvière church, the fabric museum, the Guignol (puppet theater), the fountain in the Place des Terreaux, the Place Bellecourt. The Banks of the Saône, the Ile Barbe, and at Rochetaille (3 miles away) the automobile museum.
AE – Diners cards honored
Tel: (7) 822.01.40

they slowly and lovingly prepared their dishes, refreshed with champagne or wines unknown to the public.
This very book might never have been written without Paul Bocuse; this self-made man has created a culinary aristocracy and given another dimension to an art that is based on the ephemeral and that must attain perfection and impose itself solely by strength of the memory left on the diner by a dish or meal or by the evocation of a soup *à la jambe de bois* or an *oreiller de la Belle Aurore*.

L'Auberge du Père Bise

*In the unique setting of an inn on the lake of
Annecy, Charlyne Bise and her daughter Sophie carry on the
traditions of this establishment, withdrawn from the
bustle of the highway but opening out onto the splendors of the
lake and the Alps.*

A cascade of flowers on the banks of Talloires bay. The deep, sun-speckled waters of the lake surrounded by snow-capped mountains, the greenery high up on the Semnoz, a horizon of medieval chateaux silhouetted on the Duingt peninsula, the peaks of la Tournette or the Dents de Lanfon. Such is the exquisite Alpine setting of the Bise family inn on the outskirts of Annecy. For four generations, the Bises have labored in the service of their clientele, improving the décor and comfort, installing luxurious Baccarat chandeliers, warmer-looking wood panels or an astonishing leaded-glass window graced by a peacock in all his resplendent glory. And each day sees a renewal of the ritual gestures in the kitchens. On the death of François Bise, his widow Charlyne took over the running of the restaurants. She was only twenty years old when she started her restaurant career. Hers was the fate of a daughter-in-law faced by a father-in-law who was a harsh taskmaster. Before she was engaged to François, she had already learned the essentials of working in a kitchen and restaurant management. While the father looked after the wine cellar, Sophie, at the age of twenty, in turn made her entry into the kitchen as others would enter a convent. She received a man's apprenticeship with Madame Fernand, mother of Marie-Claude Rostand, wife of Michel, at Saint-Martin-le-Vinoux, the two-star Parisian restaurant. She then spent two six-month periods with the suppliers – butchers and fishmongers – to learn all about the products. This was followed by her true culinary education: with Gaertner and Aux Armes de France at Ammerschwir in Alsace and with Peyrot, one of the geniuses of the kitchen; at Le Vivarois in Paris; the Bise tradition has been preserved. Nothing has changed at the inn despite the turmoil provoked by the decision of the *Guide Michelin* concerning its third star. Nothing? That really isn't exactly true. There is now a will to transform the appearance of the establishment and to transcend the dishes that have been unjustly described as simply classic ones. Gilles Furtin, the chef, has good credentials – Avallon, Beaulieu – and he has at his disposal a fantastic tool, his kitchen opening on the lake, airy and modern. The Auberge never deviates from its goal. Invention and classicism go hand-in-hand, the sauces are both simple and rich. A dish christened "the marriage of the sea and a lake" symbolizes a cuisine based on fish; the *mignonette de veau Mère Bise* relates the family tradition and the *chausson de queues d'écrevisses* evokes the swiftly-running streams of the Alps. The cheeses offered also remind us of the Alpine pasturelands, the slow migrations of the herds toward the tender grass, the cream metamorphosed into Roblochon or a Vacherin with all the farm flavors intact. Seconding Furtin is pastry chef Eric Girert. His "Marjolaine" cake alone would make a stop at l'Auberge du Père Bise mandatory for a self-respecting gourmand. Every restaurant has its own recipe for this delicacy. The one served at Point is world-famous. Girert acquired his skills from his teacher, André, who in turn had been trained by the great pastry chef Petit-Pierre at Vienne in the Isère region. The ingredients are known to all: crème au beurre, almond paste, chocolate, kirsch, but the secret lies in the way Girert handles the proportions. And he fully intends to keep this secret to himself with the tenacity of a medieval alchemist. But the enduring fame of l'Auberge du Père Bise rests upon the char, the undisputed sovereign of the fishes of the lake. Maurice Marucco, the Auberge director and its perfect host, with thirty-two years of service at the hotel (he began his Auberge career at the age of fourteen), knows all that needs to be known about this salmonid. According to the seasons, he knows the depth of the water in which the char has taken refuge, the temperature preferred by the fish in these cold waters, waters now restored to their original purity by herculean efforts. He knows the names of the remaining fishermen on the lake of Annecy who still have the right and privilege to bring up from the depths with infinite precautions this very special fish. He knows the fragility of its flesh, the death by decompression when a sudden raising to the surface damages the tissues and bursts the blood vessels. Once this happens, the char loses its special qualities. He knows all the varieties, all the subspecies. He has absolutely no use for the "false" chars – those raised in breeding ponds. Perhaps he might have a kind word to say for a char caught in a lake in the Auvergne, as savage and noble as those from "his" lake. He'll tell us all these stories to make us appreciate the marvelous dish which created the renown of the Auberge.

It's time to leave the table. Let us stroll in the pure mountain air before turning in for a restful night in the comfort of our rooms at the Auberge or in the annex, set up in an eighteenth-century house. Tomorrow morning, we'll have breakfast amid the flowers and feed the swans on the remnants of our croissants. Nothing will erase from our memories the legend of the noble char nor the reserved charm of Charlyne Bise.

14 Talloires 74290 Veyrier-du-Lac (meals in the garden, 15 rooms, 9 suites, dogs admitted). Nearby: tennis courts, golf course, horseback riding, fishing, sailing, water skiing on the lake. Closed from November 22 to February 5 and from April 19 to May 5. Annecy is 7 1/2 miles away (airport 22 miles), Mégève 30 miles, Paris 339 miles. To be seen: Annecy, pleasant lake resort city, the chateau, the Saint-Pierre cathedral (sixteenth century) in which Saint-Francis de Sales celebrated mass as a bishop. The Alps.
AE - Diners - Visa cards honored
Tel. (50) 60.72.01

From the outside, l'Auberge du Père Bise looks like a Savoyard chalet, without the mountain, concealed amid luxuriant greenery, isolated from the rest of the world by its trees and flowers. The airy and spacious kitchen, officiated over by Gilles Furtin, a chef with credentials from the finest restaurants, and Eric Girert, the pastry chef, whose "marjolaine" cake is a must for any self-respecting gourmand. Diners in the restaurant's outdoor dining area watch the spectacle of dazzling starlight on the waters of the lake as they sip champagne and converse. Breakfasts, luncheons, or dinners under the linden trees and the umbrellas of the gardens or under the Baccarat chandeliers of the beautiful dining room, the domain of Michel Marucco. Gourmand feasts, a riot of colors and lights, prolonged by the natural splendors as viewed through the bay windows.

Chicken liver mousse

Mousse de foies de volaille

<u>Serves 8 to 10:</u>
14 oz (400 g) chicken livers
7 oz (200 g) fresh pork fatback, diced and
  fried
6 ½ tablespoons (10 cl) port
1 bouquet garni, containing parsley, thyme
  and a bay leaf
14 oz (400 g) foie gras au naturel
3 or 4 tablespoons heavy cream
leaf fat
salt and pepper

Marinate the chicken livers with the fatback, port, bouquet garni, salt, and pepper overnight before cooking.

Remove the bouquet garni and chop the meat in a meat grinder or a food processor. Line a terrine with leaf fat and then fill with the ground liver mixture. Cover with a piece of aluminum foil, or with the terrine cover, and bake in a water bath (bain-marie) in a 350 °F (180 °C) oven for 30 minutes. When it is cooked, lift the terrine out of the water and set it aside to cool. Spoon off the fat from the terrine, then scoop out the contents and place in a bowl with the foie gras and stir to combine. Work this mixture through a sieve to make a smooth cream; add the heavy cream as the liver is being worked through the sieve.

Spoon the mixture into individual molds or ramekins and refrigerate for 12 hours before serving.

Serve as is or topped with truffles and a meat jelly flavored with port. The plates can be decorated with more jelly, cut into various patterns, and a rose made of tomato skins.

Crayfish gratin

Gratin de queues d'écrevisses

<u>Serves 4:</u>
80 live crayfish
2 tablespoons olive oil
4 onions, sliced
10 shallots, sliced - 1 clove garlic, crushed
2 tomatoes, peeled, seeded, and chopped
1 bouquet garni, of thyme, bay leaf, and
  parsley
3 tablespoons (5 cl) Cognac
3 ¼ cups (¾ L) white wine
2 cups and 1 tablespoon (50 cl) heavy cream
2 tablespoons grated Swiss cheese
4 white peppercorns, coarsely pounded or
  ground
salt and pepper - 1 truffle, sliced

Heat the olive oil in a large pan, add the onions, shallots, and garlic and cook to soften. Add the tomatoes, white peppercorns and bouquet garni; cook just until the liquid has evaporated (the tomatoes should not brown). Raise the heat and add the crayfish. Cook, shaking the pan frequently, until they turn red, then add the Cognac and set it on fire. Once the flame goes out, add the wine, salt, and pepper. Cover and simmer 15 minutes.

Lift out the crayfish, shell them, and place the tails in individual gratin dishes. Boil the sauce for about 20 minutes to reduce, then strain into a clean saucepan, pressing hard to extract all the flavor from the vegetables. Add the cream to the sauce and boil until the sauce is thick and creamy. Add salt and pepper as needed.

Spoon the sauce over the tails, sprinkle a little grated cheese into each dish, top with a slice of truffle and place under the broiler to brown. This dish can be served with rice à la Créole.

Braised chicken with tarragon

Poularde braisée à l'estragon

Serves 4:
1 3 lb (1.500 kg) chicken (neck, wing tips, and gizzard separated and reserved)
1 large bunch fresh tarragon
3 tablespoons (30 g) butter
2 cups and 2 tablespoons (50 cl) heavy cream
salt and pepper
tarragon, to decorate

Stuff the chicken with the big bunch of fresh tarragon and tie for roasting. Rub the skin with salt and pepper, then lightly brown the bird with a little butter in a large pot. Add the neck, wings, and gizzard, cover the pot and simmer for 40 minutes. Do not let the juices in the pot burn.
Lift out the chicken, boil the liquid in the pot until it has almost evaporated, add the cream, and simmer for 10 minutes. Strain.
Cut the legs and breast meat from the bird. Discard the tarragon stuffing. Pour sauce into each dinner plate, heap boiled rice in the center, and add the chicken, decorated with fresh tarragon.

Chocolate Negus

Négus

Serves 20:
12 egg yolks
18 egg whites
12 whole eggs
2 ¼ lbs (1 kg) granulated sugar
12 oz (350 g) butter, softened
1 ⅓ cups (180 g) flour
1 lb (450 g) semi-sweet chocolate
generous ⅞ cup (120 g) bitter cocoa powder
⅞ cup (20 cl) strong black coffee
chocolate shavings, to decorate

Beat the egg yolks and 1 lb of sugar until the mixture whitens, then stir in the flour and cocoa powder.
Beat the egg whites until stiff and fold into the batter.
Cook the cake in small individual cake pans, preferably high-sided ones or use one cake pan to make one larger cake. Lightly butter and flour the pans, pour in the batter, and bake in a slow oven (225 °F to 250 °F/100 °C-120 °C) until toothpick inserted in the cake comes out clean. Remove from the oven and allow to cool before turning out.
Make a chocolate filling by melting the chocolate in a saucepan with the coffee. Place the whole eggs in another pan (preferably a copper one), add the remaining sugar, and whisk over low heat until the mixture thickens. Add the chocolate-coffee mixture and leave to cool, then stir in the butter to make a smooth filling. Cut the cakes in half through the middle. Fill with the chocolate cream, sprinkle shaved chocolate over the cakes and serve.

Note: in the photo the Negus is served with ice cream and a selection of cookies.

CHÂTEAU DE LA CHÈVRE D'OR

*A succession of courtyards, the charm of a chateau perched
high and surrounded by the village of Eze, patios with fine
colonnades, the quality of the light: all these aspects
charmed owner Bruno Ingold as surely as the blue
of the Mediterranean skies and the legend of the Chèvre d'Or.*

Enchanted by the village of Eze with its flinty architecture carved out of the mountainside and by the scented flowers, the celebrated American violinists, Joyce and Slato Balakovitch, decided on a summer night in 1924 to make Eze their home. The huddle of houses and the tangled network of narrow streets were still untouched by the tourist rush that now is experienced every summer. There were no art galleries or craftsmen's shops. Did Joyce, the Californian, know that the Phoenicians had raised a temple to Isis in Eze? Did she, like the Egyptian divinity, want to restore life to the village? When she first saw it haloed by the dying rays of the sun with only a grazing goat in view, it seemed to her to be made of gold and she decided that their house would be called la Chèvre d'Or (the Golden Goat) and that it would be constructed there on the site of the chateau of the counts of Eze. Like the ancient Ligurians, they became builders, had water piped in, dug a swimming pool out of the rocky flanks, and restored the first residence in a reviving Eze Village. Two decades later, Bruno Ingold, a Swiss diplomat, also fell under the spell of Eze. Like the Americans, he was fascinated by the sun-speckled cove 1,200 feet below, now called the Bay of the Chèvre d'Or. This cove lies at the bottom of the path walked by Nietzsche when he was in the throes of writing *Thus Spoke Zarathustra.* Now part of the Relais et Châteaux chain, la Chèvre d'Or has been able to preserve the site and that exquisite relaxed atmosphere sensed by the two American musicians on that summer night sixty years ago. A succession of small suites, most of which are duplex ones, integrated into the medieval village, independent from one another, intimate and comfortable, open out onto the infinite space surrounding the chateau. In this stony setting, color is provided by purple thickets under the patio and framing the swimming pool. Bruno Ingold, the perfect master of the manor, never forgets the courtesy of diplomacy. He is now Swiss Consul General to His Serene Highness Prince Rainier of Monaco. The restrained décor compliments the stones by adorning them with high-warp tapestries and the dark colors of polished rustic woods. The setting prepares us to participate in some pagan ceremony. The serving ritual as organized by Claude Hirt, director of the restaurant, also evokes mysterious and mystical banquets.

The goal of all these elements is to ensure a proper appreciation of the cuisine of Elie Mazot. Mazot, born in Aix-en-Provence, began his career as a pastry cook. Not enough praise can be given to this sort of training to create the sense of precision called for in cuisine. Mazot worked for a time in such important establishments as the Berkeley and the Ritz in Paris. It was while working at Mère Germaine in Villefranche that Mazot garnered his first Michelin star and recognition of his talents as a chef. He has been exercising those talents at la Chèvre d'Or for the past several years, backed up by a brigade of two pastry cooks and eight cooks and displaying particular enthusiasm for the preparation of fish recipes. This enables him to get away from the routine presentations, to innovate. As might be expected, the cuisine at la Chèvre d'Or is rooted in the classic French cuisine. But it has been lightened and purified. The audacious touches are clearly evident. Each dish has a perfection traceable to the choice of the product. The market is quite a distance away; the baskets of oysters and the marvelous cuts of Sisteron lamb are carried up to the restaurant. Aromatic, but not excessively so, the cuisine praticed by Elie Mazot makes full use of regional produce. Garlic is present, but is never allowed to dominate, and even in the famous squabs with garlic cloves it remains discreet, like the chef who is rarely seen in the dining room. Despite the Michelin star, the two "toques," and 15 out of 20 from Gault and Millau, awards, honors, Mazot knows full well that every day calls for an effort to keep them, to merit them. In our opinion, he has nothing to fear on that score. The *huitres au champage* (oysters in champagne) or the *civet de gougeonnettes de turbotin* (stew of young turbots) are enough to ensure his glory.

With a prestigious wine cellar, which a competent wine steward helps the diner to discover, and the serving of the dishes performed with the precision of a Swiss watch, a meal at la Chèvre d'Or is total bliss. Ever since he was sent by the Swiss government to aid in the post-war reconstruction of France, Bruno Ingold has known all the great personages of this world. He knows exactly how to give each of his guests the correct amount of attention to the point that the welcome offered becomes an art. He also knows how to preserve the privacy of the family of Prince Rainier on a neighborly visit from Monaco or of a star wishing to remain anonymous and at the same time recognized and admired. Jacques Chirac, the mayor of Paris, Roger Moore, Gilbert Bécaud, Jackie Stewart, David Niven and Yves Piaget, the celebrated jeweler, have followed in the footsteps of Walt Disney, one of the earliest regulars at la Chèvre d'Or. Claudia

Elie Mazot, the chef, born in magnificent Aix-en-Provence, accustomed to beauty from childhood, familiar with Michelin star ratings and film and stage stars, reigns over the kitchens of la Chèvre d'Or. The delicate architecture of an imitation cloister, the dizzying sheer drops of the cliffs, the superabundance of flowers, and the swimming pool give one the impression of being in a Roman villa or a Phoenician temple. Everything at Eze contributes to the airy, plunging, fragmented vision the château gives us. La Chèvre d'Or is only a statue and the weeds of the years of misery have become geraniums.

15 rue du Barri 06360 Eze-Village (swimming pool, tennis courts, 6 rooms, 3 suites, bar-lounge, dogs allowed, golf course 6 miles away). Closed from mid-November to mid-February. Monaco is 5 miles distant, Nice 7 miles (Nice airport 10 miles), Paris 961 miles. To be seen: the old village of Eze, the ruins of the chateau and the chapel of the Pénitents Blancs (sixteenth century), the exotic gardens. The medium-level cliff road with its panoramic view on the coast. Cap d'Ail, open-air theatre decorated with mosaics by Jean Cocteau.
Diners - Visa cards honored
Tel: (93) 41.12.12

Cardinale, Gina Lollobrigida, and Mireille Mathieu impart the feminine touch to this nest perched on the heights of Eze. The presence of these stars barely diverts our attention from what is being served or from a look at the horizon line with Cap Ferrat lying like an exclamation point on the sea. Eze has seen other famous persons over the centuries. And the stones send back to us just the muffled conversations of contented people.

Lobster cream with green bean sauce

Bavarois de langouste au coulis de haricots verts

Serves 4:
1 live lobster (about 2 ½ lbs/good kg)
⅔ cup (15 cl) heavy cream, whipped
    until it peaks
1 teaspoon gelatin
1 tablespoon cold water
4 egg yolks · 8 teaspoons Cognac
1 cup plus 1 tablespoon (25 cl) white wine
1 cup plus 1 tablespoon (25 cl) water
1 stalk of celery · 1 onion
1 carrot
3 cloves garlic, sliced fine
2 bay leaves · 1 sprig thyme
2 tablespoons tomato paste
½ lb (250 g) green beans
6 ½ tablespoons (10 cl) olive oil
salt and pepper
chervil (optional)
tomato, to decorate (optional)

With a large knife detach the head from the tail of the lobster; detach the claws as well. Chop the head into large pieces. Dice the onions, celery and carrot. Heat ⅓ cup of olive oil in a large frying pan, add the lobster and vegetables and cook to lightly brown. Add the Cognac and set it afire. When the flame dies, add the garlic, thyme, bay leaves, tomato paste, white wine, and water. Season with a little salt and pepper, bring to a boil, then lower the heat and simmer for 15 minutes.

Make a green bean purée as follows: cook the green beans in a large pot of lightly salted boiling water until tender. Drain, then puree the beans in a blender; add the remaining olive oil to the beans; salt and pepper. Pour into a bowl and store in the refrigerator.

Strain the lobster's cooking liquid into a clean saucepan and boil until there is no more than 1 generous cup of liquid left. Dissolve the gelatin in cold water. Remove lobster liquid from the heat and stir in the egg yolks and gelatin, place back over the heat, whisking constantly, to warm (do not boil) for a minute or two, then remove from the heat.

Remove the shell from the tail and claws of the lobster and slice the tail meat into thick slices. Lightly oil four individual ramekins. Place some of the sliced pieces of tail in each ramekin. Dice the remaining lobster meat, and stir it into the sauce made from the cooking liquid. Gently stir the whipped cream in as well, then finish filling the molds with this mixture. Refrigerate for 2 hours before serving.

To serve, spoon some of the green bean sauce onto each plate and turn a ramekin out onto the center of each one. Decorate with fresh chervil and diamond-shaped pieces of tomato (if desired), and serve.

Turbot in red wine with onions and potatoes

Civet de gougeonnettes de turbotin

Serves 4:
1 small turbot weighing about 2 lbs (800 g)
1 bottle red wine, preferably Fleurie
1 carrot, sliced · 1 onion, sliced
1 stalk of celery, sliced
1 bay leaf · 1 sprig thyme
scant ⅔ cup (140 g) butter
4 ½ teaspoons flour
1 cup and 1 tablespoon (25 cl) water
12 baby potatoes, peeled and shaped like
    olives
32 baby onions, peeled
8 small pieces of bread, cut into heart shapes
chervil · salt and pepper

Fillet the turbot and cut the fillets into strips about 1 ¼ inches wide and 4 inches long. Flatten them slightly under a knife, then refrigerate.

Place the bones of the fish in a large saucepan with 1 tablespoon of butter and the following sliced vegetables: onion, celery, and carrot. Add thyme and bay leaf to the saucepan and cook over moderate heat until the vegetables are tender, then add the flour, wine, and water and boil slowly until three quarters of the liquid has evaporated. Strain the liquid into a clean saucepan, pressing on the bones and vegetables with the back of a spoon to extract all their flavor. Add a little salt and pepper to the strained liquid and set it aside.

Steam the potatoes. Cook the onions in a pan with 2 teaspoons of butter and a little water until tender. Brown the onions in the butter once the water has evaporated. Remove the onions from the pan, add another tablespoon

of butter, and brown the pieces of bread to make croutons. Keep warm.

Reheat the fish stock and poach the strips of fish in it for about 4 minutes, then drain and arrange them on hot dinner plates with the onions and potatoes. Keep warm.

Whisk the remaining butter into the fish stock little by little. Season with salt and pepper if needed, then spoon over the fish. Garnish with the croutons and a little fresh chervil, and serve.

Baby pigeons with puff pastry and pasta

Suprême de pigeonneaux en feuilleté, pâtes fraîches

Serves 4:
4 young pigeons (squab)
4 squares of baked puff pastry
1 oz (30 g) truffles, chopped
1 cup and 1 tablespoon (25 cl) meat stock
8 teaspoons Cognac
1 onion, chopped fine
½ lb (200 g) mushrooms, sliced
¾ cup (180 g) butter
4 ½ teaspoons (15 g) flour
½ lb (200 g) freshly made, uncooked pasta
salt and pepper

Prepare the pigeons as if for roasting. Season with salt and dust with flour, then brown them in a large pot with a tablespoon of butter. Cook 10 minutes to brown–they should be eaten rare.

Cook the pasta in a large pot of boiling salted water, drain and toss with 3 ½ tablespoons butter.

Brown the onion in a small saucepan, add the mushrooms, salt, and pepper, and cook over high heat, stirring constantly for 5 minutes. Keep warm.

Cut the legs and breast meat from the pigeons and slice the breast meat. Keep warm. Coarsely chop the carcasses with a cleaver and brown in the fat that was used to cook the pigeons. Once the bones have browned, pour off the fat, add the Cognac and set afire. When the flame has died down, add the meat stock and cook for 10 minutes. Strain the liquid through a sieve, pressing on the bones to extract all their juices. Place the strained liquid into a clean saucepan, add all but a teaspoon of the truffles and whisk in the butter little by little.

Just before serving, warm the pieces of puff pastry in a hot oven, place them on dinner plates, cover with some of the mushrooms, then place the breast meat and legs of the pigeons on top of this. Spoon over the sauce and serve with the pasta sprinkled with the remaining truffle just before serving.

Pear gratin

Gratin de poires William

Serves 4:
4 large peeled pears, poached in sugar syrup
4 thin slices of Genoese cake

For the almond cream:
¼ lb (125 g) butter, softened
generous ½ cup (125 g) granulated
  sugar - 2 eggs
1 cup (125 g) powdered almonds
2 ½ tablespoons (25 g) flour

For the sauce:
4 egg yolks
4 tablespoons (50 g) granulated sugar
6 ½ tablespoons (10 cl) heavy cream,
  whipped until it peaks
8 teaspoons (4 cl) pear brandy

Cream the butter and sugar together, then beat in the eggs, almonds, and flour.

Make a pear sauce by beating together the egg yolks and sugar until the mixture turns lemon-color, then fold in the whipped cream and the pear brandy.

Spread the pieces of Genoese cake with the almond cream, brown under the broiler, then place on the dessert plates.

Slice the pear and place slices on top of the Genoese cake, spoon over the sauce, and place back under the broiler to lightly brown. Serve immediately.

Note: a more elaborate presentation in shown in the photo, where the Genoese cake is in the center, covered by slices of pear and decorated with raspberries and fresh mint after browning the sauce under the broiler/grill.

CHÂTEAU DU DOMAINE SAINT-MARTIN

*At the Domaine Saint-Martin,
the chateau and the ruins are invisible from the road,
lost in the oleanders and bristling with cypresses.
And yet it is a gourmand empire, jealously watched over
by René Leroux, wine steward and perfect host.*

Bernard Frank, one of the finest French authors of the present generation, is also one of its truest gourmands. He disputes this title with Robert Sabatier and a handful of other sybarites of the writing profession. It was in his company and in part thanks to him that I traveled along the winding roads past the ruins of the twelfth-century Templar castle with its old drawbridge, its centuries-old olive trees and up to this Relais-Château with its little country houses on the other side of the road to Coursegoules, all facing the magnificent landscape of the hills of Vence. The imposing dining room dominates a grandiose panorama of villages perched on sheer cliffs. It is flooded by that special luminosity found only in the skies of Provence.

René Leroux, one of the greatest wine stewards on the Riviera, and president of the Riviera Wine Stewards Association, advised us to order a Corton Renardes' 79 as the wine most worthy of accompanying the cuisine of Dominique Ferrière. Although still young, Ferrière already worked under Pierre Laporte at the Café de Paris in Biarritz and André Daguin at the Hôtel de France in Auch (two highly colorful culinary personalities) before going on to the Savoy and Berkeley in London. His training gave Ferrière a taste for imaginative dishes, a respect for regional products without falling into the trap of summer folklore presentations, a fondness for the expensive products of the southwest (truffles, *foie gras,* sea perch) and a passion for exact cooking times. From his master-chef father he learned and retained a precision of gesture and aptness for the trimmings offered with the dish.

It is a pleasure to find vegetables accompanying the fish here when many other chefs do not offer them. The region and the small truck gardeners supply him, in season, with the remarkable purple asparagus, the various ingredients for the *mesclun* salad (purslane, oak leaves, *trévise,* and many others to be found at Provençal markets), and fragrant melons served with Pineau des Charentes.

This cuisine in no way resembles that of the luxury hotels. It is more intuitive, more youthful. Certain dishes permit all sorts of extravagances. Ragoût of fresh noodles with truffles, a royal dish, a juicy biscuit of hog fish with basil, a *saint-pierre* (a fine fish) grilled with a mustard coating, a rave-evoking *petite nage de poissons aux légumes* (very much like the *marmite dieppoise* but enlivened with the Herbs of Provence), cranberries accompany-ing a roast Challans duck or a paradoxical *pot-au-feu de saumon sauvage* (wild salmon boiled dinner), in which the salmon has an unsuspected tenderness due to precisely timed cooking, or a hazelnut-glazed soufflé. Served on blue tablecloths, evoking the sky and the blue Mediterranean nearby, this cuisine conserves an exceptional freshness – an impression reinforced by the large bay windows, the glass walls, the space, and the light. The bar-lounge has a comfortable British air about it. The lobby is not that of a hotel but of an inhabited house, one of great luxury and restraint. Polychrome wooden statues, Shiraz rugs hung on the walls, antique furniture, old Flemish tapestries against the background of white stone, form a highly harmonious, refined whole. Chancellor Adenauer called the Château du Domaine Saint-Martin "the antichamber to paradise." A paradise to which Raquel Welch, a "regular," adds a slightly pagan touch. The spirit of Saint-Martin, who passed this way in a.d. 350, still haunts the old stones overgrown with oleanders. The present chateau was built in the 1930s by the father of the current owners, Daniel and Edouard Genève.

The exceptional distinction of this Provençal-style hotel complex, the comfort and privacy of the apartments spread out over the hill or around large silent courtyards are more precious treasures than that of the Templars, which, according to legend, is buried under the hill. Midway between the Baou des Blancs, a small summit riddled with unusual grottos, the great stone gate, vestige of past glories, is no longer the obligatory passage point of Saint-Martin pilgrims. Other paths now lead to the tennis courts or to the Hollywood-style swimming pool. Here again, the presence of numerous movie actresses in Mack Sennett bathing beauty attitudes adds to the Californian atmosphere. The hedges offer shade, the sweet scents of summer, and break up the space, deliberately complicating the labyrinth surrounding the hotel as if to delay the time for sitting down at the dining room table. It's a bit of a voyage from the villa-apartment to the restaurant, and the dining room of the Genève brothers has the look of one on a luxury liner. Passengers on a stationary cruise, we hope that it will last indefinitely. Just so long as Dominique Ferrière is there to provide the gustatory pleasures, playing with us as he does with the flavors.

The day continues its unruffled pace in this peaceful setting, disturbed only by the chirping of the cicadas or the distant rustle of the leaves.

All that Provence offers in the way of flowers, rock gardens, and trees is concentrated on the terraces and in the gardens. The large dining room, protected from the sun by red-striped awnings, is bathed in a rosy-hued light contrasting with the clear blueness of the skies over the Col de Vence down in the valley. In the kitchens, chef Dominique Ferrière labors over one of his inspired culinary specialties. The spotless corridors ending in elegant rotundas offer the beholder a profusion of beautiful art treasures, antique furnishings, and Persian rugs.

16 Route de Coursegoules 06140 Vence (rooms for receptions and seminars, 16 rooms, 10 villa-suites, dogs admitted with an additional charge, swimming pool, horseback riding, golf course). Closed from November to March and on Wednesdays in the off season. Antibes is 12 miles away, Nice (airport) 12 1/2 miles, Paris 575 miles. To be seen: Vence, the Matisse chapel, the Peyra gate, the cathedral. Tourette-sur-Loup (4 miles), fortified village. The panoramic view from the Col de Vence (6 miles), St-Paul-de-Vence, the ramparts, the Fondation Maeght art museum.
AE – Diners – Visa cards honored
Tel: (93) 58.02.02

Mixed fish plate
with baby vegetables
and butter sauce

Petite nage de poissons

Serves 4:
7 oz (200 g) monkfish (anglerfish) fillets
7 oz (200 g) sea bream or porgy fillets
7 oz (200 g) John Dory fillets
a 10 ½ oz (300 g) sole, filleted
4 red mullet, filleted
4 mussels
4 clams
4 sea scallops
4 baby turnips, peeled
4 baby carrots, peeled
4 baby leeks, whites only,
  cut into julienne strips
1 tomato, peeled, seeded, and cut into strips
1 bunch chervil
1 bunch parsley
2 shallots, peeled and chopped
2 cups and 2 tablespoons (50 cl) fish stock
  made with the bones of the fish
⁷⁄₈ cup (20 cl) white vermouth
⁷⁄₈ cup (200 g) butter, softened
juice ½ lemon
salt and white pepper
green peas and asparagus tips (optional)

Cut the fillets of each fish into four pieces. Rub the pieces with salt and pepper and place them in the refrigerator. Boil the bones to make a fish stock. Finely chop all but a few leaves of the chervil and parsley. Sprinkle the chopped herbs into a large frying pan, add the shallot, vermouth, and fish stock. Bring the liquid to a boil, then remove from the heat and allow to cool.

Cook the remaining vegetables (except for the tomato) one by one in a large pot of lightly salted boiling water. The cooking time for each vegetable will be different; test them frequently and as soon as they are tender, drain and cool under cold water. Keep warm.

Poach the fish fillets 10 minutes in the pan with the wine-stock mixture; do not allow to boil. Once the fish are cooked, remove them with a skimmer and drain on a clean towel.

Arrange the fish on the dinner plates and garnish with the vegetables, including the raw tomato.

Place the clams and mussels in the liquid the fish cooked in and cook over high heat until their shells open. Lift them out of the liquid, remove the flesh from the shells and place on the dinner plates. Poach the scallops in the same liquid and place on the plates as well. Strain the liquid through a cloth then boil over high heat to reduce by half then, over low heat,

whisk in the butter little by little to make a smooth sauce. Add salt, pepper and lemon juice as needed.

Place the dinner plates in a hot oven to reheat the fish and their garnish, then spoon the sauce onto the plates (be careful not to spoon any of the sand from the mussels on to the plates – if there is any, it will be in the bottom of the pan with the sauce). Sprinkle parsley and chervil over each plate and serve immediately.

Lime mousse

Mousse au citron

Serves 8:
generous 1 ²⁄₃ cups (40 cl) heavy cream
1 ½ cups (350 g) granulated sugar
14 eggs
1 ½ tablespoons (12 g) gelatin
5 tablespoons cold water
zest of 5 limes
⁷⁄₈ cup (20 cl) lime juice
1 Genoese cake
⁷⁄₈ cup (200 g) raspberry sauce
a few candied lime peels, sliced thin
mint leaves

Separate the egg yolks from the whites. Beat the yolks with a scant ½ cup sugar, the lime juice, and lime zest.

Bring the cream to a boil then pour it little by little onto the yolk and sugar mixture, whisking constantly. Place the mixture over moderate heat, and boil, whisking for 2 minutes. Dissolve the gelatin in the water. Remove the cream mixture from the heat, stir in the gelatin, and reserve.

Beat the egg whites until they are very stiff, then beat in the remaining sugar. While the cream is still warm, fold in the egg whites.

Cut the Genoese cake into three horizontally so as to have three thin layers. Place one layer in the bottom of a soufflé mold or a flan ring 3 inches high and spread with half the lime mousse. Cover with a second layer of cake and

cover with the remaining mousse, then place the third piece of cake on top and refrigerate for 2 to 3 hours.

To serve, turn out the cake (or remove the flan ring) and cut it into individual servings. Serve with raspberry sauce mixed with candied lime peel, and decorate with fresh mint leaves.

Note: a simpler presentation is shown in the photo, where the cake is simply decorated with sliced lemons.

Duck breast with cranberries, mushrooms, and potatoes

Aiguillettes de canette de Challans rôtie aux airelles

Serves 4:
1 duck weighing about 3 ½ lbs (1.500 kg)
2 oz (60 g) fresh cranberries
1 ½ oz (40 g) fresh morels
1 ½ oz (40 g) chanterelle mushrooms
1 ½ oz (40 g) boletus mushrooms
1 lb (400 g) potatoes
6 ½ tablespoons (10 cl) cooking oil
2 tablespoons granulated sugar
⅞ cup (20 cl) red wine vinegar
5 teaspoons green peppercorns
2 tablespoons (30 g) butter
⅞ cup (20 cl) cooking oil, total
2 shallots
1 bouquet garni, made with thyme, bay leaf, parsley, tarragon, and chervil
salt and pepper

For the sauce:
2 cups and 2 tablespoons (50 cl) veal stock
2 cups and 2 tablespoons (50 cl) red wine (preferably Médoc)
⅞ cup (20 cl) Madeira
⅞ cup (20 cl) Armagnac
1⅔ cups (40 cl) heavy cream
⅞ cup (20 cl) duck or chicken blood (optional)
1 bunch chervil

Place 1 teaspoon of green peppercorns and one scant teaspoon of salt inside the duck. Rub the skin with more salt and ordinary pepper. Heat 6 ½ tablespoons of cooking oil and 1 tablespoon of butter in a roasting pan on top of the stove. Place the duck on its side in the pan. When it has browned turn it over to the other side and brown. Turn the duck on its back and roast in a 525 °F (280 °C) oven for 8 minutes, basting frequently, then remove it from the oven, spoon the fat from the pan, add 6 tablespoons of Armagnac, and set on fire. When the flames die down, set the duck aside.

Cut the breast meat from the duck and keep warm. Cut off the legs and save them for another occasion.

Cut the carcass into large pieces with a cleaver or large kitchen knife and place back in the roasting pan. Heat on top of the stove to brown, then add the red wine and boil to reduce by half. Add to the pan 2 teaspoons green peppercorns, the veal stock, Madeira, and remaining Armagnac. Season with salt and pepper, add a bouquet garni, some chopped chervil, and a pinch of sugar. Boil to reduce by half, then strain the sauce into a clean saucepan. Bring to a boil, add the cream and boil to reduce by a quarter. Bind the sauce with the blood and remaining butter, whisking vigorously. Strain the sauce again, and keep warm in a bain-marie on top of the stove (it must not boil).

Make "Darphin potatoes": peel and grate the potatoes and season them with salt and pepper. Heat 6 ½ tablespoons of oil in a small frying pan, add the potatoes, flatten them into a pancake, and cook 4 minutes on a side. Turn out and keep warm.

In a small saucepan, melt 2 teaspoons of butter and sauté the mushrooms and finely sliced shallots.

Boil the vinegar with 1 ½ tablespoons of sugar for 2 minutes, then add the cranberries and cook for 2 or 3 seconds. Remove from the heat. Slice the duck breasts and arrange them on the dinner plates. Quarter the "Darphin potato" and place a piece on each plate with the duck. Garnish with the mushrooms, and sprinkle the plates with chopped parsley. Spoon some of the sauce over the duck and serve the rest in a gravy boat. Finish garnishing the plates with the cranberries and green peppercorns. Place the plates in a very hot oven to reheat, garnish with a little fresh chervil when the plates come from the oven, and serve.

Prune and Armagnac sherbet

Glace aux pruneaux et à l'armagnac

Serves 4:
4 ¼ cups (1 L) milk
1 ¼ cups (250 g) granulated sugar
16 egg yolks
1 vanilla bean
12 large prunes aged in Armagnac

You can make your own prunes in Armagnac by putting some prunes in a glass jar and filling it with Armagnac. They are best if left to marinate for two years before serving.

Cut the vanilla bean in half lengthwise and place it in a saucepan with the milk. Bring the milk slowly to a boil.

Beat the egg yolks and sugar until the mixture whitens. Pour the boiling milk onto the egg yolk mixture, whisk, pour back into the saucepan, and heat until the mixture coats a spoon. Remove the vanilla bean.

Cool the mixture in a bowl over ice, then pour it into an ice cream freezer and freeze.

Pit the prunes and cut 4 of them in half; save these for decorating the finished dessert. Dice the remaining prunes using a knife or scissors and stir these pieces into the ice cream when it is almost frozen. Stir in a few spoonfuls of the Armagnac when you add the prunes.

Serve the ice cream in scoops topped with the prunes that were cut in half earlier, and spoon a little more Armagnac over just before serving.

GRILL DE L'HÔTEL DE PARIS

In the baroque atmosphere of Monte Carlo,
in that exalted manifestation of the Second Empire,
the Hôtel de Paris, the Grill is the site
of a gourmand festival presided over by chef Sébastien Bonsignore,
defender of Monegasque cuisine.

Seen from the terrace of the Grill, the port of the principality looks like a child's toy; the yachts and luxury liners lose their impressive appearances; the roof of the casino built by Garnier resembles that of his other masterpiece, the Paris Opera. The scurrying "ants" down below on their way to offer sacrifice at the baccarat and blackjack tables or the roulette wheel hardly suspect that the ninth floor of the Hôtel de Paris contains a temple to the culinary arts. The Hôtel de Paris came into being at the same time as did Monte Carlo. But its fame required the combined effects of its location in the world's most famous gambling resort this side of Las Vegas, the enchanting gardens of the city, and the persevering efforts of the reigning Grimaldi family and, especially, those of François Blanc, its true founding father.

Neither Blanc nor Prince Charles III would recognize today the hotel they knew in 1865. And yet the Empire room still displays its original ostentatious decorations, its gold and its chandeliers, the monumental lobby its gilded woodwork and the bar its wood panelings. The visitors stroll between the marble columns dreaming about the dukes and princesses of the past and about fabulous "killings" at the casino tables. Many years have elapsed since the Baron Haussmann, Liane de Pougy or Sarah Bernhardt supped in the large dining room now reserved for banquets and special occasions. Facing the sea and carried away by a construction madness, the small principality has been forced to build vertically because of its limited area. The gourmand mode has followed suit. The successors of Folleté, the master chef and director of the hotel in 1867, have chosen to take the elevator. The Grill is located at the top of the hotel. There is never an empty table – souvenir perhaps of the memorable dinner on November 24, 1867, at which Baron Brisse, writer gastronome and the dictator of the chefs (he invented 365 menus per year) and several distinguished guests, such as the Baron James de Rothschild or the widow of Tsar Nicholas I, expressed regret that the table of Ludwig I of Bavaria wasn't occupied... Undoubtedly his mistress, Lola Montez, had had a sudden whim to go elsewhere.

By day, facing the distant panorama of the Italian Riviera, the exterior is more spectacular because of the colors of the sea; there is a constant lookout for a sunny day so as to be able to open the roof, and demand to have tables placed on the terrace. With the coming of night, the dining room becomes the spectacle. The tables are bathed in the rosy light of their lamps and everyone, especially the ladies, tries to make the grandest entrance possible. Elegance reigns over all, and Pierre Orrigo, the restaurant's director, plays the role of both chief of protocol and ringmaster. Louis Padovani, the first headwaiter, is there to assist him and offer advice. With a name like the Grill, numerous dishes offered are prepared in that manner: leg of lamb with garlic cloves, shashlik (grilled skewered lamb) flavored with herbs of Provence, and grilled spiny lobsters. But chef Sébastien Bonsignore does not confine himself to just this type of cooking. He and his brigade of forty-four cooks, not counting the apprentices – the teaching courses offered at the hotel are held in high esteem – know very well how to handle the bounty of the sea (sea perch fillets cooked with white wine and onions) or peasant fare (saddle of young rabbit with spices). The solidly built Bonsignore, a true Monegasque, has a strong preference for simple dishes, traditional ones, and what he fears most of all is a large increase in costs. He takes pride in presenting a house specialty: small noodles with smoked salmon. But the true gourmand glories on the menu are *blanquette de homard* (lobster stew) or *minute de saumon sauvage aux huîtres, à la ciboulette, blancs de poireaux, fines herbes* (salmon with oysters, chives, leeks and herbs).

The hotel-trade school in Monaco recently added a course on wine-cellar stewardship. No doubt its students learn all about the history of the cellar at the Hôtel de Paris. When the construction of the hotel was completed, in 1865, it was discovered that the cellars had been overlooked. They had to be dug on the other side of the street. A visit to them combines the features of a tour of Fort Knox and the Maginot Line, but one is ready to forgive the oversight. The several hundreds of thousands of bottles stored away there only await the occasion of a Grand Prix de Monaco to be put to good use. Dario dell'Antonia, who directs the hotel division of the famous Société des Bains de Mer, a state within a state (75 percent of the shares belong to His Serene Highness Prince Rainier or the principality), has a solid professional background acquired at luxury hotels on both sides of the Atlantic and the Channel, from the Savoy in London to the Prince de Galles in Paris. In admiring and impassioned tones, he loves to relate the fabulous adventure that transformed this craggy stretch of Mediterranean coast into a world of luxury, this empire in which gambling is the goal, means, and the source

17 Place du Casino Monte Carlo (air-conditioned, 250 rooms, 22 suites, facilities for receptions and seminars, outdoor dining area, swimming pool, dogs not admitted). Closed on Wednesdays. Menton is 6 miles away. Nice 11 miles, (the airport: 15 miles), San Remo 27 miles and Paris 595 miles. To be seen: Monte Carlo, the casino, the primitive paintings of the Nice School at the cathedral, the palace of Prince Rainier, the exotic gardens, the Oceanographic Museum, and the museum of dolls and automatons.
AE - Diners - Visa cards honored
Tel: (93) 50.80.80

of profit for five thousand Monegasques. Despite the new buildings and the omnipresent Rolls Royces, Monte Carlo remains a turn-of-the-century city. The quintessence of its luxury is reflected just as much by the Baccarat glassware reflections at the baccarat tables, the musical evenings of the Monte Carlo Symphony Orchestra, or the changing of the guard at the palace as by the lights on the tables at the Grill, where every day is a holiday.

In the kitchens or in the Grill itself, the brigade of cooks at the Hôtel de Paris busy themselves in the preparation of gigantic pieces of beef or small fish, probably caught before our very eyes–a convincing proof of its freshness. The same sophistication reigns in the Grill on the ninth floor. Be it in the bar off the lobby downstairs or in that of the Grill, an impassive bartender stands ready. Beyond the large bay windows, the panorama of the principality spreads its glories before the beholder's eyes.

Crayfish gratin with wild mushrooms and pasta

Gratin d'écrevisses aux nouilles et aux cèpes des bois

Serves 6:
3 ¾ cups (500 g) flour
3 teaspoons salt
4 whole eggs
5 egg yolks
3 tablespoons heavy cream
4 ½ lbs (2 kg) live crayfish or shrimp
4 quarts (4 L) court bouillon
1 ¼ lbs (600 g) fresh boletus mushrooms
3 tablespoons oil
2 tablespoons hollandaise sauce
3 tablespoons grated Parmesan cheese
6 sprigs parsley
salt and pepper
truffles (optional)
fish stuffing (optional)
puff pastry, to decorate (optional)

Make fresh pasta with the flour, salt, egg yolks, and whole eggs. Knead the dough energetically, then set it aside for 2 hours before rolling and cutting with a pasta machine.

Cook the crayfish in boiling court bouillon until they become bright red, then drain. Save 6 whole crayfish for decorating the plates. Remove the tail meat from the others and reserve. Save the heads of six of these, and discard the remaining shells.

Lightly brown the boletus mushrooms in 3 tablespoons of oil. Meanwhile, cook the pasta in lightly salted boiling water. Add the crayfish tails to the pan with the mushrooms and cook for about a minute.

Drain the pasta and mix with the cream. Arrange the pasta around the edge of each dinner plate.

Use a slotted spoon to place the crayfish and mushrooms in the center of each plate.

Pour off any fat from the pan in which the crayfish was cooked and combine the juices left with the hollandaise sauce. Spoon the sauce over the crayfish tails (not over the pasta). Sprinkle the sauce with grated Parmesan and place the plates under the broiler to brown the cheese.

Garnish each plate with one of the crayfish heads that have been filled with a quenelle (fish dumpling) stuffing and place a slice of truffle in the center of each plate. Garnish with little pieces of puff pastry (if desired) and a whole boiled crayfish. Place a sprig of parsley on each plate and serve.

Note: the stuffed crayfish heads may be omitted for a simpler presentation.

Sea bass braised in champagne à la Grimaldi

Loup braisé Grimaldi au champagne

Serves 4:
1 sea bass weighing 2 ¾ lbs (1.200 kg)
½ lb (240 g) mushrooms (caps only)
7 oz (200 g) fish stuffing
3 oz (80 g) shelled shrimp
8 teaspoons champagne
butter
4 crayfish
4 large shrimp, crumbed and deep-fat fried
2 shallots, chopped
4 oysters
cream sauce
champagne sauce - Nantua sauce
1 small head lettuce - 1 bouquet garni

For the salpicon:
2 rock lobsters (or large shrimp)
4 sea urchins - 1 sea scallop

Fillet and clean the fish, cutting along the backbone rather than the underside.

Stuff the fish with a fish stuffing and half the mushrooms, thinly sliced. Cut the shrimp into julienne strips and add to the stuffing before filling the fish. Close the stuffing inside the fish.

Braise the fish in a pan with the champagne (or simply white wine), butter, shallots, a bouquet garni and a couple of lettuce leaves.

To serve, place the fish on a serving platter, spoon a Nantua sauce on one side of the fish and a champagne sauce onto the other side of the plate. Garnish with mushrooms caps cooked separately, large shrimp (coated with breadcrumbs and deep-fried), crayfish, oysters gratinéed in cream sauce, the lettuce leaves and a *salpicon* garnish made with the remaining mushrooms, the sea scallop, and rock lobsters (or shrimp) in a thick sauce made from the orange meat from sea urchins.

Note: the photo shows a simpler presentation with the two sauces on either side of a smaller fish, the lettuce leaves and boiled shrimp on top and "dumplings" made by poaching some of the fish stuffing separately.

Jellied bouillabaisse with star anise

Bouillabaisse en gelée à la fleur d'anis

Serves 8:
1 lb (500 g) conger eel
1 lb (400 g) weever
2 lbs (800 g) red hogfish
2 lbs (800 g) gurnet
10 ½ oz (300 g) large shrimp (optional)
1 lb (400 g) black hogfish
1 lb (500 g) John Dory
2 lbs (800 g) monkfish (anglerfish)
4 fillets of sole - 16 mussels, debearded
1 bouquet garni
2 qts (2 L) fish stock
1 cup (25 cl) olive oil
2 onions, sliced fine
2 leeks, white only, sliced fine
2 sticks of celery, sliced
dried fennel - 3 whole star anise
4 tomatoes - 5 cloves garlic
4 oz (100 g) fish stuffing made with salmon
1 ⅓ cups (30 cl) white wine - saffron
2 ½ tablespoons (25 g) gelatin
7 tablespoons water - salt and pepper

For the garnish:
½ blooming fennel - fennel leaves
12 mussel shells - parsley
6 tablespoons rouille sauce (garlic, pimentos, and chili peppers)
12 sea urchin shells - diced tomato
6 tablespoons Nantua sauce

Heat the olive oil in a large pot, add the onions, leeks, celery, fennel, star anise, tomatoes, and garlic. Lightly brown.

Place the fish in the pot, beginning with the firmest ones : the eel, the monkfish, the hogfish, the weever, the gurnet, the John Dory, the large shrimp (if using) and the mussels, in that order.

Stuff the sole fillets with the salmon stuffing and add to the pot last.

Sprinkle saffron generously in the pot, add the white wine, and boil to reduce. Add the bouquet garni and the fish stock and bring to a boil again. Boil over high heat (it will take about 20 minutes for the debearded mussels to open). At that point the other fish should be done. Lift out all the fish once they are cooked. Continue boiling the cooking liquid until it thickens, then strain it through a sieve into a clean saucepan. Spoon off any fat from the surface of the strained liquid, add the gelatin, and boil for one minute, stirring constantly. Add salt and pepper to taste and set aside to cool. Before the liquid starts to stiffen, slice the stuffed sole fillets in half and use them to line individual ramekins or one large dish. Spoon in a little of the cold liquid and refrigerate. Remove the bones and skin from the other pieces of fish and shell the shellfish. Place some of each fish and shellfish (except the large shrimp) on top of the jelly that has now stiffened in the mold(s), sprinkle in some uncooked diced tomato and fresh fennel in julienne strips, then finish filling the dish(es)

with the remaining cold liquid. Refrigerate for 12 hours before serving.

Turn out and serve surrounded with the shrimp (if using), the mussel shells filled with rouille sauce and sea urchin shells filled with Nantua sauce. Decorate the jellied bouillabaisse with a tomato rose and parsley, and serve.

Note: a selection of other white-fleshed saltwater fish may be used to make this dish if the ones mentioned are unavailable.

Hot raspberry soufflé

Soufflé chaud aux framboises

Serves 4:
6 ½ tablespoons (10 cl) milk
3 ½ tablespoons (45 g) granulated sugar
3 tablespoons (30 g) flour
4 egg yolks - 3 egg whites
½ pint (100 g) raspberries
1 teaspoon butter - confectioner's sugar
4 whole candied raspberries (optional)

Boil the milk. Beat the egg yolks and 3 tablespoons of sugar until the mixture becomes lemon-colored, then whisk in the flour and the hot milk little by little. Pour into a saucepan and cook over moderate heat 2 minutes or until thick, then pour this pastry cream into a bowl and reserve.

Puree the raspberries and strain the juice.

Beat the egg whites until quite stiff, stir in the raspberry juice, then carefully fold this into the bowl, of pastry cream.

Butter a soufflé mold; sprinkle the inside of the mold with the remaining sugar to coat the sides then fill with the raspberry cream up to

the edge of the mold. Bake in a 475 °F (250 °C) oven for 15 to 16 minutes.

Remove from the oven, sprinkle with confectioner's sugar, and decorate with candied raspberries.

Serve with stewed raspberries flavored with a little Grand Marnier and red currant jelly.

LE MÉTROPOLE

Almost exotic, a palace out of the Thousand-and-One
Nights or Florence in all its glory, the Métropole at Beaulieu-sur-Mer
basks languorously beside the beach.
Jean Badrutt, the director, enjoys a moment of relaxation in front of
the trompe-l'œil décor on the dining room wall of his luxury hotel.

An Italian *palazzo* in ocher-beige colors that make its white balustrades stand out in sharp contrast, surrounded by centuries-old trees and exotic palms, with one side facing an almost motionless sea periodically traversed by the currents that fleck its surface with traces of white foam: such is the Métropole, still lively despite its ninety years of existence. This Relais-Château is frequented by an elegant clientele. Everything is muted, peaceful, and the large communicating rooms extending the bar, the domain of Alex Deppo, are in pastel colors that contrast with the claret and black rug. The coffee tables and the brown leather chairs and couches shine in the sunlight or under the sparkle of the large chandeliers. Paintings of brightly colored bouquets adorn the walls, a touch of green is provided by the plants, trompe-l'œil scenery covers the dining room walls, the terrace is extended by a delicate awning. Everything here offers the guests refreshing coolness. The overall silence is made up of silken rustlings, a sort of interior music. This may be why the conductor Seiji Ozawa is a regular guest at the hotel, a spot loved for the same reasons by Jacques Brel and Josephine Baker.

This perfection, the refusal to become careless, the elegance of the table, the courtesy of its regular customers and its hosts recalls the pre-World War I Beaulieu. It was and still is the most esteemed winter resort on the Riviera even if nowadays it is the summer, the sun, and water sports that are more in favor with the public. The terrace looks down on a sea iridescent with "imperceptible shivers as if one had thrown it a thousand pinches of fine sand" (Guy de Maupassant). A dock is there for mooring the motorboats that tow the water skiers or take the guests off in a spume of foam to Cap Ferrat or Menton.

The pedal-craft enthusiasts maneuver around the miniature port of the Métropole. And around the swimming pool, heated in the winter, latter-day naiads and tritons bronze themselves before a wall of greenery. Amid cactuses and dwarf palms, the colors of the flowers rival those of the sails on the silvery sea. Jean Badrutt has the calm air of a mountaineer. Member of a Swiss family with a long tradition in hotel operations (they were the ones who created and launched Saint Moritz), he knows how to be unobtrusively omnipresent in his role as director of his dream palace. With each passing season he is on the lookout for ways of improving the comfort offered and the minutest details of the décor. Over the years, his guests have become his friends. He is as much in demand at their tables as a captain of an ocean liner. Monsieur Outhier, the headwaiter, is a distant cousin of the great Outhier of l'Oasis at Napoule. Highly attentive to the habits or desires of his guests, he performs splendidly an apparently insoluble task: to reconcile the classicism of the establishment and the clientele accustomed to international luxury hotels with a prejudice in favor of a cuisine with strong regional and local influence, but not falling into the folklore trap. Such a cuisine is that of chef Pierre Estival. In this land of fruits and vegetables, a veritable Garden of the Hesperides, Estival knows the importance among his brigade of assistants of the "dessert preparer." An herb expert is also a necessity because it takes the skill of a Linnaeus to find one's way through this profusion of garden products. Estival waxes lyrical and long when he speaks of the different sorts of squash, eggplant, fennel, broccoli to be found in the region. His table is truly an orchard and one is never sure whether he is more delighted by the aromas or the colors of its fruits. The horticultural bounty from the truck gardens of the Nice countryside turns the Métropole menu into an Arcimboldo painting.

Fish also occupies an important place on the Metropole menu: *mousse de rascasse à l'anis* (anise-flavored hogfish mousse), *rissoles aux écrevisses sauce ciboulette* (crayfish rissoles with chive sauce), *fricassée de poissons au sabayon de Billet* (fish fricassee in a custard flavored with a local wine), *tagliarini verdi aux fruits de mer* (green noodles with shellfish) or *merlan de palangre pané* (breaded whiting). This menu is an object lesson on how to offer the widest possible gourmand sampling of all that the sea and the hills and valleys of the Var can produce. Be it an aromatic leg of lamb or a *feuillantine d'asperges à l'orange* (orange-flavored asparagus in a pastry shell), everything is aroma, everything is nuanced. At the Métropole, this abundance is transformed into enchantment and the silence into insousiance. The Meridian torpor stops miraculously at the entrance to this palace and the very sunlight is simply luminosity. This luminosity is everywhere: in the hotel rooms when the curtains let in only the glitter of the fireflies, in the lounge prolonging the impeccably-tended lawn and under the awning of the outdoor dining area. The sun worshippers take their pleasures at the swimming pool, while others simply enjoy the enchanting atmosphere and delicate freshness. A rare quality of life, airiness and peaceful contentment surround us. Under the watchful eye of Jean Badrutt, elegance is a lifestyle at Le Métropole.

18 Boulevard du Maréchal Leclerc 06310
Beaulieu-sur-mer (air-conditioned, 50
rooms, 3 suites, swimming pool, private
beach, dogs admitted for an extra charge).
Closed from December 1 to 20. Nice is
6 miles away, heliport 10 miles, Menton
12 miles, and Paris 586 miles. To be seen:
Beaulieu, the Casino, the Villa Kerylos, a
restored ancient Greek villa, the city hall
decorated by Jean Cocteau, the Moorish
villa of W. Somerset Maugham. Boating
excursions.
Tel: (93) 01.00.08

*The bar with its fawn colors and mahogany
woodwork is the realm in which Alex Deppo
prepares the classic cocktails for "his" clientele. The
painted décor of the dining room offers landscapes
of the other side of the Mediterranean. Its light-
green tones make more vivid the colors in the array
of desserts offered by chef Pierre Estival.
Luxuriating in a deck chair facing the
Mediterranean, a charming guest of the Métropole
is lost in contemplation of the blue horizon.*

Belgian endive salad with oysters

Salade d'endives aux huîtres

<u>Serves 4:</u>
24 large oysters, in their shells
6 Belgian endives - lemon juice
1 cooked beet, cut into julienne strips
1 bunch of chives (4 tablespoons, chopped)
4 small tomatoes - olive oil
salt and freshly ground pepper

Open the oysters and take them out of their shells, straining the water from their shells into a small bowl. Reserve the raw oysters and their liquid separately.
Cut the Belgian endives into julienne strips and arrange them on 4 salad plates. Place the oysters on top of the endives; spoon a little lemon juice and the oyster liquid over them. Sprinkle the beet strips over the oysters, then season with pepper and chopped chives. Last, spoon a little olive oil over each salad, decorate each plate with a rose made of tomato peel, and serve.

Sea bass Métropole

Loup au four Métropole

<u>Serves 4:</u>
2 sea bass weighing about 2 ¼ lbs (1 kg) each
2 cups and 2 tablespoons (50 cl) fish stock, total
⅞ cup (20 cl) dry white wine
4 ¼ cups (1 L) heavy cream
2 tablespoons lemon juice
4 teaspoons (2 cl) white vermouth
4 teaspoons (2 cl) hollandaise sauce (optional)
4 small mushrooms, cooked in butter
salt and pepper
2 carrots, peeled and cut into julienne strips
1 zucchini (courgette) cut into julienne strips
1 leek, white only, cut into julienne strips
1 oz (30 g) truffle, cut into julienne strips

Scale and gut the fish, cutting off the heads and the ends of the tails. Season inside and out with salt and pepper. Place them in a roasting pan with ⅞ cup fish stock and add white wine to cover. Bake in a 400°F (200°C) oven, basting frequently for 15 to 20 minutes. Drain the fish and keep warm.
Pour the cooking liquid into a deep frying pan and boil until only a thick fish glaze is left in the pan. Add the cream and vermouth and a little salt and pepper; boil to reduce and thicken the sauce. Taste, add salt and pepper as needed and a little lemon juice. Remove the pan from the heat and stir in the hollandaise, then strain the sauce through a sieve. Keep warm.
Cook first the carrots, then the leek, and, last, the zucchini in a large pot of boiling salted water. Cook each vegetable until tender, then drain and cool in cold water.
Heat the remaining fish stock in a pan with an equal amount of water. Add the truffle, cut into julienne strips, as well as the other vegetables.
Place the fish on a serving platter and spoon some of the sauce over them. Sprinkle some of the vegetables over the fish and place a whole mushroom on each one. Serve the remaining vegetables and sauce separately.
Green beans sautéed in butter and steamed potatoes can be served with the bass.

Eggplant papetons
with tomato sauce and basil

*Papetons d'aubergines à la fondue de
tomate et au basilic*

Serves 4:
4 medium size eggplants (aubergines), 2 fat
  and round, 2 long and thin
1 cup (25 cl) olive oil, total
2 eggs
1 bunch of parsley
1 teaspoon heavy cream
6 large tomatoes
1 onion
2 cloves garlic
1 small bouquet garni
⁷⁄₈ cup (20 cl) tomato paste
basil leaves
salt and pepper

Peel the 2 round eggplants and place them on a
baking sheet with all four sides raised, with a
little cold water. Cover with aluminum foil and
bake in a 400°F (200°C) oven for one hour or
until soft.
Peel, seed, and chop the tomatoes. Finely chop
the garlic and onion. Heat ⁷⁄₈ cup of olive oil in a
frying pan, add the onions and garlic, and cook
slowly to soften, then add the tomatoes,
bouquet garni, tomato paste, salt, and pepper.
Simmer for 15 minutes.
Chop the parsley. Wash the 2 thin eggplants
and cut them into 12 slices. Fry the slices in the
remaining olive oil to brown on both sides;
drain on paper towels.
Remove the eggplants from the oven, scoop
out the pulp, and chop them fine. Place the
pulp in a bowl and beat in the eggs and cream.
Add salt and pepper.
Line the bottom and sides of 4 individual ramekins with the sliced eggplant, spoon in a little
tomato sauce, then fill the molds with the eggplant purée. Place the molds in a large roasting
pan and pour enough boiling water into the
pan to come halfway up the sides of the molds.
Cover all the molds with aluminum foil and
cook in a 350°F (180°C) oven for one hour.
Reserve 2 tablespoons of the remaining
tomato sauce, then pour the rest into a blender
to purée. Spoon some of the pureed sauce on
to each dinner plate, turn out the eggplants
once they are cooked, and place one in the center of each plate. Garnish each eggplant "pape-
ton" with a bit of the reserved sauce and decorate the plates with fresh basil leaves. Serve
immediately.

Strawberry fritters with
raspberry sauce

*Beignets de fraises au coulis de
framboises*

Serves 4:
²⁄₃ cup (80 g) flour
pinch of salt - 1 egg
8 teaspoons beer
4 egg whites
28 large strawberries
6 ½ tablespoons (10 cl) Grand Marnier
2 qts (2 L) oil, for deep frying
¼ cup (70 g) granulated sugar

For the sauce:
1 lb (400 g) raspberries
1 cup (25 cl) water
2 ½ cups (500 g) granulated sugar
dash of Grand Marnier

Make a batter by combining the flour with the
salt, the egg, and the beer. Let the batter rest for
at least 2 hours, then fold in 4 egg whites beaten
until stiff.
Stem the strawberries and marinate them in
the Grand Marnier for 20 minutes.
Make a raspberry sauce. Blend the raspberries
in a blender. Put the sugar and water in a saucepan and bring to a boil. Add the raspberry
purée and boil for 2 minutes, then pour the
sauce into a bowl to cool over ice. Stir to cool as
quickly as possible. Add a dash of Grand Marnier to the sauce.
Heat the oil in a deep frier until it reaches 300°F
(150°C) on a candy thermometer. Drain the
strawberries, dip each in batter, then deepfry
until golden.
Serve the fritters on individual dessert plates as
soon as they are cooked. Pour some of the
sauce on each plate and sprinkle each fritter
with sugar before serving.

Le Moulin de Mougins

Hidden, almost timidly, in a sweet-scented valley,
the Moulin of Denise and Roger Vergé conceals treasures of luxury,
gourmand pleasures, and inventiveness behind its rustic exterior.
For us as it is for them, the Moulin de Mougins
is truly an ideal port of call.

Everything is white, the walls, the dazzling tablecloths, the Clark Gable mustache of the owner, Roger Vergé. But there is nothing in the world less ascetic than the Moulin de Mougins. A crackling fire in the rustic fireplace casts its flattering glow on the faces of the female guests and sparkles in the mirrors. Simplicity? It is to be sensed in Roger Vergé's love for his father, for the gardens of his childhood in the Allier region, for "the sweetness of the onion, the green of a tomato, the sharp taste of the spinach, the smoothness of a potato, the suave quality of the leek, the aromas of celery, celeriac and turnip, the no-nonsense scent of garlic, the sharp tang of the radish." These unpretentious vegetables are considered worthy of accompanying the culinary preparations offered at this Michelin three-star restaurant. The lavish displays of the Moulin adapt themselves to the odor of the truffle, to the richness of the sumptuous fare offered, just as they do to the modest artichoke with thyme, cooked in white wine and scented with basil. After a career divided between the rustic simplicity of his first restaurant jobs in the establishments of Commentry in the Allier and the sophisticated classicism of La Tour d'Argent and the Plaza Athénée, Vergé knows how to do anything. But most of all he is a sauce maker by instinct. In the manner of other great chefs, he purified them by eliminating the use of flour and marked the cuisine of his period more by his talent for naturalness.

After his classical training period, Vergé went into exile. He traveled all over the world, running restaurants which he rendered famous in the twinkling of an eye. Entrusted with the creation of a restaurant chain at East African airports, he trained himself for future expeditions on the other side of the Atlantic. He accompanied Paul Bocuse and Gaston Lenôtre to Disney World; he also acquired a knowledge of how to greet dinner guests and of correct restaurant management. He developed a liking for the exotic (mikado salad, Iranian caviar, sherry vinegar) and for that *cuisine de soleil* (sun-drenched cuisine) he would feature at the Moulin when he returned to France in 1969, rich in new ideas and fluent in Swahili. (How many other great chefs can make this claim? – even though he makes very little use of it these days.) It is a cuisine founded on herbs such as savory and mint. He even used the term "cuisine de soleil" as the title of his book. And the sun is omnipresent in his cuisine down to the fresh tomato in his *omelette à la façon du Moulin.*

Vergé ranged from the Caribbean to Morocco in his globe-girdling travels, successfully carrying off his experiments with an ease which made light of the difficulties involved: a sense of application, exceptional research, and meticulousness. From what trips did he bring back the idea for his frog soup with mint leaves, a deluxe version of the *phô,* specialty of Tonkinese kitchens? Or the use of orange and lemon to scent the local sea bream? The gardens of Provence are sources of inspiration both for Vergé and the Moulin chef, Serge Chollet, his son-in-law and backup man, who sprinkles chives, squash blossoms, and rosemary on dishes to the point that one is at a loss to say whether they were created by Vergé or Chollet. Vergé holds that "one should create dishes every month because cuisine exists to be changed." In keeping with this line of thinking, the menu is in constant evolution with dishes being replaced, created, or reinvented, to the everlasting joy of the diner. One should not come to the Moulin solely to savor the creations that made it famous: the *suprême de loup Maître Auguste Escoffier* (sea perch) or the *fricassée de langouste au Sauternes et à la crème* (spiny lobster fricasseed in a Sauterne and cream sauce). A *provençale tartine de purée d'ail* (bread spread with garlic purée), a *truffe de grillon sous sa croûte de sel* (truffle coated with salt and cooked in ashes) or the popular *pieds-paquets à la marseillaise* (pig's feet in tomato sauce) are other good reasons to come and sample a cuisine that sweeps you along with its profusion of aromas and old wines. There are no wings on this mill, but its fare gives them to the diners. The welcome offered by Denise Vergé, who doubles as herbalist in the Moulin's souvenir and gourmet specialty shop, is in keeping with this establishment and its refusal to consider the partaking of the delights of the table not as a moment of meditation but as pleasant moments spent in agreeable company. The impeccable quality of the service, the homey comforts, the luxurious details exclude neither a touch of fantasy, nor humor. Like the time Vergé, who is on intimate terms with many film stars, brought Danny Kaye into his kitchens. The sight of the comic transformed into a chef complete with toque and long white apron inspired Vergé to commemorate the event by naming a dish *filet de bœuf à la Mathurini.* For the sake of any future historians of twentieth-century cuisine, it should be stated that the Mathurini referred to is not a famous chef but an Italianized version of the name the French give to Popeye the Sailor and, of course, spinach is a prime ingredient in the dish. The cuisine is paramount at the Moulin and bears the mark of Vergé in its

In the kitchens, chef Serge Chollet, son-in-law to the Vergés, invents, reinvents, and complements in his own register the talents of Roger Vergé. In the winter, in the comfort of the soberly furnished white-walled dining rooms, in the summer under the trees in a garden buzzing with the song of the cicadas and scented by the herbs of Provence, our gourmand relaxes and takes a new lease on life. The glow of a single candle or the shade of a light awning are propitious to the banquets, be they a luncheon in the sun or a midnight tryst for lovers.

19 Notre-Dame-de-Vie 06250 Mougins (air-conditioned, 3 rooms, dogs allowed). Closed Sunday nights and Mondays out of season (November 15 to December 23). Cannes is 4 miles away, the Nice airport 21 miles and Paris 560 miles. To be seen: the celebrated beach resort of Cannes, the sea-front promenade of La Croisette, the Cannes Festival palace, the hill of Suquet, the Castre museum. At Grasse, the Frago-nard museum (the famous artist was born there), the museum of Art and History of Provence, the perfume factories and shops.
AE – Diners – Visa cards honored
Tel: (93) 75.78.24

slightest details. He creates it while dreaming of extraordinary gardens. Isolated in its scented valley between the sea and Grasse, the Moulin de Mougins seems to be in hiding, withdrawn into itself, but in reality it's opened to the world, to the whole world. There, amid its recesses, its different construction levels, its rough-cast white walls, its refreshingly shaded areas, Roger Vergé, a combination of an Indian army major and the captain of a gourmand yacht, awaits with his usual discreet graciousness all those to whom he wishes to offer a bit of happiness through his cuisine.

John Dory fillets with cream and vegetable sauce*

*Blancs de saint-pierre
à la crème de petits légumes*

Serves 2:
2 lbs (800 g) John Dory (or other fish, e.g.,
    sole, sea bass, flounder)
1 medium carrot
1 leek, white only
1 small stalk of celery, heart only
1 medium potato
20 very thin green beans
1 bunch of chives, chopped
6 ½ tablespoons (10 cl) heavy cream
2 tablespoons (30 g) butter, total
salt and pepper

Fillet the fish and cut the fillets into thick strips. Cut the carrot, leek, and celery into thick julienne strips (about the shape and thickness of the prongs of a fork).
Peel and dice the potato, place in a saucepan with cold water, add salt, and boil until soft enough to be mashed. Drain and mash the potato.
Put the julienned vegetables in another saucepan with ½ cup of water, a pinch of salt, and 2 teaspoons of butter. Boil for about 10 minutes or until all the water has evaporated and the vegetables are just barely cooked. Keep warm.
Cook the green beans al dente in a large pot of lightly salted boiling water. Drain and add to the other vegetables.
Place the strips of fish in a pan, pour in the cream, salt lightly, and bring to a boil. Cook for 2 minutes.
Place a strainer over a mixing bowl; pour the fish and cream into the strainer. Stir the strained cream into a the blender with half of the mashed potato then blend to make the sauce. Once the sauce is smooth, add the remaining mashed potato (only if the sauce isn't thick enough) and the remaining butter. Salt and pepper if needed.
Pour the sauce into a saucepan, add all the vegetables and the pieces of fish and bring to a boil. Serve immediately in soup plates and sprinkle with chopped chives.

Tenderloin with currants à la Mathurini

Filet de bœuf aux raisins à la Mathurini

Serves 2:
2 tenderloin steaks, about 7 oz (200 g) each
⅓ cup (40 g) currants
2 tablespoons coarsely ground or cracked
    black peppercorns
2 teaspoons butter, for the steaks
3 tablespoons butter (50 g) softened and
    broken into 4 pieces
3 tablespoons (5 cl) Cognac or Armagnac
3 tablespoons (5 cl) beef stock or bouillon
salt

Drop the currants into 2 cups boiling water. Boil for 5 minutes, then drain.
Salt and pepper the steaks and roll them in the peppercorns. Fry the meat in 2 teaspoons of hot butter for 2 to 3 minutes on a side, or more if you prefer them well done.
Place a small dessert plate upside down on a dinner plate, lift the meat out of the pan and place it on top of the smaller plate so that it won't be in its juices. Cover both plates with an inverted mixing bowl.
Pour off the butter used to cook the steaks, add the currants and Cognac to the pan, and boil to reduce over moderate heat. Add the beef stock to pan and boil 2 minutes, then, shaking the pan, swirl in the butter a piece at a time. Salt and pepper to taste.
Serve the steaks on dinner plates, spoon over the sauce and garnish with buttered spinach and individual corn pancakes.
Note: in the photo the meat is served with a few glazed baby carrots, a tiny zucchini stuffed with buttered spinach, and the corn pancake.

* There is no photo for this recipe.

Lamb stew with garlic bread

*Estouffade de gigot d'agneau
avec les tartines d'ail*

Serves 6 or 7:
1 leg of lamb, weighing about 7 lbs (3 kg)
  boned and pared of fat
1 lb (400 g) salt pork
10 ½ oz (300 g) fresh pork rind
6 ⅓ cups (1,5 L) red wine
½ lb (250 g) onions, peeled and coarsely
  chopped
4 cloves garlic, peeled and crushed
1 lb (400 g) tomatoes, peeled, seeded,
  and chopped
1 bouquet garni (parsley, celery, bay leaf,
  orange peel, thyme)
3 tablespoons olive oil
1 ½ cups (200 g) flour
1 tablespoon coarsely crushed peppercorns
salt

For the garlic bread:
5 garlic bulbs
3 tablespoons olive oil
1 loaf French bread
salt

Cut the leg of lamb into cubes about 2 inches on a side. Place them in a pot with the onions, garlic, tomatoes, bouquet garni, pepper, wine, and oil. Stir to mix, then leave to marinate in a cool place (do not refrigerate) for 4 hours.

Remove the rind from the salt pork and cut it and the other pieces of rind into little squares. Cut the salt pork into strips about 1 inch long and ¼ inch thick. Drop the pieces of salt pork and rind into a large pot of boiling water and boil for 5 minutes, then drain and cool under cold running water.

Put the salt pork and rind into the pot with the lamb when it has finished marinating. Add water to the pot so as to cover the meat by about ¾ inch of liquid.

Mix flour and water together to make a soft dough; roll it out, using your hands to make a long "sausage". Place the dough all around the edge of the pot, then firmly set the top of the pot in place.

Place the pot in a very slow (220 °F/100 °C) oven and bake for 3 hours.

When ready to serve, break open the pot (the dough will have hardened) and spoon off the fat from the surface of the stew. Remove the bouquet garni, add salt and pepper as needed. Serve the stew in hot soup plates with slices of garlic bread made as follows. Peel the cloves of

5 garlic buds, split each clove open, and cut out the greenish sprout if there is one. Place the cloves of garlic in a saucepan with 2 quarts of cold water, bring to a boil, boil 5 minutes, and drain. Put the garlic back into the pot with 2 quarts of cold water, and repeat the operation for a total of 4 times. The last time, boil the garlic until soft, then drain and purée in a blender. Add the oil and salt to the purée.

Slice the bread into about 30 slices and toast each, then spread each piece with the garlic purée and brown under the broiler. These are delicious dipped into the sauce of the stew.

Note: in the photo the lamb is cooked and served in individual terrines instead of the large pot called for here.

Anisette parfait

Parfait glacé à la liqueur d'anis

Serves 4:
6 egg yolks
⅔ cup (150 g) granulated sugar, total
4 tablespoons (6 cl) Anisette or other anise
  flavored liqueur
⅞ cup (200 g) heavy cream, refrigerated
  in a mixing bowl
6 tablespoons water

Dissolve all but 2 tablespoons of the sugar in 6 tablespoons of water over high heat. Remove from the heat and keep warm.

Put the egg yolks into the top of a double boiler and whisk for 7 to 8 minutes, pouring the sugar syrup into them little by little. Once the mixture has become thick and foamy, remove it from the heat and continue whisking until it has cooled.

Remove the whipping cream from the refrigerator and beat it until it begins to thicken; sprinkle in the remaining sugar and heat until the cream forms soft peaks.

Beat the egg-yolk mixture for 2 minutes more, adding the Anisette as you do so, then fold the whipped cream into it.

Pour the parfait into a one-quart ice cream mold and place in the freezer for 6 hours before serving.

To serve, dip the mold into a bowl of warm water for a few seconds and turn out onto a serving platter. The parfait may be simply served as is, or as shown in the photo on a bed of semi-sweet chocolate shavings with an anise-flavored custard sauce and decorated with a sprig of mint.

Note: to make an anise-flavored custard sauce, follow the directions for making a vanilla sauce given in the recipe for Crêpes with Orange Soufflé Filling on page 131. In this case, however, omit the vanilla and simply bring the milk to a boil before pouring it onto the egg-yolk-sugar mixture. Proceed as described to thicken the sauce, remove from the heat, stir in a tablespoon (or more if desired) of Anisette and pour into a sauce boat.

L'OASIS

*Is it because the long white apron he wears under
his Master Chef jacket gives Louis Outhier the air of a soldier monk
that we consider him to be the most austere of the great chefs?
Don't you believe it; the master of the Oasis and his daughter Françoise are
very much in the modern mainstream.*

The patio of the Oasis calls to mind the deambulatory of a cloister in which thousands of cyclamen bloom in profusion up to the very edge of the well. Can this be the reason why Louis Outhier seems to be the most mystical of all the great chefs? An almost religious faith, devoid of neither grandeur nor mobility, motivates him. "The crucifix is not out of place in the kitchen" is the way he puts it. Let us simply imagine the number of miracles that must take place each day when out of one hundred and eighty customers at least one hundred express their joy and contentment. As befits a Michelin three-star restaurant, salmon-pink walls, lacquered ceilings, and a sparkling silver service with a beautiful purity of line have replaced the humdrum interior decoration and equipment of the family pension Louis and his wife took over as managers in 1954. In a little over two years, the reputation of Outhier extended well beyond a small circle of regular customers. And little by little the boarders were replaced by a transient trade. Since then, Outhier has gathered around him a staff that shares his belief that it is the cuisine that counts above all other things; a staff that knows how to welcome guests, offer discreet advice as to what to order, serve them promptly and correctly, and leave them delighted at having partaken of an exceptional cuisine. It is a cuisine replete with references to Ferdinand Point and to the profound and sincere friendship for colleagues such as Paul Bocuse and Roger Vergé, with whom he trained. Despite his retiring manner, his almost timid appearances in the dining room to greet his guests without ostentatious gestures, Louis Outhier is one of the most impressive and unforgettable chefs in the trade today.

Originally from Belfort, Outhier is less accustomed than some of the other great chefs to the demands of public relations. He remains faithful to the Jura region of his birth through the inclusion on his menu of a *Saint-Pierre au Château-Chalon,* a local wine rarely used by chefs other than those from the Jura. His cuisine is characterized by a sense of balance and a touch of alchemy. From very early in life, Outhier was determined to become a chef. His path to this goal from his initial training under Denis Micheland (one-time chef at the Court of St. James) at the Grand Hôtel de Tonneau d'Or in Belfort includes stops at very few establishments. The exoticism manifested by his use of ginger in the *escalope de foie gras* or the *petite langouste aux herbes thaï* (spiny lobster with herbs) was not the result of frequent trips abroad. Although the mark of Outhier is ever-present, his cuisine displays an obvious affinity of taste between the product and the spice. Watching him at work in his kitchen, Scandinavian in appearance because of its light woods and precise lines, hung with its shiny copper ustensils that recall his apprenticeship at Lucas-Carton or at Point, the sight of the way he deftly carves up an oyster for his egg-oyster dish or the precise instructions to an awestruck apprentice on the cooking of a *poularde aux morilles* (fattened pullet with morels) allows the observer to grasp the full significance of the word "presence". It is a matter of abstracting the essential amid a richness of details. In a twentieth-century echo of *Le Rotisseur et le Cuisinier* by Brillat-Savarin, James de Coquet wrote that "being a restaurant keeper and being a chef are not one and the same trade." Who else in this establishment of a prelate of the "grande cuisine" is capable of discerning the showiness of a *brioche* or the republican virtue of a *délice de poularde vendémiaire* (the first month in the revolutionary calendar)?

Off the beaten track taken by the mass of visitors to the Riviera on a road bordering the sea, away from intrigues and quarrels between chefs, Louis Outhier made a felicitous choice when he named his restaurant *L'Oasis.* It took me a long time to discover all this because Outhier is not one to volunteer such information. This same reticence is apparent in his cuisine. No poetic names for his creations. At most the designation "surprise" for a preparation of truffles. The other dishes bear names that are self-apparent. Everything seems simple, everything is thoroughly worked out, nothing is left to chance.

For Outhier, each meal is an opportunity to resolve his doubts. He wants to review everything: to verify the freshness of the mushrooms, the correctness of proportions established over two generations earlier. On these occasions, his anguish is almost metaphysical, but it does not provoke the outbursts witnessed in other kitchens where the roaring of the chef causes the flames on the stoves to tremble and sows panic in the hearts of the apprentices and busboys. The tension simply rises during the course of the meal and is dissipated only by the contented smile on the face of a known and respected customer. The self-control of the master of the Oasis is legendary. Where does talent end and genius begin? Is it manifested by these dark sauces, those mixtures of exotic flavors and local herbs, the wine list on which the Burgundies occupy a prominent place, or is it rather in the constant need to outdo, to transcend oneself?

20 06210 Mandelieu-la-Napoule (air-conditioned, patio and garden, dogs admitted. Golf course at the Cannes-Mandelieu club, yatching). Closed Monday nights and Tuesdays and from the end of October to December 20. Cannes is 5 miles away, Nice (airport) 25 miles, and Paris 558 miles. To be seen: the port of Napoule, Cannes, the isles of Lérins. Sainte Marguerite, the Vauban fortress (in which the Man in the Iron Mask was imprisoned), Saint-Honorat, a Cistercian monastery. Juan-les-Pins, Cap d'Antibes. Antibes: the Grimaldi palace containing the Picasso museum. The Esterel massif.
Tel: (93) 49.95.52

A meticulous care in the presentation of the dishes and the pastries. The dessert cart at the Oasis is one of the richest, most prestigious to be found. The cheese platters, well-balanced geometrical compositions lending a rustic touch to a spot given over to supreme luxury, wait in a cool area to be served at the end of the meal. The same care is lavished on the accessories: the admirable silver-encrusted ewers or the profusion of flowers in the cloister-like dining area. An observer present at the early morning ceremony of watering the garden can detect the same precision of gesture on the part of the gardener, the same love and delicacy as with the pastry cook putting the finishing dollop of cream on one of his ephemeral masterpieces. It is thanks to these combined efforts of everyone that when it comes time to sit down at the table, without lost time or abruptness, a well-oiled mechanism is set in motion so that at the same instant two, three, and, at times, four dishes with different cooking times are ready and presented to the diners. In the summertime, the dining area is moved out of doors and the meals are accompanied by the rustling of the leaves, the coolness given off by the well, and the shade of the colonnaded passages surrounding the restaurant.

Truffle surprise

Truffe surprise

Serves 1:
1 ½ oz (40 g) foie gras
½ oz (15 g) truffles
6 ½ tablespoons (10 cl) Madeira-
flavored meat jelly

Form the foie gras into a ball about the size and shape of a truffle, cover it with slices of truffle, and glaze it with several coats of Madeira-flavored meat jelly to make it shiny. Serve in the center of a dinner plate.

Author's Comment: There's nothing surprising about the way the most mysterious and secretive of the great chefs in this book decided to marry these two prestigious products. It would, on the other hand, have surprised us very much had Louis Outhier decided to complicate a preparation unnecessarily or, on the contrary, present truffles and foie gras without any treatment at all.

The simplicity and sophistication of this preparation pleased us by both its "hidden meaning" and its ingenious use of two formidable gastronomic symbols- such a preparation justifies the admiration of those who so admire Outhier's cooking.

Crayfish salad

Salade d'écrevisses

Serves 4:
24 crayfish - court bouillon
2 slices of prosciutto
1 slice of fresh fig (or strawberry) per person
4 mushrooms - 1 carrot - 1 cantaloupe
mixed greens for salad, preferably including
  some rocket - pepper

For the dressing:
½ teaspoon Pastis
¼ teaspoon soy sauce
¼ teaspoon nuoc-man (thick soy sauce)
2 teaspoons lemon juice
2 teaspoons vinegar
4 teaspoons sesame seed oil
3 tablespoons (5 cl) peanut oil
salt and pepper

Garnish each dinner plate with the mixed greens.

Cut the carrot into julienne strips and parboil; use to decorate the edges of each plate.

Cut the melon into little cubes and place them in the centers of the plates. Season generously with black pepper.

Arrange the crayfish tails (previously poached in a court bouillon, and shelled) around the center of the plates and spinkle with thin strips of ham.

Place a slice of fig (or strawberry) in the center of each plate and finish decorating with the mushrooms, cut into julienne strips, and the crayfish claws. Mix together the ingredients for the salad dressing, season the salad, and serve.

Foie gras and mango with ginger sauce

Escalopes de foie gras au gingembre

Serves 4:
1 ginger root
1 mango
1 foie gras of duck
  weighing about 1 lb (600-700 g)
⅞ cup (20 cl) chicken stock
a little carrot, onion, leek, and celery to
  flavor the stock
a dash of vodka
salt and pepper

Slice the onions, carrots, leek, and celery and place in a saucepan with the chicken stock; boil to reduce by half. Strain and reserve.
Cut the foie gras into 4 slices; season with salt and pepper.
Peel the mango, cut into quarters, then slice thin. Place the slices on a buttered baking sheet and place under the broiler to brown lightly. Set aside.
Peel the ginger and cut it into thin julienne strips.
Fry the slices of foie gras then remove from the pan and place on a platter. Pour the fat from the pan into a bowl and reserve.
Deglaze the pan with the reduced stock, add the ginger, and boil to reduce still further. At the last minute bind the sauce with the fat saved from cooking the foie gras, add salt and pepper and a dash of vodka.
Spoon the sauce onto the dinner plates. Place a slice of foie gras on each plate, garnish the plates with the sliced mango, and serve.

Squash blossoms stuffed with John Dory

Saint-Pierre fleur de courge

Serves 4:
1 John Dory (or flounder) weighing about
  3½ lbs (1.300 - 1.500 kg)
16 fresh squash blossoms, pistils removed
2 carrots - 1 leek - stalk of celery
1 onion - 2 cloves garlic
1 bouquet garni
½ bottle white wine
4¼ cups (1 L) water
butter - cardamom - lemon juice
salt - cayenne pepper

Fillet the fish and cut the fillets into 16 pieces. Place the bones from the fish in a large saucepan with sliced carrots, leek, celery, onion, and a clove of garlic. Add a bouquet garni, wine, and water to the pans and boil until the liquid has reduced by three quarters. Strain and reserve.
Stuff each squash blossom with a piece of fish then sauté them in a pan with a little butter–do not allow to brown. Lift them out of the pan and reserve.
Deglaze the pan with the strained fish stock and add a little cardamom. Boil to reduce, then whisk in some fresh butter little by little and finish seasoning with lemon juice, salt, and cayenne pepper.
Serve as shown in the photo.

OUSTAU DE BAUMANIÈRE

From its opening to the succession of grandson
Jean-André Charial, the Oustau de Baumanière
has known only a single will: that of Raymond Thuilier.
Aided by Jeanne Moscoloni, he created this paradise
in the Baux-de-Provence.

The mineral universe of the Baux region, this scree of rocks and stones, has always exercised a fascination in which fear and affection are combined. According to a legend, Dante drew his inspiration for the *Inferno* from the Entrée du Val, where for the past three centuries has stood the Provençal farmhouse converted by the indomitable will of Raymond Thuilier into the Oustau, one of the foremost inns in France. By day, the only sound to be heard in the desolate countryside is the wind stirring amid the boulders and the rocks or rustling the leaves of the fragrant vegetation. With the coming of night, another universe is revealed–one petrified in time–by the illumination of the fabulous mass of the village, whose walls prolong the steep escarpment rising from the valley below. The lights play upon, impart life, seek out the hidden recesses, and penetrate like a thousand moons the huddle of houses, and the old citadel and its neighboring mountain become one. Is it because of the whiteness of the stony surroundings that Raymond Thuilier, who has become a painter of canvases almost as famous as his cuisine, prefers vivid colors? Is that the reason why the interior decoration of his Oustau has such warmth, classical elegance, luxurious sobriety, and unobtrusive comfort? Rooted as it is in the area, the cuisine served at the Oustau makes full use of the resources of the Alpilles region: herbs, game in season, and the local lamb with as famous a reputation as that of Mont-Saint-Michel. The *pâté de gibier en croûte* (game pâté in pastry crust), *the mousse de grives* (thrush mousse) and *selle de chevreuil sauce grand veneur* (saddle of venison with a pepper-game stock sauce) are in the great hunting tradition of the seigneurs of the Baux. With his grandson Jean-André Charial installed in the kitchen, Raymond Thuilier has deftly ensured the continuity and renewal of the cuisine offered by the Oustau. The grandfather admits being greatly indebted to Fernand Point for his culinary success. The grandson has had a thorough training in some of the finest restaurants in France. This training has allowed him to acquire a knowledge of a lighter, more aromatic modern cuisine but one which dovetails perfectly with that featured on the Oustau's menu. It goes without saying that nothing needs to be added or changed in the *gigot d'agnelet en croûte* (leg of spring lamb in a pastry shell), but the airy lightness of the *feuilleté de turbot aux pointes d'asperges* (turbot in puff paste with asparagus tips) or the flavor of *filets de rouget au vin rouge sur fond de poireaux* (mullet fillets in a red wine and leek sauce) indi-

cate clearly that less butter and cream is being used. On a clear day, the sea can be seen sparkling in the distance from the heights of the village. On the journey from habitat to table, the fish undergoes a land change: it becomes impregnated with the herbs of Provence. It is flavored with pistou, or basil, which is the modern declension of the same word, the first scholarly, the other the common designation. Be it an elaborate dish or a simple *bœuf en gelée* (jellied beef), the menu is packed with temptations for all tastes. The whole country is represented: a provençal cream soup of green peppers, a Bresse fattened pullet, or lobsters from the Atlantic. Such an embarrassment of riches makes it hard for the gourmand to make his choice. The amusing and rustic *gâteau de lapin* (rabbit in crust) with its *terrine de légumes* (vegetable terrine) should appeal to the hiker returning famished after an envigorating march. The jaded epicurean will rediscover the joy of living when faced with the veal kidneys and chicken livers in sherry sauce. Those interested in the art of cooking will take their delights in the *aiguillettes de canard aux cèpes* (duck fillets with wild mushrooms) and *les cuisses confites* (preserved duck legs). It is always a source of amazement to see the rosy-pink fillets and the delicately preserved legs arrive at the table. There is a bit of a mystery involved. The entire duck is first lightly cooked, the fillets are then removed, and the legs continue to simmer with the carcass, which transmits all its juices and flavor. We could explain the process, but, as Einstein put it, "any explanation only deepens the mystery." This mysterious aspect is elsewhere. It is in the respect for the seasons, for the products used in their natural forms, in not employing chervil, dill, or any other ingredient to excess, but above all it resides in respect for smallest details so as to adhere faithfully to the truth sought by all dedicated cooks. Without the impeccable service, the perfection in the welcome offered, or the courtesy displayed, the Oustau would simply be a luxury dining spot. Matching the eternal youth of the old patriarch with his own, a worthy successor has been found in Charial. He is as restrained as his grandfather and just as enthusiastic. Raymond Thuilier is endowed with the same solid faith of the conquering soldier monks. Jean-André Charial has that of the seminarians, the seekers. As regards the culinary certitudes of his grandfather, he offers a less pragmatic approach. But the two men complement one another admirably. And the affection between them is not the least of the charms of this family.

Nowhere else on earth is the alliance between the mineral and vegetable kindgom, the spiritual and material, more discernible than at Baux-de-Provence. In order not to alter this landscape, the Oustau hides away on a bend in the road, with its guest accommodations scattered around in the valley. Within its white stone walls, the hostelry recreates another way of life. The hanging gardens, suspended as much in space as in time, participate in the festive atmosphere, offering their greenery as shade at the edge of the swimming pool or in the bouquets placed on the tables.

21 13250 Les Baux-de-Provence (air-conditioned, 15 rooms, 11 suites, dining terrace, facilities for receptions and seminars, dogs allowed, swimming, tennis-courts, horseback riding, helicopter landing strip). Closed Thursday noons and on Wednesdays from October 15 to March 31. Arles is 12 miles away, Avignon 22 miles, Nîmes 27 miles, Marseilles-Marignane airport 37 miles, and Paris 446 miles. To be seen: Les Baux-de-Provence, the chateau-monument of Charloun Rieu, the Place Saint-Vincent, the rue de Trencat, the Paravelle tower and the Image cathedral.
AE - Diners - Visa cards honored
Tel: (90) 97.33.07

Red mullet mousse

Mousse de rouget

Serves 4:
4 red mullet weighing about 7 oz (200 g)
  each
1 bulb Florence fennel, chopped
6 ½ tablespoons (10 cl) white vermouth
6 ½ tablespoons (10 cl) dry white wine
salt and pepper
3 ½ tablespoons (50 g) butter
3 tablespoons (20 g) flour
3 tablespoons (15 cl) heavy cream

For the sauce:
⅔ cup (15 cl) heavy cream
5 drops sherry vinegar
lemon juice
tarragon, chopped fine
salt and pepper

Clean and scale the fish. Place them in a roasting pan with the fennel, vermouth, white wine, salt, and pepper. Bake in a 400 °F (200 °C) oven for 12 minutes.
While the fish are cooking make a roux in a small saucepan by melting the butter, stirring in the flour, and cooking, stirring constantly until it begins to brown; remove the pan from the heat.
Take the fish from the oven and lift the meat from the bones. Coarsely chop the fillets.
Beat the cream until it peaks.
Place the saucepan with the roux back on the stove and strain into it the liquid from the roasting pan; whisk until smooth. Season with salt and pepper and add the chopped fillets to the pan. Work the resulting mixture through a fine sieve and measure the purée obtained. Measure the whipped cream. Add one third as much cream to the fish purée as there is total purée: e.g., for ¾ cup of purée add ¼ cup of whipped cream.

Spoon the resulting mousse into a bowl and refrigerate for several hours.
For the sauce, beat the cream until stiff, add the vinegar, a little lemon juice, salt, pepper, and a lot of finely chopped tarragon.
Serve the mousse in a bowl, with toast and the sauce separately, or serve spoonfuls of the mousse and sauce on each plate as shown in the photo.

Red mullet fillets with red wine sauce

Filets de rougets au vin rouge

Serves 4:
4 red mullet weighing about 7 oz (200 g) each
2 leeks
4 cloves garlic
bones from one salmon (or other large fish)
1 onion, diced
1 carrot, diced
1 leek, diced
1 stalk of celery, diced
2 anchovy fillets, chopped fine
8 ½ cups (2 L) red wine
  (preferably Côtes du Rhône)
4 handfuls vermicelli
4 tablespoons beef consommé or stock
⅓ cup (85 g) butter
salt and pepper

Begin by making the sauce. Melt 1 ½ tablespoons of butter in a large saucepan, add the diced vegetables, and cook to soften. Add the bones from the salmon, the tomatoes (peeled, and seeded), and the garlic (crushed). Stir, then add the wine and boil slowly to reduce for 1 hour, skimming off any foam that surfaces. Just before the cooking time is up add the finely chopped anchovies to the sauce, then work the sauce through a sieve into a clean saucepan. Just before serving, whisk 1 ½ tablespoons of fresh butter into the sauce.
Make the leek cream: cut the leeks into small pieces and cook 10 minutes, covered, with a little water and a tablespoon of butter. Purée the leeks in a blender, season with salt and pepper, add a tablespoon more of butter and reserve. Keep warm.
Melt a tablespoon of butter in a frying pan, add the vermicelli and chopped garlic and cook to lightly brown, then spoon them into generously buttered custard cups. Pour a little consommé, or beef stock, into each mold and bake 10 minutes in a very hot oven.

Fillet the fish, carefully removing any little bones. Season with salt and pepper then steam for about 3 minutes.
Turn out the vermicelli onto dinner plates, spoon a little of the leek cream onto the plates, then place a fish fillet on top of the leek cream. Spoon the sauce around the fish, and serve.
Note: you can also garnish the fish with a little onion cooked until soft and carrot balls cooked until tender, as shown in the photo.

Crêpes with orange soufflé filling

Crêpes soufflées à l'orange

Serves 4:

For the crêpe batter:
¼ cup (40 g) flour
3 teaspoons (10 g) granulated sugar
¼ teaspoon salt
1 egg, whole - 1 egg yolk
6 ½ tablespoons (10 cl) milk
1 tablespoon (15 g) butter

For the filling:
6 egg whites
7 teaspoons granulated sugar
½ cup (130 g) pastry cream
1 oz (30 g) candied orange peel, chopped fine
  or pounded to a paste
6 ½ tablespoons (10 cl) Grand Marnier

For the syrup:
⅔ cup (15 cl) Grand Marnier
  or other orange liqueur
4 tablespoons (60 g) granulated sugar

For the vanilla sauce:
2 cups (50 cl) milk
1 vanilla bean, split in half lengthwise
5 egg yolks
¾ cup (150 g) granulated sugar

Marinate the orange peel in 6 ½ tablespoons of Grand Marnier for 1 hour.

Make the crêpe batter by combining the flour, salt, sugar, and egg. Whisk the milk in little by little. Strain the batter through a sieve and stir in the butter (which has been lightly browned in a saucepan). Cook the crêpes in a small ungreased pan. Make eight crêpes and keep them warm.

Beat the egg whites until stiff, then add the sugar. Stir the orange peel–Grand Marnier mixture into the custard sauce, then gently fold in the egg whites. Spoon some of this mixture onto half of each crêpe and fold over the other half to enclose it.

Place the crêpes on a baking sheet and bake in a 425 °F (220 °C) oven for 12 to 15 minutes. Do not open the oven door while they are baking. Make a syrup by boiling the remaining Grand Marnier and sugar until the mixture coats a spoon.

To make the vanilla sauce, place the milk and vanilla bean in a saucepan and bring to a boil; remove from the heat, cover, and allow to infuse for 10 minutes. Beat the egg yolks and sugar together until the mixture is lemon-colored, then whisk in the hot milk. Place the mixture over low heat and cook, stirring constantly with a wooden spoon, until it coats the spoon; do not allow to boil. Strain into a sauce boat.

As soon as the crêpes are done, remove them from the oven and place two of them on each dessert plate. Spoon the syrup over them and serve immediately, with the sauce boat of vanilla sauce on the side.

Spring lamb en croûte

Gigot d'agneau en croûte

Serves 4:
1 leg of milk-fed spring lamb, about
  2 ¼ lbs (1 kg)
2 lamb kidneys
2 tablespoons (30 g) butter
thyme
rosemary
5 oz (150 g) puff pastry
1 egg yolk
⅓ cup (7 cl) Madeira
salt and pepper

Remove the bone from the thickest part of the lamb leg.

Cut the kidneys into large cubes after removing all traces of fat and gristle. Cook them quickly in a pan with a little butter, then deglaze the pan with Madeira, add thyme and rosemary, and boil for a few seconds.

Stuff the leg with the kidneys and their seasoning. Sew up the lamb so as to enclose the stuffing perfectly. Rub the outside of the lamb with salt, pepper, and a little butter, then roast in a 500 °F (260 °C) oven for 15 minutes. Remove from the oven and leave to cool completely.

To finish cooking, wrap the meat in a sheet of puff pastry. Brush the outside of the pastry with a little beaten egg yolk and bake in a 400 °F (200 °C) oven for 10 minutes.

Slice and serve the meat with some of the pastry and gratinéed potatoes.

LA RÉSERVE DE BEAULIEU

A motionless vessel, an elegant silhouette
on the shores of the Mediterranean,
La Réserve de Beaulieu has its crew, "skipper" (director Henri Maria),
and first mate (chef Gilbert Picard), all initiated
in the cult of Amphitrite.

It is very hard today to imagine the Riviera as it existed when Guy de Maupassant wrote *Sur l'eau,* the first tourist and yachting guide to the region. It was the time of winter vacations for English lords and ladies, Russian grand dukes, and boyars. Nowadays, Beaulieu-sur-Mer is an oasis in that wall of concrete that stretches from Cassis to Ventimiglia, one of the few landscapes to have been preserved: peninsulas of greenery, "prodigious gardens scattered between two seas in which bloom the most beautiful flowers in Europe." The setting at times has the air of a scene off a candy-box lid, with its pastel-colored villas and Italian-style balconies reminding us that the area was once under the rule of the House of Savoy. We should not forget that tourism in the area is a phenomenon that goes back only a little over one hundred years. Before the advent of regular rail service, the traveler to Beaulieu had the choice between the bumpy road from Nice or the steamer *Vent Debout* to reach the bay, much favored by the English and the Americans. But even in those days, La Réserve, just a restaurant then, went to great lengths to ensure the comfort of its distinguished guests. Even so, water had to be brought in on men's backs from Nice, and it was only through the efforts of a faithful customer, James Gordon Bennett, the publisher-founder of the *New York Herald* who sent Stanley off in search of Livingstone, that a telephone was installed on the premises. The number assigned to La Réserve is still 1, embellished with several zeros to flesh out the dialing process. All the royal courts of Europe had a high esteem for La Réserve and knew that its name came from the reserve of fish and shellfish kept alive in cement tanks located under the glassed-in veranda. The coming of the telephone was almost as much of an event as the visits of Queen Victoria, the ill-fated Sissi (Elisabeth) of Austrio-Hungary, the future Edward VII, and many other crowned heads.

The Oyster Bar, perhaps the first created on the Riviera, attracted the lovers of the bivalve and the serious drinkers and, over the years, other monarchs, other millionaires, other stars, like Mistinguett, made La Réserve one of the refuges for the gentry. If La Réserve still operates during the winter, it is the summer that sees a crush of the great of this world in its suites, in the terrace gardens, or at the swimming pool that juts out over the sea and the yacht basin. Along with the reigning or fallen sovereigns, other industrial leaders and theatrical or cinematic luminaries have continued to maintain the fame of the hotel: Henry

Ford II, Charlie Chaplin, David Niven, Elizabeth Taylor, Orson Welles, as well as Marc Chagall, have been guests of the Laroche family, owners of the establishment. On sunny days, the swimming pool looks like a California campus. The bar today is presided over by Michel Girardet, who startled the rather reserved and sedate clientele with his creation of the bourbon-based Billy the Kid cocktail. Here at La Réserve one still dresses for dinner, the tweed suit replacing the sport shirt and jeans. And courtesy requires you to offer your arm to your feminine companion, as is done in good company and not simply among long-time married couples. The director, Henri Maria, a member of an old Nice family who was trained on the Riviera at, among other places, the Eden Roc, has been at La Réserve for more than twenty years. His chef, Gilbert Picard, comes from Lorraine. Named Meilleur Ouvrier de France in 1979 after having received other awards and prizes, Picard has been in the establishment kitchens for more than two decades. He loves to cook fish, especially those of the Mediterranean, *daurade royale, mostelle, pageot,* red mullet, and will not hesitate to remove from the menu any of the fish for which the asking price has become prohibitive. In the luxurious ocean-front dining room enclosing an interior garden like the half-deck of a boat, the diners savor with delight the "Lady Curzon" turtle soup. The *mostelle,* a local fish, is served *à l'anglaise.* For the initiates, this means deliciously and lightly breaded or "bread crumb and butter" as maître d'hôtel Lanteri prefers to put it. Picard is in the classic mold. But this does not mean he is old-fashioned. His vegetables have a garden-fresh flavor. The green beans are *al dente* and the eggplant is scented with thyme or marjoram. The wine sauces, Mercurey or white Mâcon, are thick and light and the cooking times precise and correct. All this makes La Réserve worthy of the two white toques from Gault and Millau or the Michelin star. The fact that there are two employees for every room at La Réserve speaks volumes as regards the quality of the service.

The Americans have remained faithful to Beaulieu-sur-Mer and La Réserve. Their presence in the summer imparts a different animation and dimension to the establishment. The atmosphere is more relaxed, more communicative. These jet-set descendants of Gordon Bennett increase the carefree days of the 1920's. The Scott Fitzgerald hero rubs elbows with a Hemingway adventurer about to set off on a big game-fishing jaunt. But it

The summer is highly suited to the exotic Réserve. However, the sunshine sought after, desired, can produce serious burns on the skins of bathers. As in the days when the Riviera was a winter resort, this fear of the sun pushes us under the multicolored sunshades on the terrace or under a vermilion parasol. When the sun casts huge shadows of the palm trees on its ocher walls, the very beautiful and very classic dining room offers us the perfect spot to indulge in gourmand pleasures.

22 Boulevard du Maréchal Leclerc 06130 Beaulieu-sur-Mer (air-conditioned, 50 rooms, 3 suites, garden, swimming pool, facilities for receptions and seminars, dogs allowed). Closed from December 1 to January 10. Nice is 6 miles away, the heliport 10 miles, Menton 12 miles, and Paris 586 miles. To be seen: Beaulieu, the casino, the Villa Kérylos, Villefranche-sur-Mer, the old city with its splendid view on the road, the "obscure" street completely vaulted overs the fishing port. Nice, the famous Promenade des Anglais, the old quarters, and, in season, the carnival. Tel: (93) 01.00.01

isn't easy to leave this enchanting setting, except perhaps for a visit to the casino to experience the fleeting excitement of trying to break the bank.

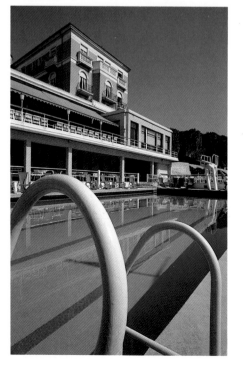

Vegetable salad niçoise

Salade niçoise

<u>Serves 4:</u>
2 large tomatoes, peeled, seeded,
  cut in wedges
4 spring onions, sliced - 2 hearts of lettuce
4 raw baby artichokes, sliced lengthwise
1 lb (500 g) baby broad beans, shelled
½ red pepper and ½ green pepper, sliced
½ yellow pepper and 1 bunch
  of radishes, sliced
3 stalks of celery, sliced - 2 hard-boiled eggs
8 anchovy fillets - 1 small can of tuna fish
parsley, chervil, and chives, chopped
12 to 16 black olives

Cut the hard-boiled eggs into wedges.
Put the lettuce, tomatoes, baby broad beans, and all the other vegetables into a large salad bowl. Add the hard-boiled eggs, olives, anchovies, and tuna. Sprinkle in some coarsely chopped chervil, parsley, and chives.
Make a vinaigrette by whisking together 6 tablespoons of olive oil, 2 tablespoons of cider vinegar, 2 teaspoons of Dijon mustard, salt and pepper. Spoon over the sauce just before serving and toss the salad at the table. Serve immediately.

Sea bass mousse with asparagus tips

Mousseline de loup aux pointes d'asperges

<u>Serves 4:</u>
1 sea bass weighing about 2 ¼ lbs (1 kg),
  filleted
4 sprigs of chervil
4 ¼ cups (1 L) heavy cream
1 lb (500 g) asparagus tips
1 lb (500 g) butter, softened
2 tablespoons lemon juice
4 fish-shaped puff pastries
salt and pepper
cayenne pepper

Make a fish mousse: pound the fish fillets in a mortar then work through a sieve to make a smooth purée. Measure the purée and combine with an equal amount of cream – it is best to combine the ingredients in a mixing bowl over ice, since the mixture should be very cold. Season the mousse with salt and pepper and spoon into individual lightly buttered ramekins. Place the ramekins in a roasting pan, pour in enough boiling water to come halfway up their sides, then bake in a 350°F (180°C) oven for 15 to 20 minutes. Meanwhile, boil the asparagus tips, drain and keep warm.
Make the sauce by boiling the rest of the cream in a saucepan until it coats a spoon, then add lemon juice, salt, and pepper to taste. Remove the pan from the heat and whisk in the butter little by little.
Turn out the fish mousse ramekins onto dinner plates; spoon the sauce over and around them. Place several asparagus tips on top of each mousse, decorate each with fresh chervil and a puff pastry fish and serve.
Note: the mousse can also be garnished with potatoes as in the photo.

Duck in red wine sauce

Civet de canard au Mercurey

Serves 4:
2 ducks weighing about 4 lbs (1.800 kg) each
1 bottle red Burgundy (preferably from Mercurey)
1 lb (500 g) salt pork
1 lb (500 g) mushrooms, caps only
1 lb (500 g) baby onions
6 ½ tablespoons (100 g) butter, softened
¼ cup (50 g) flour
4 tablespoons (50 g) butter, for the vegetables
salt and pepper

Bone the ducks and slice off the leg and breast meat. Season with salt and pepper, then marinate in the red wine for 48 hours. Meanwhile, use the duck carcasses to make a duck soup stock.

Peel the onions. Heat a little butter in a frying pan. Cook the onions in the butter until tender, remove from the pan, then cook the mushrooms in the same pan. Add a little water to the pan when cooking the onions and mushrooms if needed. In a separate pan, brown the salt pork, cut into finger-sized strips.

Lift the slices of duck out of the wine and place them in a roasting pan. Pour in enough marinade and duck stock to cover, then bake in a moderate oven (350 °F to 375 °F/180 °C) for 40 minutes.

Remove the duck slices from the pan, pour the cooking liquid into a saucepan, bring to a boil, and skim off all the fat.

Cut the batter into the flour with a fork.

Boil the cooking liquid to reduce, then whisk in the butter-flour mixture. Bring the sauce back to a boil, whisking constantly. Add salt and pepper as needed.

To serve: reheat, if necessary, the mushrooms, onions, and salt pork strips, place some of each on a hot dinner plate with the duck slices, spoon over the sauce, and serve with fresh pasta.

Raspberry gratin

Gratin de fruits rouges et son coulis

Serves 4:
1 lb (500 g) fresh raspberries or strawberries
6 ½ tablespoons (10 cl) sugar syrup, flavored with kirsch
4 egg yolks
2 cups plus 2 tablespoons (50 cl) heavy cream, cold
⅔ cup (100 g) confectioner's sugar
1 Genoese cake
4 sprigs mint

For the raspberry sauce:
1 cup (25 cl) raspberry pulp
1 scant cup (200 g) granulated sugar
2 tablespoons lemon juice

Make a raspberry sauce by boiling the crushed raspberries with the sugar and lemon juice. Boil until the sauce coats a spoon, then strain the sauce and set it aside.

Cut the Genoese cake horizontally into four layers. Brush the top of each layer with the kirsch-flavored sugar syrup. Place one slice of cake on each dessert plate, then cover the cake with the fresh strawberries or raspberries. Sprinkle generously with confectioner's sugar. In a double boiler, heat the egg yolks with 1 tablespoon of water, whisking constantly until the mixture thickens. Remove from the heat and allow to cool completely, then stir in the cream. Spoon some of this sauce over and around the pieces of cake and fruit, then place the plates under the broiler to brown the sauce. Spoon the raspberry sauce around the cake when the plates come from the oven. Decorate with fresh mint leaves and serve immediately.

L'ENCLOS MONTGRANIER

Hermits of a gourmand monastery,
Claude Destenay and his chef, Richard Assimon,
have chosen to live an exalting adventure
in the splendor of a residence restored to life
by the will of an impassioned restaurant-keeper.

For Lawrence Durrell, Sommières, an old town built on the site of an ancient Roman city "with its belt of medieval walls and ravelins, its humpbacked Roman bridge over the green waters of the Virdoule... surpasses in beauty all the other villages of the Languedoc." Located at the junction of the Provence, Camargue, and Cévennes regions, Sommières always has had political, military, and commercial importance. L'Enclos Montgranier, a seventeenth-century hunting rendezvous point, a little off the road, dominates the protected landscape of the Vidourle valley, an immense area of vines, pine tracts, strewn with low sparse vegetation, meadows and streams. The highly imposing façade of grouted white stones, the hand-constructed terra-cotta terrace, the old fireplaces separated by the monumental staircase (restored with loving care by the Compagnons du Devoir), combined with the sumptuous tapestries, paintings and contemporary furniture symbolize the holy alliance between the past and the present, between the stone and nature.

A country residence converted into a restaurant, l'Enclos has a soul and presence, bearing witness for over three centuries to the sensitivity and tact of man. Therefore, it was inevitable that one day this privileged location be consecrated to an art, this new art which allies inspiration with manual dexterity: the culinary art. Claude Destenay, the head of the establishment, and Richard Assimon, the chef, are not typical meridionals with expanded waistlines and the gift of gab. Sober as the rocky surroundings, enamored of authenticity, they are men who truly have the vocation. Claude Destenay, a former photographer, an Alsatian raised in a family which made a cult of the table, always knew that one day he would be a restaurant owner and would make full use of the experience acquired as a customer during his reporting assignments. Younger than he looks, at the age of twenty-five chef Richard Assimon nevertheless already has ten years of experience behind him and acknowledges that he owes a great deal to what he learned working with Alain Senderens, one of the leaders of the "nouvelle cuisine" at the latter's Parisian restaurant, L'Archestrate. Assimon trained under Michel Rostang and, particularly, under Bernard Loiseau at the Côte d'Or in Saulieu. His intense concern for work well done, his refusal to resort to trickery, a mystical passion shared with Destenay for l'Enclos are fully evident in what he presents at the diner's table. The daily trips of over one hundred miles to the various markets are justified by a will to offer the best of the Languedoc and a love for the product for its own self. Destenay travels to Grau-du-Roi to meet the incoming trawlers so that he can choose his fish; he selects the famous lambs of Nîmes at the slaughterhouse and his ducklings at a duck-raising farm, the address of which he jealously guards. A pond in the Cévennes provides him with his crayfish, and it is to the neighboring hills he goes for his *cèpe* mushrooms, cranberries, or game. Everything comes from the region, from the neighboring villages: truffles, strawberries, peaches, asparagus, melons ripened to perfection in the sun. Even the snails are gathered by wine-grape pickers on the low walls or on the banks of the Vidourle, a stream given to sudden rises in its level resulting at times in the flooding of the meadows surrounding the Enclos. In their kitchen integrated into the countryside, open to the sun and space of the Languedoc, Assimon and Destenay decide how to make the best use of the marketing efforts, while preparing the snacks (fresh truffle slices on toasted country bread scented with olive oil) to be served on the terrace with the pre-dinner drinks made with a rosé de Costières, muscat de Lunel, and walnut alcohol, a refreshing change from the traditional champagne-raspberry concoctions.

The menu at the Enclos is a pleasant reflection of this rustic simplicity, a bit naive but refined, offered by people who have chosen to live apart from the trends, to neglect the conventional methods and attitudes that often make so many tables in France resemble one another. Warmth and freshness are shared, making a diner hesitate between a warm chicken liver pâté or an asparagus-tip salad with an asparagus sauce or thin tuna slices in a tomato and black-olive sauce. Evoking a more contemporary aspect of the rich Provençal cuisine, the light *daube de canette* (braised duckling), served with fresh home-made noodles and a purée of turnips clearly illustrate the Assimon style, while the thyme-scented angler-fish tidbits are full of marine flavors, consummate sophistication with a simple fisherman's dish. The area is rich in local cheeses, in particular the *pélardons* from Cévennes, the rare *tommes* from Arles, scented with bay, pepper, thyme. All are present on the cheese platter offered gracefully by Madeleine Destenay, the unobtrusive hostess with the most charming of smiles. The extraordinary finely prepared desserts radiate sunshine and lightness.

As intended by Claude Destenay and his wife, this cuisine is neither ethnic nor artificial folklore, but the true essence of the Languedoc: great art, executed naturally.

23 Route de Gallargues 30250 Sommières (dining terrace, facilities for receptions and seminars, dogs admitted). Closed on Sunday evenings from October to May. Lunel (TGV Train) 4 miles away, Nîmes (airport) 15 1/2 miles, Montpellier 15 1/2 miles, Paris 466 miles. To be seen: Sommières, the lower marketplace, the ruins of the chateau, the Tour Carrée, the banks of the Vidourle. Aigues-Mortes, the old city with its ramparts (17 miles away). Montpellier, the Favre museum, and the old urban center with its private homes dating from the seventeenth and eighteenth centuries.

AE card honored   Tel: (66) 80.92.00

The successful cuisine at a restaurant is rarely due to the efforts of a single person. Destenay and Assimon associate an entire team with it in the true spirit of the old workmen's guilds. From the creation of the menu on the basis of the produce available at the markets to the meals taken in common to unite even further those who animate this converted country house amidst the wild vegetation of the Languedoc. Their life together is evident in the restored centuries-old stones, their collaboration under the light-colored ceiling vaults, in the successful marriage of the contemporary with the almost monastic austerity of L'Enclos Montgranier.

Red bell pepper terrine with olive oil

*Terrine de poivrons doux
à l'huile d'olive*

<u>Serves 6:</u>
3 ½ lbs (1.500 kg) red bell peppers
2 teaspoons gelatin
4 tablespoons hot water
1 cup and 1 tablespoon (25 cl) heavy cream
2 tablespoons Cognac
3 tablespoons olive oil
a pinch of sugar
several lettuce leaves
salt and pepper

Cut the peppers in half; remove the stems and seeds. Place the peppers in a saucepan with a little water, salt, and sugar. Cover and cook for 10 minutes to soften, then pour into a blender and purée. The mixture should be like smooth cottage cheese. If it is too liquid, pour it into a frying pan and boil until it reduces and thickens, then work it through a sieve.
Measure the pepper puree, then add half as much heavy cream. Whisk the mixture until it stiffens and peaks. Dissolve the gelatin in hot water, then stir it into the peppers. Fold in the whipped cream. Add salt, pepper, and a dash of Cognac.
Line a loaf pan with aluminum foil, then fill it with the pepper mixture. Refrigerate for at least three hours (it can be kept refrigerated in this form up to two days).
Slice the lettuce, season it with olive oil, salt, and pepper, and place it on salad plates. Turn out the pepper mousse onto a separate plate and cut it into 12 slices. Place 2 slices on each plate.
Serve with hot toast brushed with olive oil.

Scalloped tuna with tomato sauce and olives

*Escalopes de thon, fondue de tomates
aux olives noires*

<u>Serves 4:</u>
2 ½ lbs (1.200 kg) fresh tuna (preferably from near the tail), skinned, boned and cut into thin scallops
8 tomatoes
2 cloves garlic
1 bouquet garni (thyme, bay leaf, 1 sprig of parsley)
24 black olives, pitted and sliced
8 tablespoons (120 g) butter
parsley, chopped
a pinch of sugar - salt and pepper

Peel, seed, and chop the tomatoes. Melt 1 ½ tablespoons of butter in a saucepan, add the tomatoes, garlic, bouquet garni, sugar, and a little salt.
Simmer for 20 minutes, stirring occasionally, then remove the bouquet garni and the garlic. Whisk in 6 ½ tablespoons of butter and add the olives to the sauce. Season with salt and pepper.
Place the tuna on a baking sheet and put the sheet under the broiler (about 8 inches from the heat) for 2 minutes (do not turn the fish over while it is cooking).
Spoon some of the sauce onto each dinner plate, put a piece of tuna on top, garnish with a little chopped parsley, and serve.

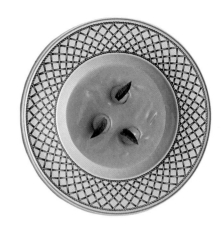

Duckling in red wine sauce with turnips

Daube légère de canettes à la purée de navets

Serves 4:
2 small ducklings
4 ¼ cups (1 L) red wine
1 ½ tablespoons (20 g) butter
2 onions, sliced
1 carrot, sliced
2 cloves garlic, whole
1 sprig of thyme
2 bay leaves
2 ¼ lbs (1 kg) turnips, peeled and sliced into very thin circles
salt - pepper

Clean the ducklings and save the livers for making the sauce. Cut off the wing tips and the necks and chop them into large pieces. Brown them in a saucepan with 2 teaspoons of butter, then add 4 ¼ cups hot water, a little salt, and boil until there is no more than ⅞ cup of liquid left. Strain the liquid and reserve for stock. Brown the ducks in a large pot (do not add any oil or butter). Turn the birds, using wooden spoons so as not to puncture the skin.

Add the carrot and onions to the pot and continue cooking the duck until it is perfectly brown, then pour off the fat. Add red wine to the pot, bring to a boil, and add the garlic, bay leaves, thyme, salt, and pepper. Boil for 15 minutes, add the stock prepared earlier, and cook 20 minutes. Check the duck to see if it's cooked by pricking one of the thighs with a knife point or needle. If the juice that comes out is pink, the duck is done (if you like it rare). If you prefer the duck well done, cook it until the juice is clear.

Make a turnip purée while the duck is cooking.

Peel and slice the turnips, place in a saucepan, and add cold water to barely cover. Add a little salt and cook until the turnips are tender but don't fall apart. Blend them in a blender. If the purée is not stiff enough, put it into a frying pan and boil rapidly, stirring, to evaporate the excess water. Add salt, pepper, and 2 teaspoons of butter.

Once the ducks are cooked, lift them out of the pot, cover loosely with aluminum foil, and keep warm. Boil their cooking liquid until there is only 1 cup left. Remove the bay leaf and thyme. Lift out the garlic and place it in a blender with the raw duck liver. Blend to a purée.

To serve: finish making the sauce by spooning some of it onto the liver-garlic mixture, then stirring this into the pot with the remaining sauce. Slice the breast meat from the ducklings into thick slices. Place the slices of duck on hot dinner plates, and garnish with the turnip purée.

Fresh pasta may be used as a garnish instead of the turnip purée.

Cantaloupe sherbet soup

Soupe de sorbet melon au muscat de lunel

Serves 4:
1 (or 2) cantaloupes weighing about 2 ½ lbs (1.200 kg) total
juice of ½ lemon or ½ orange
⅞ cup (20 cl) muscate or other sweet, strong wine
1 ½ cups (300 g) granulated sugar
⅞ cup (20 cl) water
sugar

To decorate:
1 small cantaloupe, cut into melon balls
sugar, caramelized
mint leaves

Place a 2-quart metal mixing bowl (or large saucepan) in the freezer to chill.

Mix the sugar with ⅞ cup water and boil to dissolve. Once the sugar syrup has cooled, stir in the lemon or orange juice.

Peel and seed the melons. Purée the pulp in a blender and strain. Add the purée to the sugar syrup. Pour the mixture into the chilled mixing bowl and replace in the freezer. Beat the mixture with an electric mixer once an hour for three hours.

A half-hour before serving, remove the bowl from the freezer and place in the refrigerator. Place 4 dessert plates in the freezer to chill. Just before serving, whisk the sherbet and pour in the wine little by little. The finished sherbet should be about the consistency of whipped cream.

Spoon it onto the cold plates and garnish with melon balls dipped into caramel and topped with fresh mint leaves.

LES PRÉS D'EUGÉNIE

*Christine and Michel Guérard have successfully
transfigured the hotel in which the Empress Eugénie
stayed. If perfection exists here on earth, it is undoubtedly at
Eugénie-les-Bains that our gourmand will find it, in this
most luxurious and delightful setting.*

Eugénie-les-Bains would have remained a forgotten spot on the map of France had it not been for Michel Guérard. The very unobtrusive spa and the rural hotel at which the Empress Eugénie stayed when she came for a thermal cure was dozing its way into oblivion under the warm sun of the Chalosse region. Michel Guérard had already reached the heights of glory at the Pot-au-Feu in Asnières. To succeed in getting the Parisian smart set to come to eat in a suburban bistro is not something within the powers of just any chef. The announcement that he intended to set up a new operation more than five hundred miles from Paris stupified his faithful following. All the more so since he coupled the news by stating his intention of creating a "slimming village" on the premises to satisfy one of the current preoccupations of many gourmands. This dietetic aspect of the future gourmand palace was sure to please and reassure. To be able to indulge in the pleasures of the table while respecting sound principles, what better definition could be given to the true final goal of the art of eating? Besides, it is not at all unpleasant to be subjected to a spartan diet menu amid the reconstituted splendors of a turn-of-the-century spa or, on the contrary, to defy fate and sit down at a table in one of the most exquisite residences in France and partake copiously of the fare offered by Michel Guérard. The grounds with its tall plane trees, the Italian-style swimming pool, the harmonious shapes of the statues with their touch of roguishness, the nightly fountain light show or the bandstand, symbol of carefree holidays, ready to delight the ear with Fauré or Ravel, lead us pleasantly to the doors of the beautiful hostelry.

Christine Guérard, who met her husband during his service at Troisgros in Roanne, has a family connection with spas, her father having been the administrator of a health resort chain. She and Michel were enchanted by the gentle beauty of the region, the richness of the soil, offering within a small radius all that a chef could desire. Applying her excellent taste and undeniable talents, she labored hard to transform the hotel, decorating it, embellishing it with a multitude of objects and simplifying it through the use of simple, light colors. In the chimney corner that serves as a combined bar and lounge, the comfort is cozy and the white carpeting is pleasingly thick underfoot. Glancing into the kitchen, the guest's eyes are greeted by an array of glittering silver objects, symbols of gourmand pleasures and adventures. Each decorative element, the antique regional furniture,

brightly polished and glowing, the splendid silver-decorated crystal ewers, subtly erotic, so suited to the smoothness of the Sauternes and the feminine qualities of the Margaux, the eighteenth-century English paintings add to the charm of the setting. All is softness and, on the colonial terrace, reminiscent of Louisiana complete with a superb magnolia tree, all is lyricism. The two proposed menus, the city one and the country one, as in a fable of La Fontaine, the wrought-iron balconies evoke the Vieux Carré of New Orleans, the chaises longues in the gallery and lounge invite the guests to surrender to the *dolce far niente* of the spot. What Christine Guérard conceived, loved, and thought out bespeaks a joy of living, a romantic gaiety.

Everything Michel chose is an affirmation of the picking of wild mushrooms, the netting of ring-doves, or the market choice of those livers, plump, glossy to the point of appearing glazed and offering the promise of unimagined succulence. Because laurel and roses scent the air of the grounds, because immense bouquets of lilies and arums fill the rooms, because the inventiveness of the cuisine daily creates a new aria with the fecundity and genius of a culinary Bach, improvising ad infinitum on a theme of *foie gras* and truffles, because Guérard knew how to communicate his faith, his enthusiasm to all those who work with him, nothing is too beautiful. The garden in which grow the savory herbs and the simple ones dispenses its benefits under the names of hyssop, sage, camomile, black henbane, verbena, because the infusion prolongs the evening scents. As the seasons change, we gourmands pass from the tender pigeon on its bed of fresh green cabbage, to sublime ravioli with mushroom butter and morels, to the suprême of roast duckling *à la bécassine,* to the lobster roasted and smoked in the fireplace, or a tomato butter with parmesan overtones, not because of its cheese content, as subtle as it is unobtrusive, but for its velvety violet color. After having partaken of the gourmand menu, we smoke our cigars in the soft night air under the trees which would have delighted Pocahontas, daughter of the Indian chief Powhatan, who saved the life of Captain John Smith, one of the first Europeans to set foot in the New World, the source of the tobacco in our cigars. Each time we visit Les Prés d'Eugénie, we are struck anew by the immense talent, the creativity and the sensitivity of Michel Guérard. The attention lavished on the guests, the natural perception of the beautiful surroundings or the hospitality are not there simply to cover up imperfections.

24 Eugénie-les-Bains 40320 Geaune (facilities for receptions and seminars, 28 rooms, 7 suites, dogs not admitted, swimming pool, tennis courts, spa). Closed from November 2 to March 25. Pau is 33 miles away (airport 28 miles), Dax 43 miles, and Paris 465 miles. To be seen: Pau, the Boulevard des Pyrénées, the chateau (fourteenth-fifteenth-century), which houses the Henri IV museum (of special interest here: the legendary cradle of Henri IV: a turtle's shell), the Beaux-Arts museum. The Pyrénées mountain range.
AE card honored
Tel: (58) 58.19.01

They are there to set off the harmony of flavors, the fifteen vegetables used in the frothy soup, the oh-so-precise cooking times of an Adour river salmon or those of the other fish cooked in a stock of seaweed, the "low-calorie" menu, a match for the gourmand one, both impregnated with the preoccupation for lightness of Michel Guérard.

*Has the influence of the "cuisine minceur" of
Michel Guérard found a new extension in the
airy setting of the Prés d'Eugénie? Blending
with the pure colonial-style columns and
tender green of the grounds is the languorous
charm of a spa.... Each decorative element,
each piece of furniture, each flower falls
perfectly into place. In this refuge of the rich
Chalosse region, miraculous herbs and the
rarest tree species, tangles of ampelopsis or
tropical magnolias and sparkling fountains
serve to set off the whiteness of the décor. A
delightfully old-fashioned bandstand amid
the trees offers us a remembrance of things
past. The* madeleine, *so dear to Proust, has
its place on the breakfast table to accompany
the homemade jams full of their succulent
summer flavors, summoning up a thousand-
and-one memories.*

Lobster salad with baked tomatoes

Salade de homard aux tomates

Serves 2
2 live lobsters, preferably female
2 qts (2 L) court bouillon
4 small tomatoes
½ lb (200 g) very thin string beans, boiled
fresh chervil
1 teaspoon granulated sugar
⅓ cup (8 cl) olive oil
1 clove garlic, finely chopped
1 sprig thyme, chopped
1 egg yolk - ½ teaspoon Dijon mustard
6 ½ tablespoons (10 cl) peanut oil
  (for the mayonnaise)
1 teaspoon lemon juice
1 tablespoon catsup
1 teaspoon Armagnac - salt - white pepper
1 tablespoon chopped tarragon and chervil,
  mixed

Peel the tomatoes, cut in half horizontally and squeeze out the seeds. Brush a baking dish with some of the olive oil, place the tomatoes in the dish, and spoon over the remaining oil mixed with salt, pepper, and a little sugar (to counteract the acidity of the tomatoes). Place in a 250°F (120°C) oven and bake for 1½ hours. Remove and allow to cool.

Bring the court bouillon to a boil in a large pot, drop in the lobsters, head first, and boil for 10 minutes. Lift out, drain, and leave to cool. If they are female lobsters, scoop out the coral-colored eggs and keep for decorating the plates.

Cut open each tail down the length of the underside with kitchen scissors and remove the meat. Cut each tail into six slices. Crack the claws and remove the meat. Save the lobster heads for decorating the plates.

Beat the egg yolk in a mixing bowl with the Dijon mustard, then whisk in the peanut oil little by little to make mayonnaise. Season with a little lemon juice (added little by little),

catsup, Armagnac, salt, pepper, and the freshly chopped tarragon and chervil.

To serve, place a tomato in the center of each salad plate, sprinkle with chopped garlic and thyme, and put the slices of lobster around it. Put the meat from the claws in the center of each plate. Decorate the plates with string beans, as shown in the photo. Last, coat each piece of lobster with some of the mayonnaise and a little fresh chervil. Garnish each plate with a lobster head and with lobster's eggs, if possible, and serve.

Grilled salmon with asparagus tips

Saumon grillé à la peau, beurre de verveine et pointes d'asperges vertes

Serves 4:
4 slices of salmon weighing about 5 oz (150 g)
  each, preferably cut from near the tail
8 langoustines (or large shrimp), tails peeled
  and heads reserved
3 tablespoons (5 cl) olive oil - salt and pepper

For the sauce:
2 ½ tablespoons shallots, finely chopped
3 tablespoons water
3 tablespoons red wine vinegar
½ lb (250 g) butter, removed from the
  refrigerator 15 minutes before
  making the sauce
2 teaspoons fresh verbena leaves, chopped
salt and pepper- 1 teaspoon lemon juice

To garnish:
24 asparagus tips, boiled
4 small bunches of verbena leaves
4 langoustine shells

Make a foamy butter sauce as follows. Boil the shallots, vinegar, and water in a small saucepan for about 6 minutes or until there are about 2 tablespoons of damp shallot mixture left in the pan. Lower the heat and vigorously whisk in the butter little by little; lift the pan off the heat frequently so that the butter won't brown. Beat the sauce faster toward the end and raise the heat slightly to compensate for any cooling of the sauce. Season with salt, pepper, lemon juice, and a few chopped fresh verbena leaves. Keep the sauce warm in a bain-marie on top of the stove or on a heat diffuser where the temperature of the sauce will not go beyond 40°F (60°C).

Salt and pepper the pieces of salmon and brush them with olive oil. Heat a grill over very hot charcoal embers. Place the salmon slices skin side down on the grill, running diagonally from corner to corner. Cook for 3 minutes then turn the fish 90° to make X-crosses where the skin touches the grill. Cook 3 minutes longer.

Salt, pepper and brush the langoustine tails with olive oil and grill for 2 minutes, turning

over once during this time. Reheat the asparagus.

Spoon some of the sauce onto each plate, place a piece of fish on top of the sauce, and garnish with the langoustine tails and heads as well as the asparagus.

Note: the sauce can be flavored with other herbs such as rosemary or tarragon and strained before warming or serving.

The salmon may be cooked under the broiler/grill. Place it skin-side-up toward the flame; since the skin will not touch the grill, it will be unnecessary to change the position of the fish as it cooks.

Quail pastries with boletus mushrooms

Feuillantine d'ailes de cailles "truffées" de cèpes

Serves 4:
2 quails
¼ lb (120 g) chicken livers, cut
  into large pieces
3 tablespoons (40 g) lard
4 oz (100 g) boletus mushrooms, chopped fine
8 shallots, sliced
6 oz (175 g) ordinary mushrooms,
  chopped fine
⅞ cup (20 cl) heavy cream - lemon juice
⅞ cup (20 cl) Cognac, total
1 tablespoon olive oil
1 carrot, coarsely chopped
1 small onion, chopped - 2 bouquets garnis
1 clove garlic - 1 juniper berry
6 ½ tablespoons (10 cl) red wine
6 ½ tablespoons (10 cl) red wine vinegar
1 tablespoon black peppercorns
⅞ cup (200 g) butter
12 oz (350 g) puff pastry - 3 oz (80 g) foie gras
1 lb (500 g) small potatoes - salt and pepper

Cut the legs off the quail and bone the breasts; discard the carcasses. Marinate for 10 hours in 6 ½ tablespoons red wine, 3 tablespoons Cognac, and 1 tablespoon olive oil, to which are added 1 sliced carrot, 1 chopped shallot, 1 clove of garlic, 1 juniper berry, and a bouquet garni. Make a stuffing as follows: heat the lard in a frying pan, add the chicken livers and the shallots and cook until the shallots soften. Add the boletus mushrooms and ordinary mushrooms. Cook to lightly brown, squeezing over a little lemon juice, then deglaze the pan with ⅔ cup Cognac, add salt, pepper, and the cream, remove from the heat, and leave to cool completely.

Roll out the puff pastry into four circles about 5 inches wide and ⅛ inch thick. Put a tablespoon of the stuffing in the center of each piece of dough, a boned breast and one of the legs (not boned) on top (the end of the drumstick should stick out beyond the edge of the pastry). Place a slice of foie gras and a little more stuffing on top of the quail then fold over the pastry to enclose all but the end of the drumstick. Pinch together the edges of the pastry where they meet.

Make a sauce by browning the onion, carrot, a bouquet garni, and peppercorns in a little butter. After about 5 minutes, deglaze the pan with the vinegar and remaining Cognac and boil to evaporate almost completely. Add the red wine and boil to reduce by two thirds, then strain the sauce into a clean saucepan and whisk in 6 ½ tablespoons of butter little by little. Season with salt, pepper, and another dash of vinegar if the sauce seems to need it. Place the pastries on a baking sheet and bake in a 375°F (190-200°C) oven for 8 to 10 minutes (depending on the size of the birds).

Boil the potatoes in their skins, drain, and cut into quarter-inch-thick slices. Heat 6 ½ tablespoons of butter in a large frying pan until it just begins to brown lightly and sauté the potatoes about 2 minutes on a side.

To serve, spoon some of the sauce onto each dinner plate, place the pastries on top and the potatoes next to them.

Note: baby onions and spinach leaves can be included in the garnish, as in the photo.

Millefeuille pastry with vanilla filling

Millefeuille à la crème légère

Serves 4:
13 oz (360 g) pastry

For the pastry cream:
1 generous cup (25 cl) milk
¼ vanilla bean, split lengthwise
5 tablespoons (75 g) granulated sugar
3 egg yolks
1 tablespoon (10 g) flour
1 tablespoon (10 g) cornstarch

For the whipped cream:
⅓ cup (80 g) heavy cream, refrigerated
  several hours before whisking
2 teaspoons granulated sugar

To decorate:
3 tablespoons confectioner's sugar

Roll out the dough until it is about 18 inches long and 8 inches wide. It should be about 1⁄16 inch thick. Cut it cleanly into three rectangles of about 6 x 8 inches each, place them on a baking sheet, and prick them all over with a fork. Bake in a 425°F (220°C) oven, then remove and cool on a cake rack. The dough should have browned nicely.

Make a pastry cream by boiling together the milk, vanilla, and a third of the sugar. Beat the egg yolks until they whiten with the remaining sugar, stir in the flour and cornstarch, remove the vanilla bean from the milk, and pour the milk onto the egg yolk mixture little by little, whisking constantly. Pour the mixture back into the saucepan and boil for one minute, stirring and scraping the bottom of the pan. Pour the pastry cream into a cool mixing bowl (rinse it in cold water and dry before adding the cream). Whisk the cream to cool it more rapidly.

Add the sugar to the heavy cream and whisk

slowly for one minute then progressively faster for about 5 minutes or until the cream stiffens and peaks. Gently fold the pastry cream into the whipped cream.

Spread half of the cream filling over one of the pieces of pastry, cover with another piece of pastry, and cover this with the remaining cream. Place the last piece of pastry on top, smooth side down, and sprinkle over a thick layer of confectioner's sugar. Place the pastry on a platter and serve.

Note: the pastry can be cut into individual servings, and the sugar caramelized with a hot iron rod or skewer to make a nice crisscross design. For a more sophisticated presentation, it can be decorated with mint and served with strawberries and strawberry sauce on one side, and cooked apple slices and apple sauce on the other, as shown in the photo.

Saint-James

*Establishing himself on the edge of the vineyards
on the heights overlooking Bordeaux,
Jean-Marie Amat has given himself space as well as time,
both so necessary to his dream
of a secret and pastoral domain.*

There is something austere about Bordeaux, withdrawn as it is around its docks, its passages, or courtyards behind the classic façades of the patrician residences or the town houses of the vineyard owners. It is only a little over ten years since the city took an interest in a *grande cuisine.* And if it is inconceivable that the center of the leading wine-growing region in France still does not have one or two three-star restaurants, it is certainly not the fault of Jean-Marie Amat. He was the first to create at his Saint-James, in the Cours de l'Intendance, a delicate and old-fashioned restaurant, a cuisine of rare excellence. Others followed his lead and the stars were not coming. The Pauillacs, the Saint-Emilions, the mellow Sauternes, or the subtle Pomerols had found chefs to show them off to their best advantage, but the lion's share of the credit for this beneficial culinary awakening goes to Jean-Marie Amat.

Now his "Saint-James outside the walls" on the heights of Bouliac has given him space, air, and an assured serenity. The low villa, with its two wings forming a court of honor, looks like an old Roman home. Ausonius might very well have lived within its walls. The Roman aspect is further accentuated by the glassed-in gallery filled with strange objects, marble busts, painted wooden toys salvaged from merry-go-rounds, or a collection of dishes designed for the Saint-James with simple blue patterns, each one symbolizing a great Bordeaux vintage.

Each dining room opens onto a gallery and the terrace shaded by the large trees of the grounds. The horizon line is formed by Bordeaux and the Gironde River and the changing colors of the surrounding vineyards.

The entire décor is white and as homogeneous and free of frills as is the cuisine of Amat. The dining room is in deep orange, of Italian inspiration and in a contemporary vein. The very material used for the walls, lacquered and polished, is a cement invented in Florence, which strengthens the impression of simplicity offered by the Saint-James. The floor is made of stones of the same shade. The light pine ceiling adds further to the warm harmony of the whole, while the scattered columns give one the impression of a Greek-inspired palace. The resolutely modern furniture of the establishment is white and the very restrained menu remains in these half-tones.

Jean-Marie Amat is the preferred student of master chef André Guillot, the wizard of the Vieux Marly. It was from him that Amat learned his deftness of touch, a sense of measure, a

continuous search for perfection. From him, too, certain bourgeois cuisine dishes offered on the fixed-price menu: the rabbit terrine, the bullock cheek with carrots, the desserts, or à la carte the *blanquette de veau à l'ancienne* (veal stew with white sauce), a salad with vegetable fritters. Of Chinese inspiration is the all-duck menu, with a duck bouillon and all the delicious tidbits offered by this fowl including the crisp morsels of skin as in Beijing, the fillets served in their blood have long delighted the Chartrons (wealthy vintners) and the Bordeaux gentry. But the highly contemporary raw salmon served with its skin grilled also has its enthusiastic following.

Certain creations are of munificence worthy of the owners of the *premiers crus classés* (best vintages); a salad of oysters with caviar, sole stuffed with duck livers; others the modest pretentions of more ordinary vintages: *brouillade d'oursins* (scrambled sea urchins) or eggplant terrine scented with caraway.

The exceptional delicacy of a Graves goes admirably well with the crayfish accompanied with oyster-filled ravioli and the lightly saffroned roast pigeon from the innumerable pigeon-raising structures scattered throughout the vineyard area which serve at times for the "château" appellation of some of the wines. More than anyone else, Amat knows how to exercise his talents on vegetables. He makes as much use of the leek in the classic lamprey *à la bordelaise* as in the lobster tail with glazed leeks. The tact and graciousness of this chef as much as his talent make him worthy of a renown extending far beyond the locale of his operations. A fabulous wine cellar in which Mouton and Lafite bespeak the wisdom of the Rothschilds, Yquem the precious harvesting grape-by-grape of the most natural of elixirs or a Chevalier in his domain takes on the appearance of a king, a cellar in which one finds a whole range of the other Bordeaux, bourgeois like the Médoc, or the château-bottled ones, approaching the great vineyards in quality but not the high prices, and the even more modest Côtes de Bordeaux. This veritable wine library cannot frighten the true wine enthusiast.

The diversity of the Bordeaux region is characterized in it. The modest Entre-Deux-Mers can serve as an initiation to the future joys of the more prestigious Pauillac without any shame attached to the selection of this "little" Bordeaux which is a highly popular wine. This is also a part of the great lesson represented by Jean-Marie Amat.

25 Place C. Hosteins, Bouliac 33270 Floirac (garden terrace for meals, small dining rooms, dogs not allowed). Closed on Mondays from Sept. 15 to June 1 and in Feb. The Bordeaux-Mérignac airport is 11 miles away and Paris 362 miles. To be seen: Bordeaux and its numerous churches, including the Saint-André Cathedral (thirteenth to fourteenth century), the tower of the Grosse Horloge, the Grand Théâtre, the plaza and the Hôtel de la Bourse, the Chartrons quay. The Médoc, Château Yquem and Saint-Emilion (the cloister of the Cordeliers) vineyards.
AE - Diners - Visa cards honored
Tel: (56) 20.52.19

Does this setting resemble the villa of the poet Ausonius? Perhaps modest like this light pavilion? Perhaps opening out on barely domesticated nature? Perhaps Roman with its gallery and pedestals awaiting only the statues of the Lares and the Penates or of an Aquitainian Vestal Virgin? Jean-Marie Amat has simplified the forms, mixing contemporary materials and styles with the greenhouse structures, a glass house or a doll's house lost in a park. What might be taken for a music room at the bottom of a garden, with its false appearance of a country tavern, has become a rendezvous point for the Chartrons, a spot to exchange the latest bits of Bordeaux gossip, a gastronomic shrine in the Gironde region. Under the apparent coldness of the restaurant's spaciousness, which is simply an expression of the proud constraint of a still-young chef who nevertheless is influencing a whole generation of cooks, one discovers a giddy whirl of decorative ideas every bit as diversified as the culinary creations of Jean-Marie Amat. But the most striking aspect of all these efforts is the sense of measure, the balance between the dishes and the setting. A concord as important as that of the dishes with the accompanying wines.

Sole salad with rosemary

Salade de filets de sole au romarin

Serves 4:
3 sole, about 10 ½ oz (300 g) each, filleted
4 cloves garlic
1 tablespoon fresh rosemary leaves
1 ½ teaspoons (12 g) salt
1 tablespoon cold water
1 tablespoon Dijon mustard
6 ½ tablespoons (10 cl) olive oil
juice of 2 lemons
mixed salad greens: lettuce, escarole, etc.
1 small beet, cooked

For the vinaigrette:
2 tablespoons peanut oil
2 teaspoons sherry vinegar
1/2 teaspoon Dijon mustard
salt and pepper

Pound the garlic and the rosemary in a mortar until finely crushed; add the salt, water, lemon juice, and mustard. Pour in the olive oil little by little, whisking as when making mayonnaise. Season the salad with a vinaigrette dressing made with peanut oil, sherry vinegar, mustard, salt, and pepper. Toss the salad and place some on each of the salad plates. Garnish with strips of cooked beet about the size and shape of french-fried potatoes.

Steam the fillets for 3 to 4 minutes (they should be eaten al dente). Place on the salad plates when they come from the steamer. Spoon over some of the rosemary sauce, season with freshly ground pepper, and serve while the fish is still warm.

Note: tomato, peeled and seeded, may be used instead of beets as a garnish, and the salad may be decorated with little sprigs of fresh rosemary.

Sea bass fillets with herb vinaigrette

Blanc de bar à la vinaigrette d'herbes

Serves 2:
1 sea bass weighing about 1 lb (500 g)
For the fish stock:
white wine - water
bouquet garni - carrot, sliced - onion, sliced
For the vinaigrette:
⅓ cup (8 cl) olive oil
1 tomato, peeled, seeded and chopped
1 tablespoon lemon juice
4 or 5 coriander seeds - salt and pepper
fresh basil, tarragon, and parsley

Fillet the fish (the skin can be left on and removed after cooking if preferred). Poach the fillets in a fish stock made with equal parts white wine and water, flavored with the bones from the fish, a bouquet garni, carrots and onions. Drain the fillets once they are cooked. Finely chop the basil, parsley, and tarragon (you should have about a tablespoon of each), and mix with the olive oil, tomato, and lemon juice. Add the coarsely ground or cracked coriander seed and spoon some of this sauce over the fish.

Serve while the fish are still warm.

Note: the sauce can be served separately and the fish garnished with asparagus tips and an asparagus mousse.

Deep-fried chicken breasts with ginger

Blancs de volaille frits au gingembre

Serves 2:
4 small chicken breasts
2 cloves garlic, grated
1 spring onion, sliced
a 3 inch piece of fresh ginger, cut into
   julienne strips and marinated for 1 week in
   vinegar
2 tablespoons soy sauce
1 ¼ cups (25 cl) white wine
1 tablespoon Cognac
cornstarch - lemon juice
chives, chopped

For the sweet-sour sauce:
⅓ cup (8 cl) lemon juice
⅓ cup (8 cl) granulated sugar
⅓ cup (8 cl) soy sauce
1 teaspoon cornstarch
1 tablespoon cold water

Make a marinade by combining the garlic, spring onion, ginger (drained), soy sauce, white wine, and Cognac.

Remove the skin from the chicken breasts and cut them into strips about half an inch wide. Place them in the marinade and refrigerate for 5 to 6 hours.

Make a sweet-sour sauce by mixing together the lemon juice, sugar, and soy sauce. Bring to a boil, then lower the heat and simmer for 10 minutes. Mix the cornstarch and water into a paste, then whisk this into the sauce. Raise the heat and bring to a gentle boil, whisking, allow to cook for 1 minute, then pour into a sauce boat.

Lift the pieces of chicken out of the marinade but do not wipe them off; there should be bits of the marinade stuck to them. Roll them in cornstarch and deep-fry them in very hot oil until golden brown. Drain on paper towels.

Serve the fried chicken on individual dinner plates, season with a little lemon juice and sprinkle with chives, with the sweet-sour sauce served separately in the sauce boat. The chicken may be served as shown in the photo, placed on a spinach leaf, with slices of candied ginger, a slice of lime, and a slice of cantaloupe decorating the plate, or simply with a salad of mixed greens.

Coconut cream with raspberry sauce

Gâteau à la noix de coco

Serves 4:
2 ⅔ cups (200 g) grated coconut
3 egg yolks
1 ⅔ cups (400 g) condensed milk
1 ⅔ cups (400 g) milk
butter - flour - raspberry sauce

Beat the egg yolks and the condensed milk in a mixing bowl, then whisk in the fresh milk, and then the grated coconut.

Lightly butter a 10-inch cake pan, or individual ramekins and dust the inside of the pan with flour. Pour the coconut cream into the pan and place it in a roasting pan. Pour boiling water into the roasting pan until it comes three quarters of the way up the side of the cake pan. Bake 20 minutes in a 450 °F (240 °C) oven (if individual ramekins are used, 7 minutes will be enough).

Remove from the oven and leave to cool before turning out. Do not refrigerate.

Turn out the cream onto a platter and place under the broiler to lightly brown. Serve with raspberry sauce.

CHÂTEAU D'ARTIGNY

*So classic in appearance that you would swear it was constructed
in the eighteenth century, the Château d'Artigny stands amidst
its lush green grounds overlooking the valley of the Indre.
Alain Rabier, aided by his chef Francis Maignaut,
celebrates the glories of Loire Valley cuisine.*

The surrounding countryside is La Touraine, "the garden of France." Kings and powerful nobles, princesses and royal mistresses were so enamored of the region that they dotted in with chateaux. Its simple enumeration evokes the Capetian, Valois, and Bourbon dynasties. Amboises, Azay-le-Rideau, Blois, Chambord, and Chenonceaux are the most famous ones, but each of the valleys traversed by the tributaries of the Loire contains others set in the pleasant Angevin area so dear to the poet Joachim du Bellay. The land is agreeable, with numerous streams abounding in fish; the ponds and lakes are full of frogs and snails; the forests are immense, paradises for hunters and game. The vineyards offer such famous vintages as Chinon, Vouvray, Montlouis, Saumur, Côteaux du Layon, Savennières, Touraine, and Bourgueil. The orchards make a rich contribution to the table and the cheese platter, with such types as Chouzé, Ligueil, Loches, Sainte-Maure, Tournon-Saint-Pierre, Valençay and Verneuil, is fine enough to please the most important cheese merchants.

The pleasures of the table and the bottle have been honored here ever since François Rabelais held gargantuan revels here. But along with the profusion there has been the delicacy imported from Florence, and Benvenuto Cellini and Bernard Palissy still inspire the artists of the table. Overlooking one of these valleys, that of the river Indre which flows among the trees, falls, and windmills, there where the fortifications of Montbazon castle have stood on the horizon line since the eleventh century, the Château d'Artigny, transported and transposed a short distance from its former place, relates to us the history of François Coty, the famous perfumer.

He wanted to turn his residence into a family Versailles, extending his property, recreating in the 1920s an echo of the eighteenth century. Sumptuous dining rooms, lounges, and hotel rooms have been installed where Madame Coty once had placed her wardrobe with its seventy-four marquetry closets. Another splendor of the establishment is the rotunda, decorated with a still-life trompe-l'œil fresco in which the initiated can recognize the faces of members of the famous perfumer's family. Coty, born Spoturno, was still another Italian enchanted by the luminosity of the Loire Valley. Converted into one of the most prestigious links in the Relais Châteaux chain of M. Traversac, the Château d'Artigny, with its 58 quietly elegant rooms, its suites, gardens, tennis courts, and swimming pool, has been managed

for the past twelve years by Alain Rabier. Rabier, a graduate of the Ecole Hôtelière at Thonon-les-Bains, spent seventeen years on the staff of l'Oustau de Baumanière (he even held the post of deputy mayor of Baux-de-Provence). Adjoining the music room, site of the concerts of the Château d'Artigny, is the bar, presided over by Joël Mayet, with its profusion of bottled delights covering Cognacs, Armagnacs, Calvados, fruit brandies from Alsace or Champagne – truly inciting to a glorious fling. An impressive listing of eighty-four brandies and liqueurs is topped by an Armagnac Château de Percenade 1893 and runs down to the youngest one (ten years old). Reading it prepares us to tackle the wine list. Forty-five thousand bottles are slowly maturing in the cellars, and the most remarkable aspect is perhaps the predominance of the local wines alongside an interesting selection of the most prestigious vintages of France. Let us profit from our visit and listen to the advice of Guy Blanchy to discover a Bourgueil '79 from the Lamé Delille Bourcard vineyards, offering a remarkable "nose" for so young a vintage, or this Chinon '76 from Charles Joquet, vineyard owner at l'Ile-Bouchard. All these are preliminaries to prepare us for the discovery of the cuisine proposed by Francis Maignaut. Maignaut, a Gersois from Fleurance, was trained as a pastry chef and spent a period at the marvelous Chèvre d'Or in Eze before coming to the Château d'Artigny, where he worked at all the possible culinary jobs.

Amid these gentle surroundings with their rows of poplars, in the green and gold royal rotunda, under the dazzling sparkle of chandeliers worthy of a place in the Baccarat museum, the guest is now prepared to profit from his stay in the heart of France to enjoy the regional dishes. Not that the cuisine of Maignaut is exclusively a local one. A warm salad of duckling with mangoes, the admirable ravioli filled with *foie gras* and forest mushrooms or the crayfish with citronella and ginger butter have exotic and modern savors.

But we should also admit our enchantment when faced with farm-style poached eggs on a bed of celery, a truffle sauce or squash-stuffed squab with Montlouis wine and muscat grapes. The Renaissance cuisine is rediscovered with this dish of wild boar rounds with honey and five spices; we are tempted by a *sandre en filet au vin de Chinon* (perch fillet in Chinon wine), the cheese platter reminds us of the establishment's fidelity to the locale and we are literally subdued by the dessert choices, with a

An œnologist would be delighted to possess this bookcase, where the books have been replaced by the oldest, most diversified of liquors and bespeak the richness of French production. If the impressively monumental lobby and the proportions are those of a royal palace, the gentleness of the countryside, the undulating grounds succeed in imparting an intimate quality to a stay at Artigny. And, thanks to his invaluable advice, Guy Blanchy helps us to discover an exceptional cellar featuring the wine of the Loire.

26 37250 Montbazon (tennis courts, heated swimming pool, 49 rooms, 7 suites, facilities for receptions and seminars, large grounds, dogs allowed). Closed from November 27 to January 7. Tours is 7 miles away (Tours-Nord airport: 15 miles), Châtellerault 35 miles, and Paris 152 miles. To be seen: Tours, Saint-Gratien Cathedral (thirteenth to sixteenth centuries), the Tour Charlemagne, the Beaux-Arts Museum. The Indre Valley, Loche, birthplace of Alfred de Vigny, the castle, the keep and the royal apartments, the chateaux of the Loire.
Visa card honored
Tel: (17) 26.24.24

particular weakness for the *turone au chocolat amer, sauce framboise, eau-de-vie de Cognac* (cake coated with bitter chocolate and served with a raspberry sauce and Cognac).

Our stay continues, night falls, and the noble white façade stands illuminated and the absolute comfort offered almost makes one believe for a fleeting moment that he is the lover of Marie de Bretagne, Duchesse de Montbazon and unfaithful wife of Hercule de Rohan, who lived here three centuries ago.

Freshwater fish with watercress sauce

Nage de rivière au fumet de perche et beurre de cresson

<u>Serves 8:</u>
8 perch, filleted (save the bones)
4 pike, perch, or black bass, filleted
1 cup and 1 tablespoon (25 cl) white wine
  (preferably dry Vouvray)
2 cups and 1 tablespoon (50 cl) water
1 bouquet garni
1 carrot, sliced
1 onion, sliced
⅞ cup (200 g) butter
2 tablespoons heavy cream
2 bunches watercress with stems removed
  and leaves washed
1 lemon
salt and pepper

Make a stock for cooking the fish by boiling together the wine, water, carrots, onions, bouquet garni, salt and pepper; cook until the vegetables are tender. Coarsely chop the fish bones, wrap them in cheesecloth, and place in the stock to infuse, away from the heat, for 10 minutes. Strain the stock and reserve.

Just before cooking and serving the fish, place 6 ½ tablespoons of the stock in a small saucepan. Boil to reduce by two thirds, add the cream, and boil slowly, whisking constantly, to reduce by a quarter more. Whisk in the butter little by little, season with salt and pepper as needed, and keep the sauce warm in a bain-marie.

Drop the watercress into a large pot of salted boiling water, then drain immediately and cool under cold running water. Press to extract as much water as possible, then chop fine by hand or in a blender and add to the butter sauce.

Heat the remaining fish stock until it simmers (it should not boil), add the fish fillets to it, and poach for 3 minutes. Lift out the fillets and drain on a towel.

Spoon some of the sauce onto each plate, place the fillets on top, squeeze a little lemon juice over the fish, and serve. This dish should not be served too hot.

Note: plates can also be garnished with a little tomato, whole watercress leaves, and leeks, as in the photo.

Pigeons with beef marrow, truffles, and grapes

Pigeonneaux truffés de moelle aux raisins muscats

<u>Serves 4:</u>
4 young pigeons (squab)
marrow from 2 large marrow bones
¾ oz (20 g) truffles
6 ½ tablespoons (10 cl) port
3 tablespoons (5 cl) Cognac
⅞ cup (20 cl) chicken stock
20 large sweet grapes (preferably Muscat
  grapes), peeled, seeded, and marinated
  in white wine
6 oz (150 g) fresh mushrooms
  (preferably wild mushrooms, e.g.,
  oyster mushrooms, or chanterelles)
butter
oil
salt and pepper

Slice the beef marrow into 24 pieces. Cut 8 slices of truffle (save the rest of the truffle for later). Slide the slices of marrow and truffle under the skin of each bird, being careful not to tear the skin. Tie the birds for roasting without piercing the skin, brush each one with a little butter and oil, and roast in a 475°F (250°C) oven for 12 minutes. Let the birds sit for 10 minutes after roasting, then cut off the legs and the breast meat. Keep warm.

Coarsely cut up the carcasses and place in a large frying pan. Heat to lightly brown, then add the port and Cognac and boil to reduce by half. Add the stock and continue boiling 10 minutes.

Finely chop the remaining truffle, place in a clean saucepan, and strain the stock into the pan. Heat slowly to warm, then add the grapes and remove from the heat. Keep warm.

Cut the mushrooms into large pieces and sauté them in a mixture of oil and butter until they begin to brown. Place mushrooms in the center of each plate, with pieces of pigeon around them. Spoon the sauce onto the plates and garnish with the grapes. Serve immediately.

Note: the plates can also be garnished with a little peeled and seeded tomato and fresh chervil leaves.

Rabbit salad with figs and wild mushrooms

Emincé de lapin de garenne aux figues et aux cèpes

Serves 4:
saddle of hare (or rabbit)
³/₄ lb (300 g) fresh boletus mushrooms
8 fresh figs
5 tablespoons olive oil
1 tablespoon sherry vinegar
1 tablespoon red wine vinegar
oil and butter, for the rabbit
salt and pepper

Whisk together the olive oil, vinegars, salt and pepper.
Wipe the boletus mushrooms with a damp towel to clean, then thinly slice and place in a baking dish. Pour the vinaigrette over them and leave for 15 minutes, then pour off the vinaigrette.
Peel the figs, slice them into rounds and place in a second baking dish.
Rub the rabbit with butter and oil, cover with aluminum foil, and roast in a 400°F (200°C) oven for 10 minutes. The rabbit should be slightly pink inside when it comes from the oven. Season with salt and pepper.
Cut the meat from the bone, slice it and place the slices back into the roasting pan. Lower the oven temperature to 250°F (120°C) and place the three pans (one with rabbit, one with figs, and one with the drained mushrooms) back in the oven. After about a minute, take out the pan with the mushrooms and arrange them on warm salad plates; two minutes later, take out the rabbit and the figs, and finish garnishing the plates. Serve warm.
Note: a little curly endive and peeled tomato can be added to garnish each plate.

Chocolate cake with raspberries

Turone au chocolat, sauce framboise

Serves 20:
10 eggs, separated
1 ¼ cups (250 g) granulated sugar, total
1 ½ cups plus 1 ½ tablespoons (225 g) flour
³/₄ cup plus 2 tablespoons (120 g) bitter cocoa
2 ½ tablespoons (25 g) cornstarch
1 ¼ lbs (575 g) semi-sweet cooking chocolate
2 ½ cups (60 cl) heavy cream (for whipping)
6 ½ tablespoons (10 cl) heavy cream
  (for the filling)
4 tablespoons kirsch-flavored sugar syrup
6 ½ tablespoons (100 g) butter, softened
½ lb (200 g) fresh raspberries, for the cake
2 cups plus 1 tablespoon (50 cl) rosé wine
2 cups plus 1 tablespoon (50 cl) pureed
  raspberries
1 generous cup (25 cl) sugar syrup
  (cooked to about 230°F/110°C)
3 tablespoons lemon juice
butter, for the baking sheet
flour, for the baking sheet

Make a batter as follows: separate the yolks and whites of the eggs. Beat the whites until stiff, adding ½ cup sugar (or sugar syrup made with the same amount of sugar and 3 tablespoons of water) when the whites are almost stiff.
In a separate bowl, beat the egg yolks with the remaining sugar until the mixture turns lemon-colored. Mix the flour, cocoa, and cornstarch together, stir into the egg yolk mixture, then fold in the egg whites.
Butter and flour a baking sheet, then spread the batter out onto it to make a rectangle about 11 x 16 inches. Bake in a 350°F (180°C) oven for 15 minutes, then remove and allow to cool.
Make a filling by melting 13 oz of chocolate in a double boiler. Beat the whipping cream until it peaks and stiffens. Remove the chocolate from the heat and fold in the cream.
To make the icing, place the remaining chocolate in a saucepan and melt over low heat, then stir in the butter, little by little, and then the remaining cream. Remove from the heat and reserve.
Place the cake in an 11 x 14 x 3 inch pan. Brush the cake with kirsch-flavored syrup to lightly soak it then spread half of the chocolate filling over it. Place the raspberries on top of this, then cover with the remaining chocolate filling. Refrigerate for 2 or 3 hours before finishing the cake.
To finish, take the cake from the pan and cover it with the chocolate icing. Sprinkle the top of the cake with cocoa powder. Serve with a raspberry ice made as follows: Mix the pureed raspberries, wine, sugar syrup, and lemon juice in a metal mixing bowl. Place in the freezer for several hours and serve, using a spoon that has been dipped into hot water.
Note: the photo shows an individual portion of this cake served with the ice, raspberry sauce, and fresh mint leaves.

CHÂTEAU D'AUDRIEU

Few people can boast, as do Irène and Gérard Livry-Level,
that their family has lived in the same spot
for ten centuries.
The Château d'Audrieu, a jewel of a mansion in Normandy,
confirms their assertion.

It was because the personal chef of William the Conqueror stood off a horde of Saxons armed only with a ladle that the Audrieu land tract was awarded to him. Or so the family legend goes. The story is perhaps a mite too pat and hotel-oriented and Jean de Percy was probably more deft at wielding a broadsword than a larding-needle. The fief later became a barony under Louis XIII, once more after a feat of arms by Jean de Seran, descendant on his mother's side of the heroes of Hastings. Later on, it was thanks to the ladies that the Seigneur de Fontaine became proprietor of the chateau. He had one daughter, the great-grandmother of the present owner. Gérard Livry-Level and his wife, Irène, continue the tradition. They have five daughters. Gérard was born at the chateau and, all in all, his family has lived in Audrieu for over ten centuries.

His father, an industrialist, was a navigator in the R.A.F. during World War II and, during his missions above occupied France, flew over his chateau scores of times. After the war, he represented the Calvados region in the Chamber of Deputies. Now it was Gérard's turn to take the air. He did so in a hot-air balloon bearing the coat of arms of Audrieu, gold indented on a black background coupled with three crescents on a blue background, in which he participated in competitions, or offered passengers unusual views of the Norman countryside, the D-Day invasion beaches, the spires of thousands of churches, and the roof of the chateau.

The beautiful eighteenth-century residence offers no reminders of its past glory and almost nothing remains of the building that preceded it. And yet there is an impressive and dark nobility, a perfect balance and classical elegance about its central building crowned by a triangular pediment ending in a U-shaped court of honor created by the two large wings, the whole opening onto the gentle Norman countryside.

An unassailable serenity pervades the chateau and its grounds, sheltered behind centuries of existence, a majestically simple entrance gate and moats have long since lost their warlike functions. Sixty-two acres of wooded grounds, calm and peaceful, gardens in which Irène Livry-Level gathers the bouquets for the tables, the orchards of a farm that is a manor in itself, a green domain to ensure tranquility. The chateau has kept some of its eighteenth-century furnishings, as well as the wood panelings in all its rooms. The Regency style prevails in the main drawing room, complete with ancestral portraits.

It is suspension in time, a lesson in the sense of measure. Few chateaux-hotels have had the extraordinary luck of possessing such a balance, extending even to the rooms. With a chateau so rooted in the Norman soil, it was imperative to find a native son to run its kitchens. Gilles Tournadre is from Rouen and naturally did his apprenticeship at La Couronne, on the place du Vieux Marché. After that, he worked chez Albert, Lucas-Carton, l'Auberge des Templiers at Bézards and, finally, an irreplaceable training period with Claude Deligne at Taillevent. His gourmand menu, *amuse-bouche,* scalloped duck liver, fish, guinea fowl with vinegared juices, and hot goat cheese and peach soufflé with raspberry sauce and petits-fours is a model for this type of meal. Another one, the *menu-dégustation,* offers seven dishes subject to his inspiration of the moment, the seasons, and the market.

His cuisine is not limited simply to the usage of cream and butter, though Normandy produces the best in the country, and local products like cider. And yet there is enough available in the neighboring countryside to supply a royal table. But Tournadre is also oriented toward a cuisine based upon impulses and related spiritually to the new generation of creators.

Thus, we find on the menu *foie gras frais de canard, mousses de foie blond,* ginger and tomato butter, the duck fillets, thyme blossoms, the *blanc-manger* from Taillevent and the *pannequet aux pommes.* There is no shame attached to such a situation. On the contrary, Tournadre excels in displaying a mastery in this style of cuisine: his sea scallop ravioli with cabbage and scalloped salmon with apples and honey are essentially Norman but treated in a thoroughly modern manner.

Normandy is also very well represented in the admirable cheese platter, which is very often accompanied by a bottle chosen from the well-stocked cellar in which the Burgundies are in the majority.

Let us salute the Château d'Audrieu, Gérard and Irène Livry-Level and rejoice to see that there is a smoking room, so that smokers do not offend those who, by choice or necessity, are not lovers of Havanas. (Such attention to detail is rare enough to merit mention.) But let us thank them above all for the perfect assimilation into the hotel field of a family universe and an ancestral tradition. The pleasures of the table have been well honored since Hastings.

In an age in which artists and artisans never created the same piece of furniture twice, each generation of chatelaines at Audrieu has bequeathed to posterity, as witness to the good taste of its period, the furnishings and paintings still to be found in every room of the chateau. Gilles Tournadre, as Norman as the owners of this Relais-Château hotel, enjoys the rare privilege of finding on the spot, in the gardens or on the rich plains of the small farms in the Audrieu region, a good portion of the products for the luxurious table he offers the guests at the chateau.

27　D 94 Audrieu 14250 Tilly-sur-Seulles (11 miles from the sea, 18 rooms, 4 suites, facilities for receptions and seminars, heated swimming pool, dogs admitted for an additional charge). Tennis courts (2 1/2 miles away), horseback riding (6 miles away), and a golf course (25 miles away). Closed from December 15 to February 15. Caen is 10 1/2 miles away (airport 6 miles), Bayeux 15 1/2 miles, and Paris 106 miles. To be seen: Arromanches and the invasion beaches. Caen, the Abbaye aux Hommes, the Trinité church, and the Château. Bayeux: the famous tapestry of Queen Mathilde and Notre-Dame cathedral.
AE - Visa cards honored　Tel: (31) 80.21.52

Turbot with candied onions and apples with cider vinegar

Blanc de turbot à la compote d'oignons et aux pommes au vinaigre de cidre

<u>Serves 4:</u>
1 ¾ lbs (2 kg) fillets from a turbot or other
  flat fish
2 ¼ lbs (1 kg) onions, medium size
2 tablespoons (30 g) granulated sugar
4 tablespoons honey
3 cups (70 cl) cider vinegar, total
1 large green apple, sliced thin
8 shallots, chopped fine
1 ⅓ cups (30 cl) fish stock
10 ½ oz (300 g) butter, softened, total
salt and pepper
chervil for garnish

Place the whole, unpeeled onions on a baking sheet and bake for 45 minutes in a 475°F (225-250°C) oven (they should blacken). Remove and allow to cool, then peel and slice the onions.
Slice the fish fillets into thin slices. Refrigerate. Melt 3 ⅓ tablespoons of butter in a small saucepan, add the onions, sugar, and half the honey, stir and cook over low heat to candy the onions. When the onions have begun to fall apart, add to the pan 4 tablespoons of vinegar and the apple. Continue cooking until the apple slices have softened but are not falling apart. Keep warm.
Make a sauce by boiling the shallots, 6 ½ tablespoons of vinegar, fish stock, and the remaining honey until the shallots have softened, then whisk in ½ lb of butter little by little. Season with salt and pepper. Remove from the heat. Heat the remaining butter in a frying pan and quickly cook the slices of fish (literally in and out of the pan). Season with salt and pepper.
Place several fillets on each plate with some of the apple-mixture between each pair, spoon the sauce around the fish, decorate with a little chervil, and serve.

Foie gras with asparagus-tip salad

Escalopes de foie poêlées, sur salade aux pointes d'asperges

<u>Serves 4:</u>
1 fresh duck foie gras (or calves' liver)
  weighing about ½ lb (250 g)
salad greens (curly endive, escarole, etc.)
40 small green asparagus tips

<u>For the vinaigrette:</u>
3 tablespoons walnut oil · salt and pepper
1 tablespoon sherry vinegar
chopped chives, tarragon, and chervil

Slice the foie gras into 8 slices. Refrigerate.
Boil the asparagus in salted water, drain, and cool in cold water.
Make a vinaigrette and use all but 4 teaspoons of it to season the mixed salad greens.
Place some of the salad on each plate.
Reheat the asparagus tips and place them all around the lettuce as illustrated in the photo. Spoon the remaining vinaigrette over them. Season the slices of foie gras with salt and pepper and fry in a nonstick frying pan for about 45 seconds per side, drain on a paper towel, then place on top of the salad and serve immediately.

Rabbit with apples and cream sauce

Râble de lapin cauchoise

Serves 2 :
saddle of 1 rabbit (apx ³/₄ lb)

For the marinade:
2 carrots, sliced - 1 large onion, sliced
8 shallots, sliced - 2 sticks celery, sliced
2 cloves garlic, chopped
bouquet garni - 8 peppercorns
2 cloves
4 ¼ cups (1 L) white wine
1 cup (25 cl) vinegar - 1 cup (25 cl) oil

For the sauce:
1 tablespoon lemon juice
2 tablespoons heavy cream
3 tablespoons (5 cl) apple brandy (Calvados)
2 tablespoons onion purée (onions cooked
    gently in butter and blended) - 1 apple
2 tablespoons butter, for cooking apple
salt and pepper

Make a marinade with the ingredients listed and marinate the rabbit for 24 hours.

Lift out the rabbit and brown it in a little hot oil in a roasting pan on top of the stove then lift out and drain.

Strain the marinade over a mixing bowl. Put the vegetables from the marinade in the pan in which the rabbit browned, put the rabbit back in the pan, and cook, uncovered, for 8 minutes in a moderate oven. Lift out the rabbit and keep warm.

Place the pan with the vegetables back on the stove, deglaze with the apple brandy, a small ladleful of the liquid used in the marinade, and the onion purée. Heat, add the cream, and bring to a boil. Add a little lemon juice, salt, and pepper, then strain the sauce into a clean saucepan, pressing on the vegetables to extract as much sauce from them as possible.

Peel and slice the apples and brown them in a little butter.

Remove the meat from the rabbit and cut it into thin slices. Arrange the slices on each plate with a little of the rabbit's kidney on top of them. Garnish the plates with the apples. Spoon over the sauce and serve.

Apples in pastry with raspberry sauce

Douillon aux pommes

Serves 6 :
6 large apples

For the dough:
1 ³/₄ cup (250 g) flour
1 ½ teaspoons salt - ¼ lb (125 g) butter
1 tablespoon granulated sugar
1 egg yolk - ⁷/₈ cup (20 cl) water

To stuff the apples:
½ lb (250 g) butter, softened
4 tablespoons (50 g) granulated sugar
2 teaspoons powdered cinnamon

Make an ordinary pie dough with the ingredients indicated. Roll it out and cut it into large circular pieces, each big enough to enclose a whole apple completely. Save any scraps of dough for decorating.

Core the apples using an apple corer. With the tip of a knife, draw a little line around the top quarter of each apple to keep it from bursting when baked. Fill the center of each apple with butter mixed with sugar and cinnamon. Wrap each apple in a piece of dough and decorate with the scraps of dough – cut to look like leaves, for example.

Place the apples on a lightly oiled baking sheet and bake in a 375°F (190°C) oven for 25 to 30 minutes.

Serve the apples on dessert plates with raspberry sauce.

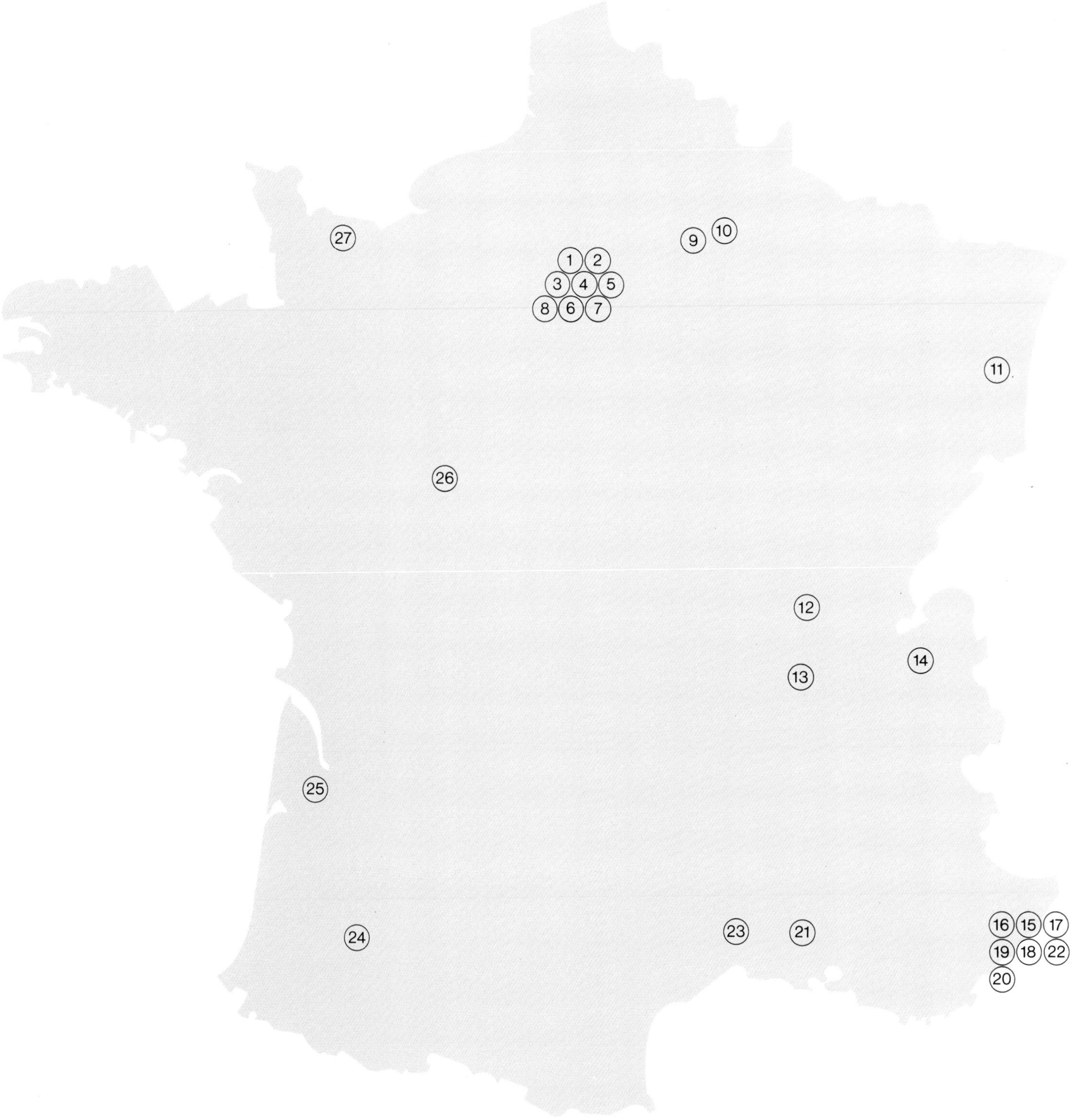

27
1
2
3
4
5
8
6
7
9
10
11
26
12
14
13
25
16
15
17
19
18
22
20
24
23
21

27 Gourmand Localities

1 *Beauvilliers*	*Paris*	*Ile de France*
2 *Fouquet's*		
3 *Le Grand Véfour*		
4 *Hôtel de Crillon*		
5 *Maxim's*		
6 *Taillevent*		
7 *La Tour d'Argent*		
8 *La Vieille Fontaine*	*Maisons-Laffite*	
9 *L'Hostellerie du Château*	*Fère-en-Tardenois*	*Picardy*
10 *Boyer les Crayères*	*Rheims*	*Champagne*
11 *L'Auberge de l'Ill*	*Illhäusern*	*Alsace*
12 *Georges Blanc*	*Vonnas*	*Burgundy*
13 *Paul Bocuse*	*Collonges-au-Mont-d'Or*	*Lyons region*
14 *L'Auberge du Père Bise*	*Talloires*	*Savoy*
15 *Château de la Chèvre d'Or*	*Eze-Village*	*Provence-Côte d'Azur*
16 *Château du Domaine Saint-Martin*	*Vence*	
17 *Grill de l'Hôtel de Paris*	*Monte Carlo*	
18 *Le Métropole*	*Beaulieu-sur-Mer*	
19 *Le Moulin de Mougins*	*Mougins*	
20 *L'Oasis*	*La Napoule*	
21 *Oustau de Baumanière*	*Baux-de-Provence*	
22 *La Réserve de Beaulieu*	*Beaulieu-sur-Mer*	
23 *L'Enclos Montgranier*	*Sommières*	*Languedoc*
24 *Les Prés d'Eugénie*	*Eugénie-les-Bains*	*Aquitaine*
25 *Saint-James*	*Bouliac*	
26 *Château d'Artigny*	*Montbazon*	*Touraine*
27 *Château d'Audrieu*	*Tilly-sur-Seulles*	*Normandy*

Some
Famous
Gourmands

Apicius	M. Gavius Apicius, fl. 25 B.C. toward the end of the reign of Tiberius.
Aron, Jean-Paul	Contemporary writer and essayist. Author of *Mangeur du* XIXe *siècle* (1973).
Archestratus of Gela or Syracuse	Fourth century B.C. The most famous chef of his age. Author of a poem on gastronomy of which only fragments remain today. Alain Senderens took the name for his three-star restaurant in Paris.
Apollinaire, Guillaume	Wilhelm Apollinaris Kostrowitsky, known as Guillaume Apollinaire (1880-1918), French poet; author of *Alcools* and *Calligrammes*.
Ausonius	Decimus Magnus Ausonius, Latin poet born in Bordeaux (circa 310-395). Tutor to the Emperor Gratian, lived at the court of Trèves. One of the most famous Saint-Émilion vintages bears his name. It is doubtful that the poet lived in a villa on the site of the present chateau, but his memory is linked with the exceptional vineyard.
Beauvilliers, Antoine	1754-1827. Victualing Officer to the Comte de Provence, the future King Louis XVIII. In 1784, he opened one of the first great restaurants in Paris. Author of *L'Art du cuisinier* (1814).
Brillat-Savarin, Anthelme	1755-1826. Magistrate and gastronome, born at Belley in the Bugey region of France, was for a time an émigré in the United States, where he worked as a musician in an orchestra in New York. Author of *La Physiologie du goût* (1826).
Carême, Marie-Antoine	1784-1833. One of the greatest of French chefs. Chef to Talleyrand, tsars of Russia, and other crowned heads. Among other works, he wrote *L'Art de la cuisine au dix-neuvième siècle* (1847).
Clause, Jean-Pierre	Born in 1757; chef to the Duc de Contades, governor of Strasbourg; credited as having created the *foie gras de Strasbourg* around 1780.
Corcellet	Famous eighteenth-century grocery shop in the Palais-Royal district of Paris, famous for the originality of products offered. Paul Corcellet continues the tradition in a shop not far from the original one.
Curnonsky	Maurice-Edmond Sailland, called Curnonsky (1872-1956). Elected Prince of Gastronomes by his fellows. One of the most famous writers on gastronomy. Author, in collaboration with Austin de Croze, of *Trésor gastronomique de la France, Cuisine et Vins de France* and many other works.
Dubois, Urbain	Born in 1818. Former chef at the Rocher de Cancale, the Tortoni, and the Café Anglais. Introduced the service *à la Russe* (course-by-course serving). Author of *Cuisine classique* (1856) and *La Cuisine artistique* (1872).
Dumas, Alexandre (père)	1802-1870. Gourmet and gourmand. Author of *The Three Musketeers* and many other novels and plays, as well as the posthumously published *Dictionary of Cuisine* (1873).
Dunand	A family of chefs. One of them chose exile to accompany Napoleon to Saint Helena; created *poulet marengo* (chicken in wine sauce).
Escoffier, Auguste	1846-1935. Chef at the Carlton of César Ritz in London, where he created the *pêche Melba* in honor of the celebrated Australian opera singer, who was singing *Lohengrin* at Covent Garden. His native city of Villeneuve-Loubet contains a museum devoted to him and his achievement.
Fraysse, Pierre	Chef, born at Sète. Created the *lobster à l'américaine* at Peter's towards the end of the Second Empire.
Les Frères Provençaux	Name of a famous restaurant in the Palais-Royal area (1786-1869).
Garin, Georges	1913-1978. French chef. Revived the fashion for purées.
Gouberville, Gilles de	1522-1578. Norman nobleman. Credited as being the first in 1554 to distill *sydre* (cider) so as to obtain an *eau-de-vie* clear spirit, which was called afterward Calvados.
Gouffé, Jules	1807-1877. Chef hired by the Jockey Club on the advice of Alexandre Dumas in 1867. Author of *Livre de Cuisine* (1867).
La Guipière	Chef to Maréchal Murat, creator of *sole Murat;* died in the snows of Russia during the retreat of the Grande Armée in 1812.
La Reynière, Balthazar Grimod de	1758-1838. Undoubtedly the most original and important personality in the gastronomy of his period. He invented everything, criticism, sampling tests, etc. His *Almanachs des gourmets* (from 1803 onward) and his *Manuel des amphytrions* (1808) are the basic reference works for any self-respecting gourmand.

Larue

Famous restaurant in the Place de la Madeleine. Founded in 1886 and taken over in 1904 by Édouard Nignon. Marcel Proust was a regular customer. Closed for good in 1954.

La Varenne, Pierre-François, Sieur de

Chef to the Marquis d'Uxelles (hence the culinary creation *d'uxelles*, originally made with a chopped mushroom base). Author of *Le Cuisinier français* (1551). His name was given to a Parisian cooking school with a strong Anglo-Saxon following.

Massialot

Author of *Cuisinier Roial et Bourgeois* (1691).

Menon

Eighteenth-century culinary writer. Some of his works are *Le Nouveau Traité de cuisine* (1742), *Cuisine bourgeoise* (1746) and *Soupers du roi* (1755). He is said to have also written *La Cuisine et office de santé* (1758).

Mongelet, Claude

1825-1888. Writer on gastronomical subjects. Author of *Lettres gourmandes* et *La Cuisine poétique*, founder of *Gourmet*.

Montagné, Prosper

1865-1948. Famous chef. One-time chef-owner of one of the greatest restaurants in France during the period between the two World Wars. Also was chef at Ledoyen. Author of *Délices de la table, Manuel du bon cuistot*, and, especially, the first *Larousse gastronomique*.

Montesquieu

Charles de Secondat, baron de la Brède et de Montesquieu (1689-1755), author of *The Spirit of Laws* and *The Persian Letters*. He once said, "I don't know whether it's my books that sell my wine or my wines that help sell my books!"

Nignon, Édouard

1865-1934. Successively chef at la Maison Dorée, le Café Anglais, Voisin, Noël Peters, Paillard, Lapérouse, Claridge's in London and the Ermitage in Moscow. Owner of Larue from 1904 to his death. Author of *L'Heptameron des gourmets* (1920) and *Plaisirs de la table* (1921).

Parmentier, Antoine Augustin

1737-1813. Agronomist, pharmacist, and soldier. Creator of the Central Bakery. Author of many works. It was he, under the reign of Louis XVI, who advocated increased raising of potatoes to counter famines and grain shortages.

Platina

Bartolommeo Sacchi, called Platina (born in Cremona). Author of *De honesta voluptate et valetudine ad amplissimum ac doctissimum* (1474).

Point, Fernand

1896-1955. Famous chef (La Pyramide in Vienne is still one of the finest restaurants in France). A good number of today's great chefs were trained by Point.

Procope

Francesco Procopio dei Coltelli, called François Procopé, one of the first to serve coffee to the Parisians. He opened a café on the rue de l'Ancienne Comédie (1686). There is to this day a restaurant bearing his name in the same spot.

Revel, Jean-François

Contemporary journalist, essayist and writer. Author of *Un festin de paroles*, a literary history of gastronomical sensitivity from antiquity to the present day.

Taillevent

Guillaume Tirel, called Taillevent (1326-1395). Chef to Jehanne d'Evreux, Philippe de Valois, Charles V, and Charles VI, author of *Viandier*, first book of recipes in French.

Tendret, Lucien

1825-1896. Born at Belley. Distant relative of Brillat-Savarin. Author of *La Table du pays de Brillat-Savarin* (1892), a work which has been a source of inspiration for many chefs of the "nouvelle cuisine."

Tortoni

Head-waiter of the Neapolitan Velloni; opened a café in Paris in 1798 and in 1804 the Café Tortoni. This last establishment attracted such customers as Talleyrand, Bismarck, Victor Hugo, Alfred de Musset and the Prince Orloff, the Russian ambassador. It was for the prince that he created the *selle de veau Orloff* (saddle of veal with soubise, mushrooms, truffles and Mornay sauce). The café closed in 1894.

Vatel

Fritz Karl Watel, called Vatel (1635-1671). Majordomo to Fouquet and Le Grand Condé; he fell upon his sword because a consignment of seafood did not arrive on time in April 1671 when his master was receiving Louis XIV.

Velloni

Famous family of Italian ice cream makers in the eighteenth and nineteenth centuries. A member of the family operated a restaurant, Le Hameau Chantilly, in the former residence of the Marquise de Pompadour; the building has since become the French White House.

Very

Restaurant originally in the Tuileries gardens and later at the Palais-Royal (1804). Used as a setting several times in *La Comédie humaine* by Balzac. Closed down for good in 1859.

Viard

Nineteenth century culinary writer; author of *Cuisinier impérial, Cuisinier royal*, and *Cuisinier républicain*. In fact, these are the same work with title changes that indicated which way the political wind was blowing. The author probably was a creation of the publishers.

Villeneuve, Arnaud de

Died in 1313. Doctor-alchemist at the École de Montpellier; author of a *Traité des vins* (Treatise on Wines). He is considered to be one of the creators of the distillation process for alcohols, a technique that actually is Arabian in origin.

General Comments about the Recipes

The recipes in this book are given to help the reader imagine the types of dishes that characterize the very personal cuisine each chef has developed. They are written as the chefs gave them and are as vague or as precise as a given chef's own instructions, but they always convey his style of cooking. They should therefore inspire and motivate both amateurs and professionals alike.

The following Dictionary of Terms and Ingredients is included to define briefly words that are mentioned frequently in the text but that may not be familiar to cooks outside France. Further details about any one of them can be obtained in almost any standard book on French cooking.

Dictionary of terms and ingredients

Bain-marie:
A bain-marie, or water bath, is used for cooking foods at low, even temperatures or for keeping prepared foods warm. When used on top of the stove it corresponds to a double boiler, consisting of a large pan of water into which a smaller pan or a mixing bowl is set. The water in the bain-marie should never boil and should just barely touch the bottom of the smaller pan or bowl. More frequently, a bain-marie is used in the oven. In this case it consists of a large roasting pan or baking dish into which boiling water is poured and into which the utensil containing the food is set. The water should come about halfway up the sides of the smaller utensil.

Bouquet garni:
A bouquet garni is a bunch of fresh herbs tied together with kitchen string; it is almost always made of a sprig or two of fresh parsley and of thyme, and a whole bay leaf. If dried herbs must be used, they should be put into a small bag of cheesecloth or other material, to hold them together.

Butter:
In France, unsalted butter is always used in cooking; it should therefore be used in making these recipes, or else the amount of salt called for should be reduced accordingly.
Clarified butter is sometimes called for. This is butter that has been heated over very low heat until all the water contained in it has evaporated and impurities either surface as a white foam or fall to the bottom of the pan. When the foam is spooned off and the clear, melted butter is poured off, leaving the remaining impurities behind, the butter is said to be clarified.

Court bouillon:
A court bouillon is an aromatic liquid used for poaching fish. For instructions on making it, see the recipe for Sea Bass Marinière, p. 79.

Deglaze:
Deglazing occurs when a small amount of liquid is added to a hot pan to detach juices that have stuck to the bottom of the pan during an earlier stage of the preparation. Generally, the pan is scraped and the liquid used to deglaze is either simply brought to a boil, or reduced to the consistency of a sauce (see **Reduce**).

Foie gras:
Foie gras is the enlarged liver of force-fed ducks or geese. In ducks it weighs about 1 to 1 ¼ pounds, in geese up to 2 pounds. A good foie gras is creamy in texture and mild in flavor.
Canned foie gras is often a mixture of foie gras and other meats used as a filler. It should be avoided unless the can is clearly labeled "au naturel" or "entier," indicating a whole, unadulterated foie gras.
Although neither chicken liver nor calf's liver tastes like foie gras, one or the other may be substituted for foie gras, depending on the recipe. While the finished preparation will not taste exactly the same as when foie gras is used, results can be excellent.

Fold:
This term is most often used when stiffly beaten egg whites or whipped cream are to be combined with other ingredients. Use a flat wooden spatula. Depending on the recipe, either the egg whites or cream will be poured over the other ingredients, or vice-versa. When this has been done, cut through to the bottom of the bowl with the spatula and lift the bowl's contents over on top of the rest. Continue cutting and "folding" in this way until a smooth, homogeneous mixture is made.

Fish stock (Fumet de poisson): See Stocks.

Genoese:
A Genoese is a round or square cake made by briefly beating whole eggs and sugar in a double boiler, then removing from the heat and beating to form a ribbon, folding in first flour, then a little melted butter. This batter, baked in a moderate oven, makes a light, airy cake somewhat like a sponge cake.

Herbs:
The herbs most frequently used in France are parsley, chervil, tarragon, and basil, always used fresh, along with thyme and bay leaf, which can be used either fresh or dried (see **Bouquet garni**). Often one can be substituted for another, although this will inevitably change the taste of the preparation. Generally speaking, if you must, you can substitute parsley for chervil and basil for tarragon.

Julienne:
Julienne strips are thin strips, most often of vegetables, used to garnish many dishes. About the size and shape of ordinary matchsticks, they are about 2 inches long and 1/16 of an inch wide.

Lardons:
Lardons are little pieces of bacon or salt pork about 1 inch long and ½ inch wide.

Meat jelly:
Meat jelly is made just as stock is, except that a highly gelatinous meat, usually calves' feet, is included when making the broth. When cooked, the broth is reduced by about half to intensify its taste, clarified by whisking lightly beaten egg whites into it and straining them out, then flavored by the addition of a strong wine like Port or Madeira or simply left as it is.
To be used, the jelly must be cooled until it thickens to the consistency of olive oil, then either poured into a mold to line it or brushed over a preparation to produce a brilliant glaze. It is then chilled until completely stiff.

Mushrooms, wild:
Boletus mushrooms are the most frequently called for among wild mushrooms in this book. When fresh, they have a very delicate taste, but when dried they can be extremely strong; this is also true of chanterelles, morels, and other wild mushrooms. Therefore, it is sometimes preferable to use ordinary fresh mushrooms when a wild variety is called for, but if you prefer, use about ½ cup of dried wild mushrooms for every ¼ pound of fresh ones called for, and soak them in warm water for about 30 minutes before cooking.

Reduce:
This term means simply to boil a liquid rapidly over very high heat until the quantity has diminished. The amount by which the liquid is to be reduced is generally indicated by expressions like "reduce by half," "reduced by three-quarters," and so on. If the term is used with no qualification whatsoever, it is generally understood to mean "reduce by half or until the liquid lightly coats a spoon."

Stocks (Meat, poultry, or fish):
All stocks are made in essentially the same way. A large number of bones (generally carcasses where poultry is concerned, bones and heads where fish are concerned) or cheap cuts of meat are simmered with water, onion, carrot, pepper, and bouquet garni until a rich broth is made. This generally means cooking times of about 1 hour for fish, up to 4 hours for beef. The solid ingredients are then strained out. The stock may be used as it is, boiled down to make a jelly (see **Meat jelly**), or boiled down further until only a thick, syrupy glaze is left in the pan. This meat or fish glaze is sometimes used to enrich sauces, and because the stock must be so concentrated no salt should be added when making it.
As a rule, about 1 quart of water should be used for every pound of meat when making stock. Some chefs will include white wine when making fish stock.

Sugar syrup:
Sugar syrup is simply a mixture of water and sugar boiled together. If no other direction is given, "sugar syrup" should be taken to mean bringing the mixture just to a boil, then removing it from the heat, using a proportion of 1 cup water to 1 scant cup of granulated sugar.

Terrine:
A terrine is an oval or rectangular baking dish of porcelain or earthenware, generally used for baking pâtés. One is pictured on page 119. Depending on the recipe, the pâté itself, or for that matter any preparation molded in a terrine may also be referred to as a terrine.

Truffle juice:
Truffle juice is the liquid that comes from truffles when they are canned and sterilized. It can sometimes be purchased separately from the truffles themselves, but if it is not available, simply use the liquid in the can with canned truffles.

Turn, to give a turn:
This concerns only puff pastry (flaky pastry). The butter is wrapped in the dough and the dough is rolled out into a band. The band is folded in thirds, then turned a quarter-turn so that the edge of the last fold is running perpendicular to the edge of the table. Each time this process is repeated (rolling into a band, folding, and turning), the dough is said to have been given a turn.

Zest:
The zest is the colored outer portion of the peel of a citrus fruit. It is most easily removed with a vegetable peeler, or if grated zest is called for, with a fine-holed vegetable grater. If grating zest, be sure to remove only the colored part of the peel and not the bitter, white pith just underneath it.

Measurements

Quantities have been given in American and metric measures (in this order).

International conversion tables often differ and are under constant revision. Recipe users may find the following comments helpful.

The metric measures came direct from the chefs and are, therefore, the most accurate. The American measures were provided by the translators of this book, who personally verified all quantities. (For Imperial measurements consult an International conversion table.)

Recipe Index

Entrées

Caviar	Caviar "alms-purses" (La Vieille Fontaine)	56
Chicken livers	Chicken liver mousse (L'Auberge du Père Bise)	88
Crayfish	Crayfish gratin (L'Auberge du Père Bise)	88
	Crayfish gratin with wild mushrooms and pasta (Grill de l'Hôtel de Paris)	106
	Crayfish salad (L'Oasis)	124
Eel	Eel and sweetbread pie with nettle sauce (L'Hostellerie du Château)	62
Eggs	Poached eggs with asparagus (Taillevent)	44
	Red and white quail eggs in cream sauce with herbs (Hôtel de Crillon)	32
Foie gras	A gourmand's tiered terrine (Georges Blanc)	78
	Foie gras and mango with ginger sauce (L'Oasis)	125
	Foie gras with asparagus tip salad (Château d'Audrieu)	166
Frogs' legs	Frogs' legs soufflé (Le Grand Véfour)	26
Lobster	Lobster cream with green bean sauce (Château de la Chèvre d'Or)	94
	Lobster salad with baked tomatoes (Les Prés d'Eugénie)	148
	Lobster with bell pepper mousse and tomato sauce (Maxim's)	38
Mussels	Mussel soup with orange (Boyer les Crayères)	68
Oysters	Belgian endive salad with oysters (Le Métropole)	112
Puff pastry	Puff pastry with oysters, scallops, and spinach (Le Grand Véfour)	26
Salad	Vegetable salad niçoise (La Réserve de Beaulieu)	136
Scallops	Scallop and spinach dainties (La Vieille Fontaine)	56
Sweetbreads	Sweetbreads and lobster in aspic (La Tour d'Argent)	50
Terrine	Red bell pepper terrine with olive oil (L'Enclos Montgranier)	142
Truffles	Truffle surprise (L'Oasis)	124

Fish

Bouillabaisse	Jellied bouillabaisse with star anise (Grill de l'Hôtel de Paris)	107
Freshwater fish	Freshwater fish with watercress sauce (Château d'Artigny)	160
Haddock	Smoked haddock salad (Fouquet's)	20
John Dory	John Dory fillets with cream and vegetable sauce (Le Moulin de Mougins)	118
	Squash blossoms stuffed with John Dory (L'Oasis)	125
Mixed fish	Mixed fish plate with baby vegetables and butter sauce (Château du Domaine Saint-Martin)	100
Porgy	Porgy with garlic and tomato sauce (Hôtel de Crillon)	32
Red mullet	Grilled red mullet escabèche (Beauvilliers)	14
	Red mullet fillets with red wine sauce (Oustau de Baumanière)	130
	Red mullet mousse (Oustau de Baumanière)	130
Salmon	Grilled salmon with asparagus tips (Les Prés d'Eugénie)	148
Sea bass	Sea bass baked in salt (Fouquet's)	20
	Sea bass braised in champagne à la Grimaldi (Grill de l'Hôtel de Paris)	106
	Sea bass fillets with herb vinaigrette (Saint-James)	154
	Sea bass marinière (Georges Blanc)	79
	Sea bass Métropole (Le Métropole)	112
	Sea bass mousse with asparagus tips (La Réserve de Beaulieu)	136
	Sea bass with truffles (L'Hostellerie du Château)	62
Sole	Sole salad with rosemary (Saint-James)	154
Tuna	Scalloped tuna with tomato sauce and olives (L'Enclos Montgranier)	142
Turbot	Turbot in red wine sauce with eggplant purée (Beauvilliers)	14
	Turbot in red wine with onions and potatoes (Château de la Chèvre d'Or)	94
	Turbot with candied onions and apples with cider vinegar (Château d'Audrieu)	166
	Turbot with lobster mousse and cabbage (Hôtel de Crillon)	33
	Turbot with maderized champagne (L'Hostellerie du Château)	63
	Turbot with mixed vegetables and champagne sauce (Boyer les Crayères)	68

Poultry

Chicken	Braised chicken with tarragon (L'Auberge du Père Bise)	89
	Chicken breast stuffed with truffles, served with leeks (Boyer les Crayères)	69
	Deep-fried chicken breasts with ginger (Saint-James)	155

174

Duck	Duck breast with lime sauce and peppery pineapple (Fouquet's)	21
	Duck breast with cranberries, mushrooms, and potatoes (Château du Domaine Saint-Martin)	101
	Duck in red wine sauce (La Réserve de Beaulieu)	137
	Duck à la Tour d'Argent (La Tour d'Argent)	50
	Duck with raspberry vinegar, turnips and glazed onions (Maxim's)	38
	Duckling in red wine sauce with turnips (L'Enclos Montgranier)	143
Pigeon	Baby pigeons with puff pastry and pasta (Château de la Chèvre d'Or)	95
	Pigeons with beef marrow, truffles, and grapes (Château d'Artigny)	160
	Squab with cabbage (Taillevent)	44
Quail	Quail pastries with boletus mushrooms (Les Prés d'Eugénie)	149

Meat

Beef	Filet mignon with green pepper sauce (Le Grand Véfour)	27
	Tenderloin with currants à la Mathurini (Le Moulin de Mougins)	118
Lamb	Lamb stew with garlic bread (Le Moulin de Mougins)	119
	Lamb with chanterelles and tarragon sauce (La Tour d'Argent)	51
	Lamb with zucchini and tomatoes (Hôtel de Crillon)	33
	Spring lamb en croûte (Oustau de Baumanière)	131
Rabbit	Rabbit salad with figs and wild mushrooms (Château d'Artigny)	161
	Rabbit with apples and cream sauce (Château d'Audrieu)	167
Veal	Stuffed calves' kidneys with truffles and spinach (Beauvilliers)	15
	Veal steaks with Marsala (Fouquet's)	20
	Veal steaks with mustard sauce and mushrooms (La Vieille Fontaine)	56

Vegetables

Eggplant	Eggplant papetons with tomato sauce and basil (Le Métropole)	113
Potatoes	Potato crêpes (Georges Blanc)	78

Desserts

Apples	Apples in pastry with raspberry sauce (Château d'Audrieu)	167

Cakes	Chocolate Alcazar (La Vieille Fontaine)	57
	Chocolate Alexandra (Boyer les Crayères)	69
	Chocolate cake with raspberries (Château d'Artigny)	161
	Chocolate Marquise (Taillevent)	45
	Chocolate Negus (L'Auberge du Père Bise)	89
	Coconut cream with raspberry sauce (Saint-James)	155
	Lime "mirror" (La Vieille Fontaine)	57
Cream	Almond cream with fruit (Taillevent)	45
Crêpes	Crêpes with orange soufflé filling (Oustau de Baumanière)	131
	"Merry widow" crêpes (Maxim's)	39
Eggs	Snow eggs with pink caramelized almonds (Fouquet's)	21
Fritters	Strawberry fritters with raspberry sauce (Le Métropole)	113
Gratins	Fruit gratin with champagne sauce (La Tour d'Argent)	51
	Pear gratin (Château de la Chèvre d'Or)	95
	Raspberry gratin (La Réserve de Beaulieu)	137
Ice	Anisette parfait (Le Moulin de Mougins)	119
Millefeuille	Millefeuille pastry with vanilla filling (Les Prés d'Eugénie)	149
	Strawberry millefeuille (L'Hostellerie du Château)	63
Mousses	Frozen mousse with fresh fruit (Georges Blanc)	79
	Lime mousse (Château du Domaine Saint-Martin)	100
	Tulip pastries with raspberry mousse filling (Maxim's)	39
Oranges	Oriental oranges (Le Grand Véfour)	27
Pie	Lemon pie with white rum (Beauvilliers)	15
Sherbet	Cantaloupe sherbet soup (L'Enclos Montgranier)	143
	Prune and Armagnac sherbet (Château du Domaine Saint-Martin)	101
Soufflé	Hot raspberry soufflé (Grill de l'Hôtel de Paris)	107

The recipes of the Moulin de Mougins, Georges Blanc, and Les Prés d'Eugénie are cited with the kind permission of Editions Robert Laffont. Because of exclusive contractual arrangements made by Paul Bocuse and the Haeberlin brothers, we were unable to offer any of their recipes.

The photographs of Fouquet's were taken by Ian Berry. Miguel Rio Branco photographed Taillevent, Georges Blanc, Paul Bocuse, L'Auberge du Père Bise, and L'Oasis. All the remaining restaurants were photographed by Gilles Peress.

Abbreviations for credit cards accepted in the restaurants are as follows:
AE   American Express
Diners Diners Club

Artistic Director:
Gérard Schneider

Photographers:
Ian Berry
Gilles Peress
Miguel Rio Branco

Assistant:
Bernard Huet

Translators:
David Lieberman
(Henry Viard's text)
Philip and Mary Hyman
(recipes)

Editorial assistant:
Barbara Stockwell